RACE/SEX

R o u t l e d g e
New York and London

RACE/SEX

Their Sameness, Difference, and Interplay

Edited by

Naomi Zack

Published in 1997
by Routledge
29 West 35th Street
New York, NY 10001

Published in
Great Britain by
Routledge
11 New Fetter Lane
London EC4P 4EE

Copyright © 1997 by
Routledge
Printed in the
United States of America
on acid-free paper.

Library of Congress Cataloging-in-Publication-Data

Zack, Naomi
        Race/sex: their sameness, difference, and interplay/
edited by Naomi Zack.
                p.   cm.—(Thinking gender)
        Includes bibliographical references (p.) and index.
        ISBN 0-415-91589-9 (alk. paper).—ISBN 0-415-91590-2 (pbk. : alk. paper)
        1. Racism. 2. Sexism. 3. Social evolution.   I. Zack, Naomi, 1944–   .
II. Series.
HT1521.R2357   1996
305.8—dc20   96-21091
                                        CIP

DEDICATION

To DJ

We must therefore abandon the hypothesis that modern industrial societies ushered in an age of increased sexual repression...[N]ever have there existed more centers of power, never more attention manifested and verbalized; never more circular contacts and linkages; never more sites where the intensity of pleasures and the persistency of power catch hold, only to spread elsewhere.

—Michel Foucault, *The History of Sexuality*,
Robert Hurley, trans., New York: Vintage
Books, 1980, Vol I: An Introduction, p. 49.

ACKNOWLEDGMENTS

THE PROJECT

Linda Nicholson invited me to submit a proposal for an anthology in her Thinking Gender series at Routledge in November 1994. Through the initial call for papers, my own editorial management of the project, and the development of its final theoretical framework she has encouraged me, advised me, left me to my own devices, and deftly intervened as necessary. As an editor's editor, Linda J. Nicholson is Olympian.

THE TITLE

My thanks to both John Pittman and Linda Nicholson for independently suggesting the title, RACE/SEX, and to John Pittman for the subtitle.

ACKNOWLEDGEMENTS

MANUSCRIPT PREPARATION

Thanks to the contributors for putting up with my irritating demands for manuscript and disk preparation. Thanks once again to Tom Reynolds for final disk management and manuscript collation—no left-handed person could wish for a better right-hand man in these matters. Thanks to Maureen McGrogan, Laska Jimsen, and Charles Hames for turning the project into a book.

REPRINT PERMISSION

I appreciate being able to reprint the following:

Anthony Appiah, "'But Would that Still Be Me?' Notes on Gender, 'Race,' Ethnicity, as Sources of 'Identity,'" *Journal of Philosophy* 77, no. 10 (October 1990), pp. 493–99.

Langston Hughes, "Silhouette," *Selected Poems of Langston Hughes.*

Nancy Holmstrom, "Humankinds," *Canadian Journal of Philosophy*, Supplementary Volume 20 (1994), pp. 49–74.

Maria P.P. Root, "Mixed Race Women," from L. Comas-Diaz and B. Greene, eds., *Women of Color: Integrating Ethnic and Gender Identities in Psychotherapy*, New York: Guilford Press, 1994, pp. 455–578.

Naomi Zack, "Race and Philosophic Meaning," *American Philosophic Association Newsletter on Philosophy and the Black Experience* 94, no. 1 (Fall 1994), pp. 14–20.

NZ
Albany, NY
April 1996

CONTENTS

CONTENTS

xii

INTRODUCTION:

Aim, Questions, and Overview

Naomi Zack

I ORIGINALLY had one vague aim for this collection. Given the present interest of feminists in racial and ethnic studies and the use of feminist insights by
racial theorists, I wanted to create a context in which race and sex (in the
sense that includes gender) could be considered together, both as a new combined subject and as a meeting ground for feminists and racial theorists.[1]

I had three two-part questions that I hoped could be answered in such a
forum. First, my ongoing project of exposing the false biological foundation
of ordinary and intellectual ideas of race had encountered resistance and criticism that I was not able to understand fully: If there is no such thing as race
biologically, then why do liberal and even radical intellectuals want to retain
the concept?[2] Given the historical and contemporary demographic reality of
mixed race, especially in the case of black and white, why do theorists who
have no practical objection to "miscegenation" want to retain fictions of racial

purity by supporting the subsumption of all 'mulattoes' under the black category, according to the American one-drop rule (i.e., the rule of *hypodescent* for blackness)?[3]

Second, can we have a "unified field theory" for combined liberatory feminist and racial theories in which both the categories of race and sex and the ways they intersect can be respected and given voice?[4] Essentialism in racial theory has entailed a false idea of inherited racial essences that are biological, cultural, or both; and essentialism in feminism has entailed a centralization and projection of the problems of the white bourgeois intellectuals who dominate scholarly feminism.[5] Can we think about the rejection of both kinds of essentialism as an opportunity to consider the common political goals of both women and nonwhites?

Third, since white men are now doing feminism and black men have had the cruelest enemies on the American battlefield of race and sex, can black male gender be critically explored in emancipatory terms within a combined race/sex forum? Specifically, can black male masculinity coexist with liberatory intent toward both black and white women?

With that vague aim and three questions, I put out a call for papers under the working title, *Comparing Sex and Race*. Most of the chapters of the book are original responses to that title; but there are always more things in philosophy than even a philosopher can dream of, and far more is at work here than comparison, though four contributors do mainly compare race and sex (Appiah, Corlett, Holmstrom, Hershel) and comparison is a subtheme that runs through most chapters.

My vague aim—to construct a forum on race/sex—has been attained here. My questions have been answered as follows. First, unified field theor*ies* are possible because we have at least six here (Corlett, Garcia, Lang, Shrage, Miles, Sterba). Second, the social reality of race is often physical in a way that overpowers the lack of biological foundation, which renders the lack of a scientific foundation for the concept of race a mere theoretical truth (Gordon, Hershel, Miles, Zack). Third, some racial theorists are willing to discuss black male gender in a context that overlaps with feminist theory (Gordon, Miles, Pittman). Furthermore, the combined discussion of black and mixed-race identity with gender allows for application of the concept of *performance*, so that both racial and gender roles can be viewed as performances in varied contexts: theatre (Giles), psychological therapy (Root), public life (Pittman), and gender change (Pittman, Shrage). As a result, race and gender can be seen to *interplay* in identity choices that would be very difficult to make if race and gender were viewed as the effects of biological essences (Pittman, Shrage).

Given these answers, the anthology has already proved hugely instructive for me, though I expect others will approach the same pages with different aims and questions and find new answers. My remaining task in this introduction is to present an editorial overview of the sections and chapters. But first, I want to note a serendipitous effect of the combined subject matter.

The passage from Michel Foucault's *History of Sexuality* at the beginning of this book suggests a theory of human sexuality as culturally *emergent*. This means that human sexuality may suddenly appear or take on new forms, given new situations of power, that is, new relationships of dominance and submission. Thus far, discussions of gender in the context of racial studies and discussions of race in the context of gender studies have dealt with different meanings and experiences of race and gender, but they have not on a widespread basis addressed sexuality. This is surprising because when the non-theorist discusses race and sex, he or she will more often than not use the non-alphabetical word order, "sex and race," and the real subject will be sexuality.

The reader will notice that the subject of sexuality emerges in different ways throughout this book. Whether that is because the focus is sometimes on "sex and race," instead of the proper alphabetical and academically abstract order of "race and sex," or is due to the addition of the subject of power to the theoretical matière is moot. The welcome effect is a further extension of theoretical discussion to bodily experience—insofar as sexuality is "of the body"—as well as the inclusion of a previously neglected topic.

THE SECTIONS AND CHAPTERS

The chapters are divided into four sections according to the methodology and apparent concerns of the authors: Analysis; Comparison; Phenomenology; Performance.

3

SECTION A: ANALYSIS

In this section, race and sex are addressed in ways distinctive of the methodologies of subsets of philosophical inquiry: metaphysics (Lang); semantics (Zack); moral theory (Garcia); social and political philosophy (Sterba). From a position within the philosophical tradition, these essays show that as subjects, race and sex are complex and intellectually engaging. Those who read and write from intellectual positions outside of the tradition of philosophy may find that these analyses address their own intellectual concerns as well, or at least that the concerns of traditional philosophy are not incompatible with theirs.

The volume opens with Berel Lang's somewhat rueful analysis of the relationship between metaphysics and racism. Lang distinguishes metaphysical racism from racism that purports to be based on biological and cultural difference. With examples from Nazi anti-Jewish propaganda and American antiblack racism, he argues that metaphysical racism, which is "nonfalsifiable" and "shameless," is ideologically prior to both biological and cultural racism. The pseudo-scientific veneer of biological racism, as well as the often-contradictory and arbitrary markers used in cultural racism, underscores the ulterior motives behind these racisms. Lang speculates that metaphysical racism is based on the Aristotelian tradition that derives individual identities from group identities that are ordered in hierarchical configurations which privilege the 'essence' of the (relevant) metaphysician's own group. He also suggests that male-biased constructions of female gender rest on analogous metaphysical commitments. However, Lang is reluctant to support an elimination of those falsely drawn racial (and presumably, as well, gender) categories which have been used to pick out recipients of Affirmative Action for reasons related to past injustices. Lang concedes that contemporary "reinscribed" racial identities that exist for the sake of entitlements are ironic, but he cautions that elimination of all racial categories may perversely support those who oppose Affirmative Action on the grounds that racism has not had harmful social consequences.

If Berel Lang's architectonic of racism is well formed, then biological racism, which is based on biological racialism—the belief that the existence of races has scientific confirmation—is only one of several façades over the underlying problem. Nevertheless, biological racialism is still widely accepted, and even when philosophers dismiss it, few take the trouble to explain exactly how or in what sense there are no biological races and what the philosophical consequences of this absence may be. In "Race and Philosophic Meaning," I apply philosophical theories of meaning to the American folk idea of biological race. As a concept, race is meaningless on the grounds of Aristotelian essentialist meaning theory, either because no essences of any kind have ever been discovered or because no racial essences have ever been discovered. The ordinary concept of race also fails nominalist theories of meaning that locate meaning in defined concepts, even though other posited 'natural kinds' have retained their meaningfulness according to revised versions of these theories. The new theory of reference, that locates meaning in entities in the world that are named by the terms for them, at first appears to rescue the ordinary meaning of 'race.' However, the individual biological foundations of 'race,' such as skin color, hair texture, and body structure, are too specific and culturally arbitrary to be used to explain or predict the presence of other specific biological traits of race. Without general racial traits whose existence can be verified in science, 'race' is meaningless according to the new theory of reference. The only philosophical meaning that folk ideas of race yield is pragmatic meaning that depends on what is valued in concrete situations in which ideas of race are invented or applied. Reading Alain Locke through Leonard Harris' interpretation, I conclude that black racial identity is probably best understood as cultural identity, which is to say that in philosophical theory, 'race' reduces to 'ethnicity.'

J.L.A. Garcia applies virtue-based moral theory to his examination of what sexism and racism are, given a consensus by feminists that sexism is like racism in important respects. Garcia rejects the models of racism which locate it in propositional beliefs or in the harmful consequences of actions to the groups about which racists are racist. Rather, he argues that racism is a matter of the heart which involves "a certain kind of ill will" or "deficit in good will." This definition of racism captures the sense in which sexism, which is also "in" the heart, is like racism. Conceived in these terms, both racism and sexism qualify for condemna-tion on moral grounds. Garcia points out that the definition of racism and sexism as a failure in the virtue of benevolence preserves the possibility that someone's actions may result in unintended harm to blacks or women, without that person automatically being a racist or a sexist; and it allows that someone may be a racist or a sexist without actually harming blacks or women. Finally, Garcia's model makes it possible to determine whether or not an individual is a racist or a sexist, independently of his or her possibly-true or possibly-false beliefs, which ought to be assessed on an independent empirical basis.

James Sterba abstracts the injustice of racism and the injustice of sexism and argues that remedies for both forms of injustice need to be pursued jointly. Racism and sexism are both based on the attachment of superiority to some group differ-ences as a justification for domination. Thus, the theoretical move from difference to superiority to domination is the same for both sexism and racism. A contem-porary racist or sexist may relinquish the idea of important and determining bio-logical differences of race and sex, but accept current inequalities which are the result of past injustice based on such ideas. The justification of this kind of accep-tance of present injustice is that its remedy would result in greater injustice. Sterba, in response, argues that both affirmative action and comparable worth can be implemented without resulting in further injustice. In addition to the theoretical reasons for pursuing racial and feminist justice together, Sterba acknowledges prac-tical considerations: black feminists have grounds to question the general commit-ment to social justice of white feminists who do not seek racial justice; both white and black feminists may doubt the commitments of advocates of racial justice who are not also concerned with justice for women; and finally, there is "the fact that 50% of those who need racial justice need feminist justice as well."

SECTION B: COMPARISON

In this section, the categories of race and sex are directly compared with intent to account theoretically for their sameness and difference. This comparison has his-torical roots in the uneasy history of alliance and divergence between white female feminists and African Americans of both sexes that goes back to the pre-Civil War abolitionist and women's suffrage movements.[6] In contemporary contexts of social criticism, "women and minorities" are conceptualized as one unit by opponents of affirmative action and "political correctness," as well as by traditional defenders of educational "canons." But within the unified target itself, similarity and difference have yet to be clearly sorted out in terms that all theorists can accept. The writers in this section contribute to this ongoing cartography of race and sex, motivated by emancipatory social goals that structure the ways they raise problems and offer solutions. Thus, the theory here is explicitly "interested": in the preservation of individual and cultural identity (Appiah, Corlett); in humanist equality (Holmstrom); and in psychological well-being (Hershel). While these essays do not read as direct attacks on racism and sexism, they strongly resist racism and sexism from more general perspectives which support individual human rights as well as social justice.

Anthony Appiah compares race, sex, ethnicity and gender, as components of individual identity in "But Would That Still Be Me?" Appiah focuses on what can be changed for a person to retain the same *ethical* identity, given (metaphysical) genetic constancy, or physical sameness according to reference theories of scientific meaning. He argues that if outwardly perceptible gender morphology is changed, the answer to "Would that still be me?" is "No," whereas if outwardly perceptible racial morphology is changed, the answer is "Yes." That is, "racial ethical identities are conceptually...less conventionally central to who one is than gender ethical identities." Appiah concludes that racial identity is not different from ethnic identity except for the false idea that races have a biological reality. Thus it is not common descent, which is the basis for assigning individuals to racial categories, that determines ethical racial identity, but shared recognition of common descent with others in the same culture, community, and, perhaps most important, family.

Angelo Corlett, in agreement with Appiah and me, begins with the absence of a biological foundation for race and notes that genetics alone also fails to differentiate gender groups. He argues that all "primitive race and sex theories" fail because they are arbitrary, incomplete, or lack significance: they pick out traits which may not be more important for group membership than those left out; they ignore the influence and importance of cultural experience for group membership; they fail to allow for degrees of membership in groups. As an alternative to these theories, Corlett proposes a *genetic-experiential* account of the categories of race and sex. His proposal includes intentional (i.e., chosen) experience as a criterion for both ethnic and gender group membership and it allows for change and variety within groups, as well as different degrees of membership. While genetics remains a component of Corlett's categories of gender and ethnicity (as they were components of race and sex in the primitive theories), it is no longer necessary or sufficient, much less determining, for group membership.

Nancy Holmstrom compares essentialist accounts of humankind, race, and gender, and argues that the idea of human nature does not have to be rejected for either political or scientific reasons, as do essentialist ideas of race and gender. Holmstrom notes that the main problem with race is its lack of a biological foundation. A biological foundation for sexual dimorphism is more secure but the difficulty in "teasing out" the exact part of that foundation which determines gender in different cultural senses makes gender essentialism indefensible. Human nature, however, is based on human biology in ways that, Holmstrom explains in an interpretation of Marx's use of the concept, determine our needs, justify our universal rights, and make possible our highest creative endeavors in different cultural contexts (including capitalism). According to Holmstrom, Marx's biological and political defense of human essentialism is, in the final analysis, a moral position that enables the struggle against the oppression of both blacks and women.

Helena Hershel directly compares the categories of race and sex in terms of recent research on childhood self-esteem. Some readers will find Hershel's analysis of empirical findings a reassuring complement to more speculative theoretical approaches, while others may view it as an opportunity for interdisciplinary comparison and criticism. In either case, Hershel's conclusions add contemporary cultural context to what most racial theorists and feminists will, I think, recognize as their own intuitions about individual development, and race and gender as social categories. Given a distinction between core or subjective self-esteem, i.e., what we think of ourselves, and public or internalized-objective self-esteem, i.e., what we think others think of us, the relevant variables are related as follows: Core self-esteem is more closely related to gender than to race in early childhood; public self-esteem is more closely related to race than to gender in adolescence; the core self-esteem of adolescent girls is more at risk than their public self-esteem and more at risk than the core self-esteem of adolescent boys; the public self-esteem of adolescent boys of color is more at risk than their core self-esteem. Generally, race is more of a social issue than gender, which is why it becomes more salient as the child develops in contexts outside of the family. Although, there are exceptions, such as parental racial self-hatred that is communicated to the child from an early age, and mixed-race children's experiences of parental or wider familial disapproval on the grounds of race. Hershel writes about the parental "gaze" as a source of validating approval for the child. In households where female gender conveys a lower status, this gaze, from either parent, may contribute to lower core self-esteem for girls.

SECTION C: PHENOMENOLOGY

The broad historical and cultural contexts of our individual lives, as well as particular situations at given times, are not subject to immediate acts of will. Still, our ability to make choices in these contexts is the basis on which we are responsible for our actions. If one could not have chosen to do something other than what one did, it makes no sense to claim that one is responsible for having done it. However, choices present themselves to agents based on how their immediate situations *seem* to them. Investigation of how things seem to be to agents in particular areas of their lives is what is here meant by *phenomenology*.

How things seem to agents is influenced by how history and one's present culture, as well as other agents, have constructed the phenomena that present themselves to consciousness. Thus constructed, the phenomena are objects about which choices can be made. When the phenomena are race and sex, the choices made about them that require the most courage may involve acceptance of oppressive social realities that cannot be changed in the time span allotted for individual

7

ZACK

action. Such acceptance may itself be an act of *authenticity*, which is the claiming of an identity that the social world has unjustly but irrevocably assigned to one.[7]

Authentic choices of racial and gendered experience, as well as authentic understanding of racism and sexism, are often beside the rational points of empirical truth and moral argument. The empirical truth may be that things are not what they seem (for example, that races do not exist or that subordinate female gender roles are not "natural"), and moral argument may conclude that people ought to be treated the same regardless of socially constructed differences in race and gender. However, empirical truth and moral argument alone cannot give us a full understanding of how things seem in the ways in which we are unable to change them given limited time and resources for action. That is, empirical truth and moral argument may be insufficient to explain the ways in which false ideas of race and gender, in social reality, influence individual bodily experience of race and gender. A full understanding of how things seem, which allows for the authentic acceptance of bodily experience in ordinary life, may proceed through varied types of phenomenology that include but are not limited to: (speculative) sociology (Gordon); post-scientific biology (Miles); genealogy (Zack); and psychology (Root).

The phenomena of race and sex in ordinary life, that is, of their physical seemings, are shaded by racism in ways that cannot be willfully removed by those who authentically claim racial and gender identities. However, phenomenology may have surprisingly liberating effects. The laying bare of social constructions of race and gender that are not supported by empiricism or moral argument is a theoretical reconstruction that facilitates detachment from racism and sexism. While such *hermeneutic* investigation neither remedies racism and sexism, nor suggests how they can be remedied, as a clarification of the mechanics of oppression, it may nonetheless be intellectually therapeutic.

Lewis Gordon builds a theory of sexuality for what he has already defined as an *antiblack* world. Gordon's worldview appears Manichean unless one reads him as a phenomenologist in the process of hermeneutically accounting for how things seem from a black perspective in American life. Indeed, his coinage of the word "antiblack" signals the seamless normality of American racism as an unavoidable structure of lived experience. In Gordon's account, the antiblackness of American life is a structure of black life that is present even when antiblack opinions are not immediately in evidence. Gordon interprets the racial terms 'black' and 'white' on a basis of Aristotelian binaries: white is hot, light, active, masculine, and virtuous, whereas black is cold, dark, passive, feminine, and lacking in virtue. The metaphysical polarities of race have gender polarities built into them and the result (crudely) is that gender in the antiblack world reduces to race. For Aristotle, there was one gender—masculine—and to be virtuous was to avoid being feminine. In our antiblack world, there is one race—black—and to be virtuous is to avoid being black. As a result, only white men can be masculine in our world and Gordon does

8

ZACK

not flinch from this consequence of his analysis: "In an antiblack world, the phallus is white skin." Moreover, Gordon maintains that the attachment of femininity to blackness means that white women can only be white at the cost of their femininity and that white men have homoerotic social relationships with black men which are fraught with violence due to their own homophobia. Gordon's analysis proceeds with schematic analyses of the permutations of black-white and masculine-feminine sexual relationships that many readers will protest. However, and this is the hermeneutic effect all need to consider, the fundamental distortion of antiblack racism renders pathological the most commonplace as well as the most highly charged social interactions.

Kevin Thomas Miles refers to feminist insights about the inability of science to adequately describe the sexual body, and he urges racial theorists to reclaim and review the racial body as a phenomenon that eludes empiricist investigation. As both sexual and racial, the body cannot be reduced to the concepts of Western *bio-logic* because science, insofar as it is a fantasy of pure reason, cannot countenance the body's pollutions, shifting boundaries, and passions. Miles rejects the reduction of race to ethnicity in the kinds of analyses and comparisons undertaken by Appiah, Corlett, and me in Sections A and B, because ethnicity is a cultural and therefore non-bodily mode of human experience. For Miles, we are mistaken to have claimed that race and sex have to be rejected because science cannot confirm their existence. Rather, it is science that has to be rejected in its failure to account for race and sex. Borrowing from Hölderlin, Miles observes that the body is "a sign that cannot be read." He builds on the observations of a number of writers who have insisted that American racial problems cannot be solved until the white association of black racial bodies with sexuality is fully understood.

In "The American Sexualization of Race" I give an account of the connection between lived racial experience and sexuality. I agree with both Gordon and Miles that race is sexualized in the United States and that the theoretical truth about race, namely, that its physical existence has not been corroborated by empirical science, does not do justice to that experience. However, unlike Miles, I assume that the connection between race and sex can be analytically understood, and unlike Gordon I preserve a distinction between race and sexuality. Applying several broad insights of Foucault's, I suggest that both sexuality and physical race are seemingly natural but socially-constructed phenomena that intersected in distinctive ways in American history, to result in the sexualization of black race. In an historical genealogical analysis, I speculate that black female race was sexualized by white slave owners due to its profitability as a medium for the reproduction of black children. At the same time, black male race was desexualized and black males denied aspects of masculine gender, due to white male dominance and competitiveness. My analysis is admittedly incomplete because it is a partial account of the sexualization of black race by white racists. The analysis of the sexualization of black race

9

ZACK

by black Americans, if it has taken place free of white racism, remains to be written.

Maria Root explores mixed-race identity within the context of psychotherapy from the perspective of both therapist and client. Working with a composite case study of a *multi-racial woman*, Root explains how uniqueness, belonging and acceptance, physical appearance, sexuality, self-esteem, and identity are prominent psychological issues for the client and therapist. These issues can be addressed in terms of healing and growth and at the same time can be read as "objective" reflections of social realities of race and female gender. The inner complexity experienced by a multi-racial woman, of the intersection of different races and the intersection of that intersection with female gender, makes it difficult for the multi-racial woman to be seen by others as she experiences herself. Root's chapter offers a phenomenology of mixed race that might not otherwise be accessible to those who are already steeped in the 'seemings' of monoracial identity. This phenomenology of mixed race is both a segment of direct experience in its own right, as well as an appearance of reality, i.e., a 'seeming' that is foreign to the reality of those (most) Americans who experience their racial identity on a basis of being one of (as in "check one"): black, white, Asian, Native American; and, Hispanic, or not Hispanic.

SECTION D: PERFORMANCE

There are varied ways in which the concept of performance can be used to describe dynamic racial and sexual identities of individuals. Analytic philosophers will remember J.L. Austin's concept of performative utterance whereby an agent is described as performing an action by saying words appropriate in certain contexts, such as "I do" in a marriage ceremony, or "I promise" in a contractual agreement.[8] Austin's analysis is persuasive partly because the ceremonial aspect of his examples evokes images of dramatic actors performing their roles before audiences. This theatrical dimension of performance reminds us that the theatre itself is a primary location for acting by speaking, and if race and gender are culturally constructed then what better place to renew or reinvent them than in dramatic art (Giles)? But just as drama on stage is influenced by the culture off-stage, so may non-theatrical performances reflect external cultural factors. As a balance to such ritualistic constraints, unique stylistic elements of individual performances of race and gender introduce elements of autonomy and caprice that underscore undetermined, playful aspects of performance (Shrage). But even serious scholarly speech and writing may become a site for discovering, inventing, and revising race and gender (Bradford and Sartwell). And, when forms or styles of race and gender are invented and performed for the sake of political goals, the concept of performance itself can be used to examine historical and cultural change (Pittman).

Generally, actors choose how to play out their unique matrices of race and gender while at the same time engaging with other performers before audiences. Much becomes illuminated when race and gender are viewed in these terms, although the question remains of whether the performer is raced or gendered when not performing. This question could be recast as whether performance of one kind or another is a constant factor in an individual's life, which would imply that private physical spaces and subjective experiences are merely different kinds of theatre: If performance in general is constant, are the performances of race and gender continual in an agent's experience? If performance is not constant, what is the player doing when not performing?

Freda Scott Giles' discussion of *methexis*, as communal experience in African-American church ritual that is recreated in womanist Afrocentric theatre, suggests that audience-interactive dramatic performance spontaneously creates power for black female performers. In this context, which overflows the Aristotelian poetic model of *mimesis* that emphasizes the separation of the tragic hero from the audience, there would be no need for private psychic or bodily space off-stage, because the performances that valorize black women at the same time create the players' identities. According to Giles, the Aristotelian play proceeds along a chronological plot-line that has imitated misogynistic patterns in the external culture at different stages in Western history. Giles explains how Afrocentric womanist theatre adds racial emancipation to feminist theatre by recasting debased stereotypes of African-American women into self-validating identities and exploding oppressive cultural scripts into non-chronological plot configurations that liberate and redefine African-American women's lives.

Judith Bradford and Crispin Sartwell speak separately as a white male philosophy professor and a white female graduate student in philosophy and together from an interwoven liberatory "we" about whether the oppressed have voices and can speak. They argue against traditions that impose silence on the oppressed; against Richard Rorty's equation of all forms of oppression with physical torture; and against the facile dismissal of the oppressed's ability to speak on the grounds that if they are speaking then they are not really oppressed. They insist that those who are oppressed can almost always speak, though those oppressors who ought to hear them are rarely able to hear them—when they are willing. Bradford and Sartwell construct 'voice' as a relational, rather than individual, product of bodies that are in every case both raced and engendered in inextricable ways. They suggest that a power grid of oppressive social norms allows for only very specific vocal forms and contents to issue from specific race/sex types, for example: white male academic voices are expected to be authoritative but neutral; white female activist voices, provided that they are properly self-effacing, may make virtuous pronouncements on behalf of other sufferers; black female novelists may be heard speaking narratives but not theory; and black male preachers may moralize. This critical sociology of American voices points to a web of external constraints on who is allowed to perform what in epistemic contexts, and it has the sobering effect of explaining exactly how performance in the academy (with or without affirmative action) cannot be fully explained in terms of individual intelligence, diligence, talent, skill, knowledge, or whatever else may in fact be a virtue of the performer when considered apart from the audience.

The word integration is not often used at present because we are acknowledged to be a pluralistic society, with a goal of equality for contending groups, instead of an ideal of equality for diverse but "assimilated" individuals. Laurie Shrage points out some of the identity problems with identity politics, and she resurrects integration as a vehicle for individual mobility across race and gender. Shrage begins by suggesting that integration is conceivable, or at the least, segregation is inconceivable. Therefore, just as transsexuals and other *queers* have liberated themselves from sexual and gender roles fixed to biological sex, so may *mulattas* liberate themselves from assigned black identities—if they choose. That is, if race doesn't have the hereditary potency it was assumed to have, then people who are mixed black and white may choose to be mixed or to take on white cultural traits. Also, racial and ethnic identities need not be construed as effects only of ancestry but could be determined by the race of one's descendants, so that a white parent with a black and white child might thereby be black or mixed, or a black parent with a black and white child might thereby be mixed or white. Shrage refers to her own experience of being more or less Jewish depending on social goals in different situations, and she suggests that racial identities, even hybrid ones, need not be constant. Shrage's kaleidoscopic view of racial and gender identities crazes the fault lines of identity politics into an intricate and undetermined mosaic, with the result that race and gender become roles that actors perform at will. Shrage's analysis is the fulfillment in terms of performance of the theoretical position that race, like gender, is a social construction, and it moves the laboratory of the theatre into real life.

The volume closes with John Pittman's presentation of Malcolm X's political performance of black masculinity. Pittman reads Malcolm's public enactment in two stages: first, a retributive autobiographical and social purification of blackness that rejected both the "white rapist" forebear of Malcolm's racial mixture and the white oppression in American culture writ large; and second, a turn toward racial toleration cut short by Malcolm's assassination. While Pittman's trope of performance is analogous to the portrayal in queer theory of gender as flexible and chosen, it adds further body to that play with gender by racializing it. Malcolm's gender is thereby understood to have been racialized in an historical project of black identity where race itself is played as resistance, attack, and exposure of (white) racism.

As Pittman indicates, it remains perplexing that Malcolm X simply inverted white notions of superiority and purity vis-à-vis blacks and that he never questioned white heterosexist male-female dominance. Giles' essay on womanist Afrocentric theatre and other recent work in black feminism suggest that emancipatory performances of black female gender need to resist and attack male-female oppression. But if, as both Gordon and I argue from different directions in Section C, American patriarchy is fundamentally white, then major elements of male-female sexual oppression are rooted in white-black racial oppression. Thus, the performance of white male gender superiority might be understood to be dependent on performances of white male racial superiority, so that once again 'sex' can be seen to emerge where power (domination and submission) is transacted (see epigraph). Therefore, if Malcolm X's black male superiority is read first as a racial inversion—he was appropriating white male superiority for black males—then his position of heterosexist male-female dominance can be viewed as part of the appropriated white male identity. Of course, mere inversion of oppressive power relations cannot be expected to hold up morally and it is not likely to succeed in cases of extreme oppression. Such inversion is nonetheless a performance of race that forcefully captures audience attention. It is also the type of performance that allows us to imagine the actor "backstage," which in Malcolm's case would be without race or gender in their performative modes. Insofar as race and gender are bodily, i.e., physical, the non-performative mode of thought, fantasy, or speech, in which an actor chooses how to make changes in race and gender, would be a level of "meta-physical" discourse or activity. Individual responsibility for choices of race or gender, as well as choices of how to perform them, would be located on that meta level and would support evaluations of performance that include moral assessment, as well as aesthetic criticism.

NOTES

1. I am grateful to Linda Nicholson for editorial clarification of how I have framed the issues in this introduction.

2. Naomi Zack, *Race and Mixed Race* (Philadelphia: Temple University Press, 1993), Chapter 2. During the past three years, I have presented the issues raised in this chapter to professors, graduate students and undergraduates, in philosophy, political science, the social sciences and literature, at the University of Helsinki, University of Albany, SUNY, Brown University, Rutgers University, University of Pittsburgh, Berkeley, UC, and American Philosophical Association conference meetings. Through a wide range of inquiry, support, and criticism from audiences, the reluctance to abandon the false ordinary idea of race has surfaced many times.

3. For multi-disciplinary discussion of contemporary mixed-race identity, see: Maria P.P. Root, *Racially Mixed People in America* (Newbury Park: Sage, 1992); idem, *The Multiracial Experience* (Newbury Park: Sage, 1995); Naomi Zack, *American Mixed Race: The Culture of Microdiversity* (Lanham, MD: Roman and Littlefield, 1995).

4. One of the ground-breaking statements of the problem of intersectionality for black women is probably Kimberle Crenshaw's "Demarginalizing the Intersection of Race and Sex: A Black Feminist Critique of Antidiscrimination Doctrine, Feminist Theory, and Antiracist Politics," *University of Chicago Legal Forum,* (1989): 139–167.

5. For these problems with feminist essentialism, see Elizabeth V. Spelman, "Simone de Beauvoir and Women: Just Who Does She Think 'We' Is?" in *Inessential Woman* (Boston: Beacon Press, 1988). For a discussion of problems with essentialism in terms of biological foundationism, see Nancy Holmstrom's chapter in this volume.

6. For an historical discussion of the conflicts between nineteenth-century abolitionists and feminists, and between white and black feminists, see Eleanor Flexner, *Century of Struggle: The Woman's Rights Movement in the United States* (New York: Atheneum, 1974).

ZACK

7. See Jean-Paul Sartre, *Anti-Semite and Jew*, trans. George J. Becker (New York: Schocken Books, 1965), p. 143–151.

8. J.L. Austin, "Performative Utterances," *Philosophical Papers*, 2nd ed., J.O. Urmson and G.J. Warnock, eds. (Oxford: Clarendon Press, 1970), pp. 233–52.

ANALYSIS

part A

METAPHYSICAL RACISM

(Or: Biological Warfare by Other Means)[1]

Berel Lang

*Is a metaphysics of race more or less serious than
a...biologism of race?*

—Derrida

chapter 1

IN THE sense that the English use the expression, "So-and-so had a good war,"
it seems undeniable that metaphysics has had a bad century. Battered in its cra-
dle by the cash values of pragmatism; squelched in young adulthood between
disciplined logical positivism and all-seeing phenomenology; torn in mid-life
by the inflationary spur of existentialism and the deflationary asceticism of
ordinary-language; forced in decline to read its own obituaries, as post-struc-
turalists and -modernists competed to have the last word (again and again).

And now, evidently, the charge of racism is to be added to the collection
of metaphysical sins and blunders. Well, Yes and No. I certainly do not intend
"metaphysical racism" as redundant—to suggest that racism is necessarily
metaphysical or metaphysics necessarily racist. Rather I mean the conjunc-
tion—racism as metaphysical—to contrast with two other versions of racism
for which, although apparently independent, metaphysical racism turns out to

be a common source, the base for their superstructure. This ground identifies group difference not in putative genetic traits or cultural homogeneity—sources for the two other (biological and cultural) varieties of racism—but in essential, that is, meta-biological and meta-cultural, features. The latter—what could they be then, other than meta-physical?—are represented as intrinsic attributes of the group's individual members and thus as invidiously distinguishing them and their group from others.

Metaphysical racism here takes on the pejorative connotation of "racism" itself, and it might be objected that the move to criticize *racism* has in either case gone too quickly; that, wherever we wind up, we have to speak first—conceptually, historically—about race itself. So, Anthony Appiah, in *In My Father's House*, distinguishes between the invidious use of racial traits or categories and the prior identification (more precisely, the nomination) of those traits or categories. These are, evidently, two distinct projects, as Louis Agassiz, the prominent nineteenth-century biologist, had earlier at least asserted: "We disclaim...all connection with any question involving political matters. It is simply with reference to the possibility of appreciating the differences existing between different men, and of eventually determining whether they have originated all over the world, and under what circumstances, that we have here tried to trace some facts respecting the human races."[2] Thus, too, Appiah distinguishes between "racialism"—which identifies characteristic features of a group in evaluatively neutral terms—and "racism" which finds in those first distinctions a warrant for invidious comparison or a set of supposedly evaluatory "facts" in their own right.[3]

This distinction is undoubtedly worth preserving, but I focus here on "racism," mainly because the racialism-racism division, which seems clear and equitable when viewed in that chronological order, has in its actual history been neither. It can be shown, I would argue, that what the distinction between "racialism" and "racism" claims as an historical sequence—the former as a condition of the latter—has in fact appeared in the reverse order. In other words (and contrary to Agassiz's statement), the search for categories of racial difference has typically been motivated by racism—the attachment of invidious weight to racial characteristics—rather than the other way round. That is, racism has been primary and racialism secondary.

This reference to conceptual motives may, of course, be held irrelevant to the legitimacy of the concept of race; nonetheless, I cite the genetic premise here because if it cannot alone decide the concept's validity, it at least illuminates the concept's structure and presuppositions which (I shall be arguing) hover between incoherence and triviality. My meaning here may be clearer from observing the two contrasting versions of racism: biological or scientific racism and (secondly) cultural or ethnic racism—as these appear as derivatives of metaphysical racism.

About biological or scientific racism certain obvious things must be repeated as a basis for others less obvious. Clearly, scientific racism has been the preeminent form of racism for the past two centuries—partly because of the hegemony achieved by science in the modern Kulturkampf for authority; partly because of developments in nineteenth-century biology and linguistics that provided an inviting metaphorical ground for describing (more accurately, inscribing) racial differentiation. I refer to that ground as metaphorical because one way of understanding the supposedly scientific category of race is as the product of a covert conceptual displacement—with distinctions by race first taken to be *like* distinctions among biological species (lacking the latter's distinguishing mark, the barrier to interspecies reproduction), then followed by a literalist shift which asserts race to be as fully determinant of the individual as its species.

With or without this rhetorical genealogy, the supposedly scientific concept of race, even detached from ra*cism*, turns out to be problematic on the very grounds it claims for itself. Only consider, for example, the conflicting numbers of races identified by biologists or social scientists who *affirm* the concept of race. These range from a minimalist two (the smallest number logically intelligible: what would a "universal" race amount to?) to a conventional three or four or five (manageable and interesting numbers), to an increasingly stressful fifty, and then on to a deconstructive sum in the thousands.[4] Discrepancies of this order amount to more than "normal" scientific disagreement—they are enough to put the question from which they set out under suspicion.

Admittedly, there is nothing new in the contention that allegedly scientific racism is only questionably scientific; that the ordering or even the distinction among races has at most the force of convention, at least, the force of force. It is invariably possible, in any large natural population, to identify sub-species; *which* sub-species are identified—that is, which traits are selected for classification below the level of species—may be explicable psychologically or functionally, but hardly in terms of the traits viewed in themselves. (Even the distinctions among species is not always so evident—as we hear Darwin himself complaining: "After describing a set of [biological] forms as [two] distinct species, tearing up my MS., and making them one species, tearing that up and making them separate, and then making them one again…I have gnashed my teeth, cursed species, and asked what sin I had committed to be so punished."[5])

I have emphasized the tendentiousness linking race to racism, and examples supporting this are plentiful—what amounts methodologically to their non-falsifiability or, in non-falsifiability's moral equivalent, their "shamelessness." The Nazi efforts to identify a scientific basis for distinguishing the "Jewish" race provide a full-scale view of this equivalence, including elements which even in that context can only be described as farcical. These range from the establishment in Germany of research institutes measuring nose lengths and chin shapes to the growth industry of genealogical shops employed to exempt clients' family-trees from any Jewish connections (for prospective S.S. members, such searches extended back to 1650. As Himmler himself soberly explains: "I will not go any further back than that…There is no point—for 1648, the end of the Thirty Years War, is mostly the limit…[of] parish records….");[6] to the bizarre decisions of the Nazis to solve the issue of racial identity posed by their Japanese allies by designating them "honorary Aryans"—or to exempt the Karaites, a community who professed not only to be Jews but to be the authentic Jews since they accept no post-Biblical Jewish texts as authoritative, from being classified as Jews (basing this decision, incidentally, on the words of a Rabbinic decision).

Beyond this arbitrariness in the application of racial categories, of course, remains the more basic issue of the specific racial definition—and here the category's tendentiousness is still more evident. In April 1933, soon after the Nazis came to power, the "Aryan-Paragraph" was promulgated that required the "retirement" of "non-Aryan" civil servants—"non-Aryan" then being defined (in a separate document) as anybody having one "non-Aryan" grandparent (there were other sufficient conditions as well, but this was the 'biological' condition). Two years later, in the specifications attached to the 1935 Nuremberg Laws, the condition of Jewish identity—the euphemism of "non-Aryan" had disappeared—was suddenly narrowed to three Jewish grandparents. Contemporary records show that the Nuremberg Laws were drafted hastily in order to provide a grand finale for the Party rally at Nuremberg, but the pressure of time does not itself explain this change in racial definition. Quite simply, the earlier definition had been too broad—in the too-large number of "Germans" or "Aryan material" it included and which would make their repression as Jews more difficult or at least awkward.

The racial definition was thus narrowed not because of evidence concerning racial differences, but for social and political reasons closely tied to the reasons for the racial categorization of Jews in the first place. And of course there remains the arbitrariness of even the narrowest definition abstracted from its history: exactly what genetic line is crossed by a single grandparent that is not crossed by a single great-grandparent? The supposedly scientific distinction that would later mean the difference between life and death was non-falsifiable—shameless—just insofar as it misrepresented a convention as nature.

In comparison to the arbitrariness of the Nazi definition of the Jews as a race, the traditional "one-drop" rule in the United States determining who is to be counted as black seems a model of consistency. On that definition (invoked, for example, in implementing laws against miscegenation and assumed in another context as recently as in a 1986 Supreme Court ruling), *any* evidence of black ancestry, no matter how remote, suffices to identify a person as black (hence the "one-drop" designation).[7] But of course this same consistency also vividly discloses the tendentiousness of the category itself. Apart from the fact that its claims are oblivious to the process of genetic transmission, the one-drop rule itself is, qua rule, so underdetermined as to be vacuous: Is there any reason in principle why "one drop" should make a person black rather than white if the same person has both "drops"? Admittedly, as soon as more than one "drop" is counted, we find ourselves on a slippery slope—but that is a practical difficulty, not one of principle. Yet the reason why principle was not admitted here in the first place was also "practical"—it was intended to reaffirm a predetermined social hierarchy.

The strongest evidence for the dissociation of racism from biological racism alone is to be found in the history of racism itself—specifically the forms of non-biological racism that both preceded the nineteenth-century analysis of speciation and persisted after its discovery. This claim is supported by evidence in both Jewish and black history, among others. The justifications for black slavery in the United States from the seventeenth to the early nineteenth centuries (including some by America's "Founding Fathers") indifferently mingle cultural and quasi-biological grounds, with the latter hardly more attentive to "scientific" evidence than the former. Stanley Elkins summarizes a standard syllogism of argument: "All slaves are black; slaves are degraded and contemptible. Therefore blacks are degraded and contemptible and should be kept in the state of slavery."[8] Some version of this argument, with all its logical and biological gaps, was nonetheless found compatible with proclaiming "liberty throughout the land" (a Biblical proclamation which ironically heralded the Jubilee emancipation of slaves) and the declaration that "all men are created equal." To be sure, skin color is in an obvious sense a biological trait. But in the long history of slavery, skin color is an inconstant and often negligible factor—further evidence that the "black" in black slavery is more a social than a biological trait. Certainly the defenders of black slavery did not wait for either disproof or reassurance from Darwin and Mendel of the quasi-biological claims they based on skin color.

Also antisemitism predates nineteenth-century biology; and although it has been argued that antisemitism of the early or medieval Church, for example, was not racist because the Church always extended the option of conversion, the discourse of racism occurs even so in the form of constant and at times intractible alienation, most familiarly in institutional forms like the Inquisition which in the end simply refused to take Yes (that is, the overt assent to religious conversion) for an answer; *conversos* remained under suspicion irrespective of what they professed.

And then, still more conclusively, the secular history of antisemitism in the past two centuries, although often employing the rhetoric of science, includes important strands which are not even superficially scientific. Admittedly, the term "anti-Semitism" itself, introduced by Wilhelm Marr in the late nineteenth century with his founding of the "Anti-Semitic League," was chosen specifically for its biologically racial connotation. (In this sense, current use of the term reinscribes a racist designation, and would be well discarded). Marr emphasized that his antisemitism was not about religious belief, but about biology—a putatively scientific ground subsequently incorporated in the more virulent expressions of Nazi antisemitism.

It is important, however, to recognize that even for the Nazis, their biological or scientific antisemitism never displaced its cultural counterpart. Whatever progress Nazi science believed it had made toward defining the racial features of Jews, it

21

hardly demonstrated the connection between those features and the (often contra-
dictory) cultural characteristics ascribed to Jews in its standard antisemitic discourse: Jews were avaricious and wealthy—and feckless and dependent; deracinee
and cosmopolitan, but also parochial and clannish; sexually potent and seductive,
but physically weak and repulsive. How to explain the contradictions among these
characteristics is a matter for the study of ideology—but quite apart from this, the
characteristics cited (*certainly the contradictions among them*) evidently come under
the rubric of social or cultural rather than genetic identity. This does not mean, of
course, that they may not also be alleged to be natural functions, as Nazi racist theory would go on to claim. But there is a difference between the explicit assertion
of a natural ground for racial distinction and the tacit reassignment of cultural features to an intrinsic "nature."

A dramatic example of the distinction between biological and non-biological
racism appears in relation to the charge of antisemitism in the "question" of Martin
Heidegger's history. In his own most direct response to that charge—in his letter
(4 November 1945) requesting reinstatement to the faculty at Freiburg—
Heidegger calls attention to what he claims had been his consistent opposition to
Nazi biological racism. In this connection, he cites the statement in his Rectoral
Address, that "The greatness of a Volk is guaranteed by its spiritual world values."
"For those who know and think," he then defends himself, "these sentences express
my opposition to [Alfred] Rosenberg's conception, according to which, conversely, spirit and the world of spirit are merely an 'expression'...of racial facts and of
the physical constitution of man."[9]

However one judges Heidegger's interpretation of his own words (*or* his antisemitism), what is most striking about this response is its premise that Nazi racism
and antisemitism stands or falls on its biological grounds—that rejecting those
grounds are proof against any such charge. That Heidegger feels able to cite in his
own defense an assertion linking the "greatness of a Volk" to its "spirit," moreover,
underscores the concept of metaphysical racism on which the discussion here
focuses—one side of the distinction Derrida mentions in the epigraph quoted earlier and beside which biological racism becomes only a subordinate and not necessarily the most consequential form of racism.

It seems arguable, then, not only that biological racism is a relative latecomer in
the history of racism, but that when it does appear, far from displacing racism's
other varieties, it serves as a cover for them. First, as invoking the authority of science for racist practice based on other grounds (if the Jews were a biological
threat—a disease, in the Nazi metaphor—the extreme measures taken against them
become plausible; if blacks were innately morally degenerate, slavery and laws
against miscegenation have an arguable ground; and so on); but then, also, in providing a cover for racism which is *not* biological, through its implication that anyone who rejects the latter basis could not be a racist. Not many people who seek
this second cover are as open about it as the English diplomat and author Harold

Nicholson when he writes that "Although I loathe antisemitism, I do dislike Jews"—but the number of those who come under this second category of racism (cultural racism) is undoubtedly larger than those in the first. This is the case because the second category includes many (arguably, I have suggested, all) members of the first, but also because its near-random specification of cultural markers lends itself even more readily to the non-falsifiability of its distinctions than do genetic traits.

Cultural racism has been at the center of so many recent discussions that I refer to it here mainly in passing from biological racism on its one side to metaphysical racism on its other. If anything, the shamelessness of distinctions asserted in cultural racism is more flagrant than that of biological racism. It is, for example, difficult to know where one would begin to argue with the words of Senator Vardaman, as recalled by W.E.B. Du Bois in his *Autobiography*, who on the floor of the United States Senate (6 February 1914) could assert with a flourish: "[The negro] has never risen above the government of a club. He has never written a language. His achievements in architecture are limited to the thatched-roof hut or a hole in the ground. No monuments have been builded by him to…perpetuate in the memory of posterity the virtues of his ancestors. For countless ages he has looked upon the rolling sea and never dreamed of a sail."[10] And what exactly would one even now say to Chauncy Tinker, the distinguished professor of English Literature who, during his tenure at Yale which lasted until 1945, successfully opposed the appointment of any Jew to the Department of English because of "cultural incompatibility…He [Tinker] did not believe that a Jew could be understanding of the English literary tradition."[11] "Polite antisemitism" thus turns out to be as little concerned about the falsifiability of its claims as it is to be polite; and no like phrase has even been applied to antiblack racism—which says something about the blatant forms that *that* has taken.

In systematic terms, it is at this point, responding to the persistence of both biological and cultural racism in the face of counterevidence—how many "master races" can there be, after all?—that the category of metaphysical racism presents itself as a presupposition, conceptually underlying the two other forms of racism cited and self-assertive as well. In my claim for this sequence—finding behind biological racism the hand of cultural racism and then behind that the hand (or head) of metaphysical racism—it may seem that other possible explanations of scapegoating or prejudice are simply ignored. But few biological racists have claimed that racist *beliefs* are biological and innate[12]—and in the absence of evidence to that effect, the presumption must be that even "simple" prejudice is not self-defining, that also its agency is part of history and culture.

How then, or where, does metaphysical racism appear? As biological racism has been proposed as dependent on cultural racism, I mean here to suggest an analogous relation between cultural and metaphysical racism. This is to say that under-

LANG

writing the tendency for asserting social hierarchy and classification by which cultural racism incites biological racist categories, a metaphysical ground serves the comparable function for cultural differentiation. Viewed thus, metaphysical racism asserts a basis for group difference not in genetic traits uniquely shared by members of a group or as a function of distinctive cultural homogeneity—but in essential (i.e., extra-genetic and -cultural) features of a group which, in one direction, are transmitted to individual group-members; and which in the other direction mark a place for the group in relation to other groups within a common ontological and hierarchical framework.

The line of argument here can be put in transcendental terms—responding to the question of how biological and/or cultural racism are "possible." Three main principles seem to me implicated in the answer to that question. The first is that human identity and activity are the function first of a group and only then of an individual—that is, the group is prior to the individual. (I think here, for one, of Aristotle's conception in the *Politics* of the relation between the individual and the polis—and the analogy he cites there of the relation between the hand and the body, with the hand's function obscure except in relation to the body.)[13] The second principle is that human group identities (and then the identities of individuals within the groups) vary not only accidentally (as in customs of dress), but essentially—in their access to or grasp of reality, moral and/or epistemic. In other words, group identities differ in respect to intrinsic moral and cognitive capacity, in their person-hood. The presupposition of this claim is that these differences occur within a single framework which itself distinguishes among them. And finally, the third principle holds that the group identities so realized are 'naturally' ordered hierarchically and evaluatively—with their various capacities corresponding to differentiated and essential values. In other words, also the rights and entitlements of groups are hierarchical. What thus results is perhaps not a great but a lesser chain of being—more precisely, a chain of lesser beings. Not by virtue of biology or nature; not, except symptomatically, in terms of comparative cultures, but as a reflection of the essences of groups and then their members.

I recognize that these principles require more elaboration than I can provide here about the assumptions they make and the evidence they draw on. But one point that has already been stressed is in any event crucial to this further work; namely, that much if not all biological and cultural racism requires the metaphysical principles or conditions stated in order to hold their own respective hierarchies up. A commitment to the two other versions of racism, in other words, is also a commitment to the metaphysical conditions cited—although not necessarily the other way round. (The latter asymmetry opens the possibility of metaphysical racism distinct from biological or cultural racism, although empirically one rarely if ever finds the one without either of the others.)

It should be evident that an analogous progression stands behind the practices of gender discrimination, although I can here only sketch briefly the terms of this

24

analogy. That the biological differences between the sexes are more extensive than the differences related to skin color seems evident. But no more than the latter do the former differences in themselves translate into cultural, let alone into metaphysical categories. In this sense, cultural ideology has been as much responsible for the construction of gender (as a concept and then in the distinctions based on it) as it has for the construction of race and *its* distinctions. The formulation in which those two hierarchical patterns are enclosed, then, is metaphysical insofar as the hierarchy does not simply display or logically derive from the ostensible biological properties cited but essentializes them, first as properties and then in their evaluative standing with respect to both specific capacity and overall worth.

Admittedly, it is awkward to subsume the metaphysical gender-hierarchy under the rubric of racism which I have more extensively discussed here. But the likeness between the process of the two constructions is evident—as is, more importantly, the metaphysical foundation that it presupposes and reaffirms in both cases. There is no common designation that has yet been accepted as applying to these two and other possible versions of metaphysico-social hierarchy. But this is a semantic problem, not a conceptual one and not (unfortunately) a matter of disagreement about the evidence. Indeed, there may be some advantage to this lack of a 'portmanteux' term for such varieties of arbitrariness or tendentiousness: as the way is thus left open to the ingenuity of prejudice for discovering new objects, it also allows for innovation or development in the reaction against them.

I want in conclusion to relate the foregoing critique of metaphysical racism (with its implication for gender prejudice) to a practical issue now dramatically present in the United States. The issue is this: Even if one supposes that racism in the forms mentioned is conceptually suspect and morally wrong, the concept of race underlying them has undeniably figured significantly in shaping group identities in our current social structure—it is integral, in fact (albeit in different degrees), to the identities of the "races" constituting that structure. Furthermore, as the repression shaping the collective memories of the groups so distinguished has diminished, allowing them to reflect on that history, an impulse in the groups themselves has emerged for joining the past to the present. What this effort to sustain continuity in an identity that was originally defined racially entails, with the irony strong and evident, is the reinscription of the same racial categories that founded the collective memory. Individual members of the group at present, responding long after the distinction was initiated and sometimes without having themselves experienced racial identity as a problem, yet wish to reassert that original identity. For however misbegotten its grounds, those grounds have indeed shaped their own history and identity.

This irony, which is severe enough as a general feature of the current discussion of racial identity, becomes still more intense in relation to specific issues of social policy. Consider, for example, the status of Civil Rights legislation and programs of

Affirmative Action in the U.S. which have been designed to address certain social—racial, gender—injustices and disparities. Admittedly, even the advocates of these programs disagree about their justification—whether they are entailed (or consistent) constitutionally or are warranted as reparations or as remedies or, more simply, as expressions of collective self-interest on the part of the body politic. But quite aside from the issue of justification stands the question of their reference—how to identify the groups to whom the policies are addressed. And it is evident that the crucial concept in any such definition is, once again, the concept of race. In order for these programs to work—for all Affirmative Action programs and for at least some programs under the broad heading of Civil Rights (like the Voting Rights Act of 1965)—the basis for deciding when and what action to take depends on the concept of race and the differences asserted in its terms between one person or group and others. In other words, in order to implement policies designed to make good on prior social injustice, categories have to be used that were in the first place responsible for that injustice—categories that are also in themselves (so I have argued) if not incoherent, then tendentious, or, at best, trivial and mischievous.

The problem here is epitomized in the superficially simple matter of the census. It is, however, on the basis of the census that regional allocations for certain social programs are made and that civil actions (concerning voter registration, for example) are initiated—once again as based on the racial categories by which respondents to the census classify themselves. There is no doubt that the question of who belongs to which of the four racial categories now presented as options should be settled by self-description—but this means also that the results are wide-open to interpretation. And still more perplexingly: even if one wanted to adhere strictly to the four categories now used, the increasingly evident occurrence of multi- or inter-racial identity makes it impossible to do so in any reasonable way. Yet on the other hand, to add other and more nuanced categories would raise questions first of how many or which should be added, and then of how to relate the new categories to the earlier ones in terms of which the injustices now meant to be redressed were committed.[14]

The irony of this practical problem is further heightened in relation to the body of opinion that holds all Affirmative Action programs and some Civil Rights legislation to be wrongful because discriminatory (in the sense of "reverse discrimination"), and thus, racist. The advocates of this view profess to will the disappearance of the social concept of race in the past and present as well as in the future—and there is unquestionably a certain consistency in that stance. But it also leaves these critics who deny the social consequences of racism in a stronger position to reject the categories of race than those who deny the biology, the culture, or the metaphysics of racial difference, but consider that justice demands a response to the past based on the reiteration of those differences. And this would replace irony with perversity.

26

LANG

NOTES

1. A longer version of this paper was presented at the Hannah Arendt/Reiner Schurmann Memorial Symposium at the New School for Social Research (October 19–20, 1994).

2. Cited in Stephen J. Gould, *The Mismeasure of Man* (New York: W.W. Norton, 1981), p. 45.

3. Kwame Anthony Appiah, *In My Father's House* (Cambridge: Harvard University Press, 1992), pp. 13-14.

4. Which is not, of course, a hindrance to dogmatism: "A combination of processes thus gave rise to the modern races, which must at the very least [!] include Mongoloids, Caucasians, Negroids, and Australoids, the native peoples of Asia, Europe, Africa, and Australia." Pat Shipman, "Facing Racial Differences—Together," *Chronicle of Higher Education*, 3 August 1994, p. B2.

5. Letter to J.D. Hooker, September 25th, 1853, in Francis Darwin, ed., *The Life and Letters of Charles Darwin* (New York: Appleton, 1898) 1, pp. 400-1.

6. J. Noakes and G. Pridham, eds., *Nazism 1919-1945* (vol. 1), (New York: Schocken, 1984), p. 495; see also on this, Berel Lang, *Act and Idea in the Nazi Genocide* (Chicago: University of Chicago Press, 1990), ch. 1.

7. On the "one-drop" rule, see Naomi Zack, *Race and Mixed Race* (Philadelphia: Temple University Press, 1994), pp. 128-130.

8. Stanley Elkins, *Slavery* (New York: Universal Library, 1963), p. 61.

9. Richard Wolin, *The Heidegger Controversy* (Cambridge: MIT Press, 1992), pp. 62, 64.

10. Cited in W.E.B. Du Bois, *Autobiography* (New York, 1968), p. 230.

11. From a letter by George Pierson, quoted in Dan A. Oren, *Joining the Club* (New Haven: Yale University Press, 1985), p. 121.

12. Paul Gilroy in *The Black Atlantic* (Cambridge: Harvard University Press, 1993) calls attention to a claim of this sort in Edmund Burke's *Inquiry into the Origin of Our Ideas of the Sublime and the Beautiful*.

13. One could move still farther back to Aristotle's metaphysics—in his claim that matter exists *only* in species (*Physics*, II:8). See Helen S. Lang, "Aristotle and Darwin: The Problem of Species," *International Philosophical Quarterly*, XXIII (1983), pp. 141-153.

14. See Lawrence Wright, "One Drop of Blood," *The New Yorker*, 25 July 1994, pp. 46–55.

27

RACE AND PHILOSOPHIC MEANING*

Naomi Zack

IT IS not always clear if a philosophic theory of meaning is meant to be descriptive or prescriptive of ordinary, scientific, or perhaps only philosophic usage. Still, theories of meaning can be applied as tests for the meaningfulness of non-philosophic terms. Something would be wrong with a term that "failed" all or most philosophic theories of meaning tests, especially those which many other terms pass—although the failed term might not be meaningless in non-philosophic usage.

I will minimally argue here that the ordinary or folk term 'race,' particularly in the cases of 'black' and 'white' as used in the United States, fails important philosophic meaning tests, according to essentialism, nominalism, and the new theory of reference. As a result, it should be clear that only pragmatic theories of meaning could render 'race' philosophically meaningful, although at the cost of the biological foundationism upon which the folk concept of race purports to rest.

Let me begin with a neutral version of the present folk meaning of "race." Roughly, there is an assumption that there are three main human racial groups (although the federal census has admitted more at different times): white, black, and Asian. These races are not as distinct as species, because interbreeding is possible, and they are something like breeds, i.e., natural biological groupings of human beings into which all individuals can be sorted, based on traits like skin color, hair texture, and body structure. Although different races have different histories and cultures, their histories and cultures are not part of the biological foundation of racial differences. This biological foundation has value-neutral or factual support from science, and if a racial term is attributed to an individual, then something factual has been said about her. In other words, the term 'race' refers to something real.

I. ESSENTIALISM AND RACE

According to Aristotelian and Thomist doctrines of essence and substance, things are what they are because they contain the essences of the kinds to which they belong: essences (somehow) inhere in individual things that are substances; and the essences of substances support their accidental attributes. Words that refer to kinds of things have definitions that describe the essences of those kinds.

The present folk concept of race did not exist when essentialist theories of ontology and meaning were widely accepted in the ancient and medieval periods.[1] And, essentialist theories of ontology and meaning were philosophically dethroned by the later half of the nineteenth century, when American scientists constructed speculative theories of the hierarchy of human races, based on philosophical essentialism. These scientists posited a unique essence or "genius" for each race that was present in all its members: in cultural and biological rank, the white race was highest, the black race lowest; the essence of the black race was infinitely transmittable from one generation of direct genealogical descent to the next, but the essence of the white race could only be preserved if the essence of the black race were not present with it in the same individual.[2]

We expect folk world views to lag behind scientific ones, but these nineteenth-century racial theories are a case study of science turning away from empiricist philosophy and its methodological implications. For example, nineteenth-century scientists of race did not attempt to isolate "racial essences" for study but merely spoke vaguely of those essences as "in the blood."[3] Insofar as a universal negation can be affirmed, it is now accepted by scientists that there are no racial essences which inhere in individuals and determine their racial membership. Nevertheless, varied combinations of ancient philosophical essentialism and nineteenth-century scientific racialism linger to this day in American folk concepts of race.

When ordinary folk would not expect to find scientific support for the existence of essences of other human traits or kinds of objects, but still speak of racial essences, they are mistaken to do so. If attributing a race to an individual means attributing the essence of that race to him, then, on those grounds, the ordinary term 'race' is meaningless. But, of course, many terms which were in the past believed to refer to essences have remained meaningful in terms of non-essentialist theories of meaning, such as nominalism. So the next step, here, is to test the ordinary meaning of race against nominalist theories of meaning.

II. LOCKE'S NOMINALISM

John Locke shaped the modern form of nominalism.[4] Locke was reluctant to talk about substance because it could not be known either from sense experience or by reflection upon the ideas of the mind.[5] In keeping with this agnosticism, Locke addressed *essence* through analyses of the meanings of terms, as opposed to something *in re*. For Locke, the essence of a (particular) thing was the idea of the kind of thing it was, which idea was "in the mind," and "made by" the mind.[6] Locke also held that those things which were to correspond to an idea could be decided without restrictions imposed by the things themselves. This meant that sorting things into kinds, including sorting beings into species, was an arbitrary process. For example, he suggested that it was a matter of stipulation whether infants with what today would be considered severe birth defects should be classed as human beings.[7] Furthermore, what counted as a species for Locke seemed to have been the result of decisions about the meanings of words. For example, he speculated that a rational parrot could not be called a man because human shape is part of the definition of 'man.'[8]

Thus, Locke did not seem to think that which beings were to count as human was determined by natural structures outside of ideas and words. Indeed, throughout his discussion of "monsters" and his account of a story about an intelligent parrot, in the *Essay* chapter "On Personal Identity," he seems to regret that human morphology is ordinarily a necessary part of what it means to be a 'man.'[9] From this, one could read Locke as denying the existence of natural kinds, or species, in any objective sense, since if there are natural kinds or species, surely the group of human beings, in their customary human form, would qualify.[10]

Even if one follows Locke in denying the objectivity of natural kind taxonomy, such extreme nominalism requires empirical and logical criteria for defining terms that are used to classify objects that are in common sense believed to exist independently of thought and language. The traditional distinction between *intension* and *extension* does some of this work: the definition of a term is its intension; the class of objects, each one of which can be picked out by the definition, is the term's extension; and intension determines extension.[11] Typically, the intension states necessary and sufficient conditions, or conjunctions of properties, that must be present for an object to belong to the extension.[12] When terms with accepted extensions

31

cannot be defined by such conditions or conjunctions, because the members of their extensions share clusters of properties or bear only "family resemblances" to one another, then the terms can be defined by disjunctions of properties. Overall, the definition of a term ought to pick out only its extension and not the extension of a term with a different intension; though, in borderline cases, precising definitions can be developed.[13] These criteria for definitions suggest that the determination of extension by intension does not preclude investigating extension in order to get intension "right." Finally, even though a definiens is analytically connected to its definiendum, the definiens cannot be vacuous: For example, it would be vacuous to define a cat as an animal with cats for parents, or to define wood as a stuff similar to other stuff called "wood."[14]

III. THE PROBLEMS WITH 'RACE' ACCORDING TO NOMINALISM

As noted earlier, races are ordinarily held to be real and racial differences are assumed to be physical differences. However, contemporary biologists and anthropologists define a 'race'—when they infrequently use the term—as a group of people who have more of some genetic or heritable traits than other groups. In scientific practice, there are no racial genes per se, but merely genes for traits that have been identified as racial traits in folk culture. Such racially significant genes are no different in principle from other physical genes, i.e., they may be dominant or recessive, combine with other genes, "blend," mutate, or result in differing phenotypes due to the overall genotypical environment. There is no defining collection of racially significant genes, for any presumptive race, that always gets inherited together, and no defining collection of phenotypical traits that all members of any race have.[15]

Thus, the failure of 'race' against nominalist meaning criteria is that there are no necessary, sufficient, or necessary and sufficient conditions of individual human biological traits, which need be present for black or white racial designation. Consider black designation, first. The group of American blacks has been estimated to have 30 percent of the genes for characteristics considered racial that the group of American whites has.[16] This overlap between the classes of designated blacks and whites is related to other problems with genetic definitions of blackness: over 80 percent of the class of blacks has some racially significant genes in common with the class of whites; there are greater racially significant genetic differences among black people than among white people; and some black people have no black racial genes (but merely at least one known designated black ancestor).[17] Also, there probably never has been a pure black or white race, and neither the Europeans who settled this continent nor the Africans brought here as chattel slaves were "racially pure." Therefore, the above descriptions of the problems with American black racial classification that presupposes pure black and white races before known mixtures are even oversimplified.[18]

RACE AND PHILOSOPHIC MEANING

There are matching problems with a nominalist account of the folk concept of white race. The absence of black genes, or of a black phenotype, is not sufficient for folk white racial designation: Rather, to be white, regardless of phenotype, an individual must have no black (or any other nonwhite) forebears. This is another way of saying that there are no positive individual biological traits for whiteness that are present in all white individuals.

If folk concepts of black and white race cannot be defined by scientific terms for non-overlapping classes of racial genes neither can they be defined by reference to phenotype or appearance: perceptions of racial appearance are unstable and too variable to be translated into necessary and sufficient conditions; many physical characteristics that people interpret as racial characteristics in others are interpreted that way only after the persons in question have been assigned to races, based on what is known about their ancestors. To put it crudely, some black people look white, some white people look black, and some white or black people look racially indeterminate—and how anyone looks racially varies among observers.[19]

In American life, ever since slavery, black and white racial designations have ultimately rested on the so-called "one-drop rule," which can be expressed by this schema, S:

> An individual, X, is black if X has one black forebear any number of generations back; An individual, Y, is white if Y has no black forebears any number of generations back (and no other nonwhite forebears).[20]

The problem with S is that blackness is indefinitely anchored because any black forebear need be black only on account of a black forebear; and since whiteness is defined as the absence of a black forebear, whiteness is a negation which rests on indefinite blackness.

If races were human breeds, there would be no reason to prevent the designation "mixed race" for individuals who have both black and white forebears.[21] But the one-drop rule prevents exactly that—mixed race people are always designated black. Regardless of how individuals may identify themselves privately, for all cases of mixed black and white race the one-drop rule is implemented officially, in law as well as public policy: Since 1915, the federal government has not recognized a category of mixed black and white race in the U.S. Census or in any federal system of racial classification;[22] in state and local record-taking anyone with a known black ancestor must be classified as black, and (except for two states) school children with recorded black and white parentage are classified as black.[23]

In the language of nominalism, the terms 'black' and 'white' purport to have mutually exclusive intensions and should therefore have mutually exclusive extensions, which they do not. But when the extensions of 'black' and 'white' overlap, that overlapping extension takes on the intension of 'black.' Either extension is determining intension, here, which should not happen, or the extension of 'black'

ZACK

is simply ambiguous because there is no way to exclude the intension of 'white' from it.

A cluster theorist or family-resemblance nominalist might propose that even though race cannot be defined by necessary and sufficient conditions, the concept has a (real) extension of individuals who share different amounts of those physical traits considered to be racial, family relations with other people in the same racial group, and self-identification as members of that group—not to mention identification by members of other racial groups.[24] While this proposal might seem to protect the folk ideas of black and white race by loosening up the classical nominalist meaning requirement of necessary and sufficient conditions, it does not preserve the *intention* behind American racial designations. It is usually intended that a racial designation of an individual say something pertaining to the biology of that individual and not about someone to whom the individual may be related. If the cluster-theory meaning were intended when an American is designated black, that is, if such a designation were analogous to calling something a game, then it would be appropriate to qualify the designation by indicating what kind of black the individual in question was. But this never happens officially and is rare socially.[25] The "life form" or game of black and white race is exclusively disjunctive, and morphological variations within blackness are not enough to give rise to subcategories that stand up on their own in racial terms, i.e., in the game of black race there are no analogues to divisions such as games of chance, games of skill, games with balls, etc. When Americans are designated white, they may qualify their racial categories with reference to national origin of forebears who are also assumed to have been white. Still, it is not clear if this practice among whites points to purely cultural distinctions or racial distinctions within the white race. (Until the 1920s, social scientists maintained that Irish, Germans, Italians, and Poles were all separate races, and until after World War II, Jews were considered a race.[26] At present, all these groups are considered white ethnic groups.)

A black person is someone with a black forebear; a white person is someone with no black forebears; some black people have white forebears: these definitions of 'black' and 'white' are more vacuous than defining a cat as an animal with two cat parents or wood as a stuff resembling other wood stuffs—a black person need not have two black parents or be similar in racial respects to other black people.

To return to Locke, before leaving nominalism, it should be noted that folk ideas of black and white are ideas of kinds, in the mind, created by the mind, and, indeed, without correspondence in their boundaries to any boundaries fixed by nature. There is no reason to believe that there are any kinds in the world which correspond to the ideas that the words "black race" and "white race" name. Up to this point, according to extreme nominalist standards, concepts of black and white race fare no worse than any other concepts of kinds. However, the problem with these racial concepts is that they do not meet the empiricist qualifications to nominalism that are met by other kind terms accepted by science and common sense, e.g., 'cat' and 'wood.' So, the ordinary term 'race' fails the meaning test of nominalism yet nominalism holds up for terms similar to 'race.' Therefore, unlike the previous case of race and essentialism, where the philosophic theory was itself defective on scientific grounds, the problem here is with the term 'race' and not with nominalism.

IV. THE NEW THEORY OF REFERENCE APPLIED TO 'RACE'

If races were natural kinds, then the new theory of reference would appear to preserve the meaningfulness of the ordinary term 'race.' I will therefore begin with an application of the new theory of reference to folk ideas of race. After it becomes clear that races do not qualify as natural kinds, according to the new theory of reference, it should be obvious that this application is bogus.

According to the new theory of reference, natural kind words are *rigid designators* that are more like proper names than terms that can be defined by the necessary and sufficient conditions which objects must meet to be part of their extensions. On this theory, 'black race' would mean, because it would refer to, as a proper name, all of the human beings who in folk terms are called "black." Thus, the failure of ordinary folk to come up with necessary and sufficient conditions for blackness, which apply to all who are, have been, or will be named by the word "black," is no longer the semantic problem it was according to the old nominalist theory of meaning. The meaning of the word "black" is simply its real world extension, and not any verbal or mental definition "in the head" (or on paper). Similarly, "white" is a name for a group of people, which does not overlap with the group that is named by "black " (or by names for other nonwhite groups). While the rules for racial sorting may not make sense according to nominalist criteria, these racial names have always been intelligently used in the American linguistic community.

Continuing with this new theory of reference interpretation of folk racial words, while it may be a matter of culture that some physical traits have been picked out as racial traits, the genes which underlie those traits, and which are clustered in different ways within each racial group, can be studied within the legitimate sciences. Those genes are scientific entities which, as in the relation of XY and XX to male and female, or H_2O to water, are necessarily related to their phenotypes. The genes for racial skin colors, for example, would be the genes for those skin colors in all possible worlds.[27] Furthermore, like the case of XX and femaleness, the technical scientific meanings of physical racial traits need not be part of the folk meaning of concepts of race. The scientific meanings may refer to underlying traits which are objects of biological or chemical study, and folk speakers may be totally unaware of them. The folk meanings of race names may thus be neutrally *stereotypical* (like part of the folk meaning of 'lemon' as "yellow and sour"), because they refer to phenotypical properties as opposed to genes. (This is in addition to how they are stereotypical in that ordinary sense of 'stereotype' which devalues.)

Finally, on this reference account of folk race words, although both the black and white racial groups have changed throughout American history, and the black group contains people who have white as well as black ancestry, folk usage of racial words as proper names is supported by the perceived correctness of this usage in the past, and the shared belief that others in the culture have the same understanding of the correctness of the usage. The change over time in the amount and distribution of racially significant genetic traits in the black race (i.e., the effects of "racial mixing"), is no different than the change in the amount and distribution of genetic traits to which varying significance is attached in the case of animal breeds, over time: Cows, for example, produce more milk than in the past and are still properly called "cows"; non-domesticated breeds of animals are subject to evolutionary-type changes. The one-drop rule whereby a person is black if she has one black ancestor, could be viewed as a *living mnemonic* in the (real world) causal process whereby racial words come to be applied correctly and confidently. This living mnemonic assures that a person who is of black descent will be labeled in a way that refers to past labeling, not unlike other forms of hereditary labels, such as "baron" or (unfortunately) "untouchable." The mnemonic also has the utility of providing an automatic rule for the racial sorting of infants, and it allows American society the stability of automatically perpetuating, over generations, its group differences based on race. This situation is similar to the mistaken common sense that tomatoes are vegetables and spiders are insects, or to older beliefs in the existence of witches. In these examples, folk names or assumptions which are not in accord with scientific reality are nonetheless meaningful, due to folk experience. And here the case rests for a new theory of reference reconstruction of American concepts of black and white race.

V. PROBLEMS WITH THE NEW THEORY OF REFERENCE MEANING OF RACE

If the scientific realism of the new theory of reference is important, and according to Saul Kripke, W.V.O. Quine, Hilary Putnam, and others of its architects it is very important, then the above reconstruction of folk ideas of race within the purview of that theory is misleading. The core problem is that races do not qualify as natural kinds, and once this is clearly understood it follows that any historical account of the causal process whereby race words function as proper names, while it might be an interesting cultural study, does not contribute to semantic knowledge that can be directly used; instead, the result is that race words can only be mentioned by informed speakers and writers.

How is it that races are not natural kinds? In this context, there is not merely the empirical point that there are no racial essences, or the empirical–nominalist point that there are no uniform necessary and sufficient conditions for the application of race concepts. The problem is the lack of evidence that there is anything specifically racial on a genetic level: Not only are there no genetic racial essences, or nominalist analogues to such essences, but there are not even any racial *accidents,* genetically. It is not merely that a person designated black or white at a certain time and place might with the same physical traits be otherwise racially designated in a different time and place, i.e., not merely that the bearer of a racial label does not bear it in all real worlds, or, a fortiori, in all possible worlds. Rather, there is no purely racial sub-structure *per se*, to which morphology that is perceived or judged to be racial on a folk level, can be necessarily or (even contingently) connected. This last failure needs to be spelled out in some detail.

Suppose one compares racial designations with sexual ones. Despite many borderline cases in sexual dimorphism, for both phenotypes and genotypes, there are large numbers of human beings who genotypically, on a chromosomal level, fit the exclusive disjunction of XY or XX. To say that an individual is XY has explanatory force in predicting both primary and secondary physical sexual traits, and this explanatory force is on a more general nomological level than statements about the genotypes or phenotypes of primary or secondary physical sexual traits. Thus, in addition to XY and XX, there are genes for testicles, ovaries, and male and female body hair patterns.[28] But, by contrast, with race, while there are genes for morphology perceived or judged to be racial, such as hair texture and skin color, there are no chromosomal markers for black race or white race (or any other race), no genes for race *per se*, and, indeed, nothing which is analogous to XY, XX, or to any of the borderline sexual-type combinations of X and Y, for instances of mixed race.

Although the genes for specific hair textures, skin colors, body structures, and facial features, judged or perceived to be racial, may be necessarily associated with those traits, the lack of a genetic racial substructure means that *race* is not necessarily associated with those traits. Although it may be argued that the folk meaning of 'race' is a cluster or family-resemblance-type of meaning, and that these kinds of meanings refer to varying accidents, as opposed to essences, the lack of any specifically racial genetic substructures means that there are no racial accidents. It is not merely the case, as Anthony Appiah has asserted, for instance, that sexual identity is an ethical matter more central to who a person is than racial identity.[29] Instead, more strongly, the sexual identification paradigm is objective or real in a scientific way, while the racial part of clusters of racial traits are solely "in the head." Race is a social construction imposed on human biological differences which are not in themselves racial—because nothing is racial which is not "in the head."[30] Again, the genes for traits deemed racial are scientifically real but there is no racial aspect of these genes which is scientifically real. And yet, on a folk level, the prevailing assumption is that race itself is physically real.

These days no one claims that human races are distinct species. But might they not be breeds—a result of human-human breeding—and in that sense natural kinds? All of the major races seem to be associated with places, which are natural (i.e., Africa, Northern Europe, Asia), and groups called races are composed of biological human beings, which are also natural. Why, then, aren't races-as-breeds natural kinds, in the new theory-of-reference sense, since they clearly are natural kinds

37

according to folk taxonomy? The answer is that, as Quine points out, in scientific taxonomy, underlying trait terms are the only analogue for the folk meaning of 'kind.'[31] It is also important to realize, at this juncture, that the term 'natural kind' does not derive from folk usage but from new theory of reference claims that meaning relies on scientific usage. In scientific usage, underlying trait terms have explanatory power—they explain structures and events described or named by "overlying" trait terms.[32] While groups from different geographical areas can be called natural kinds in a sense that accounts for their common history, culture, and in-group recognition, no explanatory power is added by adding the term 'race' to such group terms, and that zero increment may drop into minus territory when, as with black Americans, the term 'race' is applied on the basis of geographical origin of some of the ancestors of some members of the kind.

Michael Ayers indicates that without a previous definition of 'similarity,' biological beings cannot be sorted into kinds based on their similarity to beings that have already been so sorted.[33] At some point in the epistemology of taxonomy, reference to either underlying structures or history is required. The latter historical requirement brings us back to the foregoing interpretation of the one-drop rule as a living mnemonic which sorts people into the black group based on black descent. This appears to mean that the history of racial words rides on the history of individuals' families. But not all biological family members need be, or ever have been, of the same race. Indeed, American racial history is replete with stories of white and black branches of the same biological families and this means that something other than biology has divided the branches;[34] in fact, it is only black Americans for whom racial membership is positively determined by biological descent. And, as already noted, there is no way in which all black Americans are similar so that the relevant and necessary degree or kind of similarity can be specified. That is, there is no scientific way to pick out the black family members who "make" an individual black.

Therefore, no non-circular causal account of folk racial words is possible. Such words cannot be proper names because the proper name of an individual's forebear is not, in this sense of reference, the proper name of that individual, and we may not even know what—or, if anything—it was about the relevant forebear that made the proper name in question the correct proper name for him.

To be sure, there are strong American traditions about how people get sorted racially, but the only uniform empirical content to trait terms for the beings named by racial words is that they have been so named. All we can definitely say is that racial groups are groups that have had racial traits attributed to them, and that the individual members of such groups get sorted into them if their ancestors have had the relevant racial words attributed to them, or not (since a person is white if she has no nonwhite forebears).

A more (philosophically) technical way to state these problems with a causal-historical explanation of racial words is to construe racial proper name words as *attributive*, in Kieth Donnellan's sense, as opposed to descriptive or referential.[35] In this way, racial words pick out individuals who exist, regardless of whether or not they fit the descriptions attached to the racial words. The descriptions attached to the racial words (names) are stereotypes. Racial names have stereotypical connotations in terms of both physical morphology as well as value judgments.

While this new theory of reference's attributive account of racial concepts does preserve some of the folk meaning in racial concepts, like the interpretation of the one-drop rule as a precising definition on a family-resemblance nominalist account of meaning, it fails to preserve folk intentions in the use of racial words. People do not think that all they mean by race words are stereotypical names that some call others, in order to pick them out. To conclude, the new theory of reference does not preserve the meaningfulness of folk terms of race, and the fault is with those terms because the new theory works satisfactorily with the meanings of other apparent natural kind terms that have scientific analogues.

VI. PRAGMATISM AND RACE

There are two kinds of pragmatic meaning theories that could be relevant to 'race' but only the second is. The first is scientific pragmatism, which shows the purposiveness and intentionality behind all concepts, even the most exact scientific ones; the specialized philosophy-of-science form of this kind of pragmatism is an instrumentalist view of scientific theories and theoretical terms. This kind of pragmatic meaning is not relevant to race because race is insufficiently empirical: there are no confirmed scientific theories about race as it is understood on a folk level, and race is not a theoretical term in science.

The second kind of pragmatic meaning is axiological and it has some of the connotations of the folk word "pragmatic": efficient, useful, and morally compromised. The folk concept (i.e., the meaning of the word) of race is morally compromised in two ways. Its pragmatic meaning is not the kind of meaning that most folks in the linguistic community are prepared to admit is its only meaning, because they want to believe that race has a neutral, factual basis, supported by science. And, some of the purposes served by the imposition of racial categories on human beings have been evil. This is not surprising, because people lie and create illusions in order to mask wrongful motives and actions, and 'race' as it is vulgarly understood qualifies as such a lie and illusion. For example, after it became illegal to import slaves into the United States and the cotton gin intensified the demand for slave labor in the Southern economy, there was widespread "breeding" of slaves and widespread miscegenation among the slave population. By that time, only blacks could legally be enslaved, so it was pragmatic to designate the mixed-race and white offspring of slave mothers as black.[36] A second example of the axiologically pragmatic meanings of race can be found in constructions of race by nineteenth-century scientists, in which blacks always fared worse than whites in measurements of cranial size. The relevant data was manipulated to confirm the dominant ideology that blacks were "inferior" to whites.[37]

Of course, not all of the pragmatic meanings of 'race' are morally bad or compromised. While the evidence for changing the belief that culture was racially hereditary was available since the 1920s, it wasn't until the racist horrors of World War II registered in civilized global consciousness that the United Nations issued a series of position papers on the historical, rather than racial origins, of cultural difference.[38] Also, contemporary white liberal society engages in affirmative constructions of blackness that attempt to be helpful and benevolent towards blacks. Finally, it is no less pragmatic in this axiological sense that the American black emancipatory tradition has always responded to pragmatic white racist constructions of blackness with its own pragmatic constructions of blackness. Consider, for instance, the following excerpt from Leonard Harris' introduction to the pragmatic philosophy of Alain Locke:

> A social identity entails for Locke the positive valuation of an interest, an affective feeling, a method of representation, and a system or process of continual transvaluation of symbols.

> ...The Negro race and the Negro culture were for Locke two distinct phenomena that by dint of history were identified as synonymous. Loyalty to the uplift of the race for Locke was thus, *mutatis mutandis*, loyalty to the uplift of the culture.[39]

One final point given limitations of space: If Alain Locke's equation of race to culture is related to current discussion, then race will be reduced to ethnicity.

NOTES

* For criticism of previous versions of these ideas, I am grateful to my colleagues in the Philosophy Department at the University at Albany: Ron McClamrock, Robert G. Meyers, John Kekes, and Berel Lang. Thanks also to Thomas Magnell for comments on a paper I read at the 1993 International Society for Value Inquiry Conference at the University of Helsinki, and to Leonard Harris and an anonymous reviewer of the American Philosophical Association *Newsletter on Philosophy and the Black Experience*, where this article first appeared (94 no. 1 (Fall 1994) pp 14–20).

1. For discussions of whether the modern concept of race was in use in the ancient world, see: M.I. Finley, *Ancient Slavery and Modern Ideology* (New York: Pelican, 1983), pp. 97, 117–119; Martin Bernal, *Black Athena* (New Brunswick: Rutgers University Press, 1987), pp. 339–445.

2. See, for example: John C. Mencke, *Mulattoes and Race Mixture* (Ann Arbor: University of Michigan Research Press, 1979), pp. 39–46.

3. Almost any nineteenth-century reference to race makes heavy use of the blood metaphor, and even physicians believed that the blood of different races was different in "essential" ways. See, for example: Robert J. Sickles, *Race, Marriage, and the Law* (Albuquerque: University of New Mexico Press, 1979), pp. 53–4. The only empirical differ-

ence in blood types among groups of people that is credited by scientists is a somewhat geographical distribution of the four major blood types over the surface of the planet. See: N.P. Dubinin, "Race and Contemporary Genetics," in Leo Kuper, ed., *Race, Science, and Society* (New York: Columbia University Press, 1975), pp. 71–74.

4. See: Stephen P. Schwartz, "Introduction," in Stephen P. Schwartz, ed., *Meaning, Necessity, and Natural Kinds* (Ithaca: Cornell University Press, 1977), pp. 16–17; Michael Ayers, *Locke: Vol. II, Ontology* (New York: Routledge, 1991), pp. 65–7.

5. See: Peter H. Niddich, ed., John Locke, *Essay Concerning Human Understanding* (Oxford: Oxford University Press, 1990), IV,iii,5, (1–6), pp. 338–40. All quotes from Locke and *Essay* citations in this paper refer to this edition.

6. As Stephen Schwartz interprets Locke, the nominalism of the old theory of meaning is that essences are ideas, i.e., things in the mind. See: Schwartz, "Introduction," op. cit., pp. 16–17; and Locke, *Essay*, III,iii,12, pp. 414–415.

7. For Locke's stipulative view of species, see *Essay*, III,vi,27, p. 454.

8. That is, for Locke, there is no deep connection between morphology and natural kinds, or species, viz.:

Since I think I may be confident, that whoever should see a Creature of his own Shape and Make, though it had no more reason all its Life, than a *Cat* or a *Parrot*, would call him still a *Man*; or whoever should hear a *Cat* or a *Parrot* discourse, reason, and philosophize, would call or think it nothing but a *Cat* or a *Parrot*, and say, the one was a dull irrational *Man*, and the other a very intelligent rational *Parrot*. (*Essay*, II,xxvii,8, p. 333.)

For a more complete discussion of the absence of the modern concept of race in Locke's writing, see Naomi Zack, *Bachelors of Science: Seventeenth Century Identity Then and Now* (Philadelphia: Temple University Press, 1996), Chapter 12.

9. Ibid., p. 335. See also, mention of monsters in *Essay* III,vi,17, pp. 448–449, and III,vi,27, pp. 454–455.

10. See: Ayers, op. cit., pp. 85–7.

11. See: Irving M. Copi, *Introduction to Logic* (New York: Macmillan, 1961), pp. 107–112.

12. Schwartz, op. cit., pp. 14–18.

13. Copi, op. cit, p. 104ff.

14. See: ibid; also, Merilee H. Salmon, *Introduction to Logic and Critical Thinking* (New York: Harcourt, Brace, Jovanovitch, 1984), p. 330. Technically, these are circular definitions, but it is their almost comical, explicit surface circularity that I am calling vacuous.

15. For these facts about race and racial inheritance, see, for example: L.C. Dunn, "Race and Biology," in Kuper, op. cit. pp. 61–67; L.C. Dunn and Theodosius Dobzhansky, *Heredity, Race, and Society* (New York: Mentor, 1960), pp. 114ff. For a recent discussion of the conceptual issues involved in genetic atomism versus contemporary theories that genes interact with each other as well as with the overall genotypical environment, see: Ernst Mayr, "The Unity of the Genotype," in Robert N. Brandon and Richard M. Burran, eds., *Genes, Organisms, Populations* (Cambridge: MIT Press, 1984), pp. 69–86. However, it should be noted that even though genes underlying traits perceived to be racial may interact in these ways, so that an atomistic model does not apply, the interactive model does not reliably clarify racial inheritance because there is no phenotypical group of traits which can be identified in order to resort to this model for the inheritance of the gene underlying the phenotype. For example, if parents with known ancestry have a child who is phenotypically white, one would resort to the interactive genetic model only on the assumption that the child would have to be black because he or she has black ancestry.

16. For a discussion of antebellum racial mixing among the black population, see: Joel Williamson, *New People* (New York: Free Press, 1980), pp. 9–26, 125.

17. See: Debunin, op. cit., pp. 84ff.

18. Thanks to Thomas Reynolds for pointing out the oversimplification.

19. See, for example: Adrian Piper, "Passing for White, Passing for Black," *Transitions* 58, 1992, pp. 4–58.

20. For a more comprehensive discussion of this schema, see: Naomi Zack, *Race and Mixed Race* (Philadelphia: Temple University Press, 1993), chaps. 2 & 3.

21. Many dictionaries define "race" as "breed." For a discussion of human-human breeding and black and white race in the United States, see Zack, op. cit., chap. 4.

22. For details on the history of black and white official racial classification in America, see: F. James Davis, *Who is Black?* (University Park: Penn State Press, 1991), chaps. 1 & 4; Zack, op. cit., chap. 8.

23. The two states are Ohio and Georgia (legislation pending). See: *Project Race Newsletter*, April 1993, (published in Roswell, GA).

24. This is the basis on which Anthony Appiah accepts folk ideas of race. See: Anthony Appiah, "But Would That Still be Me?: Notes on Gender, 'Race', Ethnicity as Sources of Identity," *Journal of Philosophy*, no. 10, Oct. 1990, pp. 493–498 (reprinted in this volume).

25. See, by contrast, the situation of classification for Native Americans: Terry P. Wilson, "Blood Quantum: Native-American Mixed Bloods," in Maria P.P. Root, ed., *Racially Mixed People in America* (New Brunswick Park: Sage, 1992), pp. 108–126.

26. For an analysis of the history of concepts of race in the field of sociology, see: R. Fred Wacker, *Ethnicity, Pluralism, and Race* (Westport: Greenwood, 1983).

27. That is, like the case of water on twin-earth, which is not H_2O, and therefore not water, brown skin due to a sun tan or makeup rather than to a gene is not racial brown skin.

28. This is an oversimplication of the genetics of sex because the study of genotypically sex-linked, non-sexual abnormalities as well as the genetics of sexually indeterminate individuals is such an important part of the epistemology of selecting XY and XX as the paradigm of human sexual dimorphism. See, for example: Daniel J. Kevles, *In the Name of Eugenics* (Berkeley: University of California Press), pp. 238–250.

29. Appiah, op. cit., pp. 495–497.

30. This is, of course, in contrast to Hilary Putnam's arguments that meanings "just ain't in the head." See: Hilary Putnam, "Meaning and Reference," in Schwartz, op. cit., pp. 120–124.

31. W.V. Quine, "Natural Kinds," in Swartz, op. cit., pp. 174–5.

32. See: William K. Goosens, "Underlying Trait Terms," in Schwartz, op. cit., pp. 133–154.

33. Ayers, op. cit., p. 81.

34. See, for example: Patricia J. Williams, *The Alchemy of Race and Rights* (Cambridge: Harvard University Press, 1991), pp. 154–155.

35. See: Keith S. Donnellan, "Reference and Definite Descriptions," in Schwartz, op. cit., pp. 42–66.

36. Indeed, the universal human rights affirmed in the United Nations Charter do seem to support such a right to self-identification. See: Naomi Zack, "Mixed Race and Public Policy," paper read at Feminism and Social Policy Conference at University of Pittsburgh, 1993 (printed in *Hypatia* 10:1, Winter 1995, pp. 120–132).

37. See Stephen J. Gould, *The Mismeasure of Man* (New York: W.W. Norton, 1981), pp. 73–108.

38. See the United Nations' "Four Statements on the Race Question," reprinted in Leo Kuper, ed., *Race, Science, and Culture* (New York: Columbia Press, 1975), Appendix.

39. Leonard Harris, ed., *The Philosophy of Alain Locke* (New York: Temple University Press, 1989), Introduction, p. 20.

RACISM AS A MODEL FOR UNDERSTANDING SEXISM

J.L.A. Garcia

chapter 3

INTRODUCTION: RACISM AND SEXISM

ACCORDING TO the *OED*, the term 'sexism' entered English in the middle and late 1960s. It is generally allowed that the term was conceived as an analogue of racism, and the first recorded use of any cognate term makes this derivation explicit: "When you argue that since fewer women write good poetry this justifies their total exclusion, you are taking a position analogous to that of the racist—I might call you in this case a 'sexist'—who says that since so few negroes [*sic*] have held positions of importance...their exclusion from history books is a matter of good judgment rather than discrimination."[1]

Those who devised the term 'sexism,' then, took it to be the same kind of thing as racism with the notion of sex replacing that of race in marking out the victims and women replacing Black people as the most salient targets of victimization (in the actual current and historical situations, if not necessarily).[2] Sexism was held to be formally, structurally similar to racism, but with different content. What appear to be among the first recorded uses of this and related terms bring this out. Thus: "A sexist is one who proclaims or justifies or assumes the supremacy of one sex (guess which) over the other." Or, again: "Sexism is judging people by their sex where sex doesn't matter."[3] These remarks clearly adapt, to relations between the sexes, understandings of racism then (and now) current. The former formally resembles a typical definition of racism as "an explicit and systematic ideology of racial superiority," changing content by the substitution of sex for race. The latter is a formal match for the common view that racism consists in irrelevantly taking race into account.[4]

Even a quick examination of some survey literature shows that this close formal connection is still widely assumed. One social critic says racism "suggests first and foremost a negative external view, that is, a negative view held toward members of another group." She thinks both 'sexism' and 'racism' "refer...to oppressive behaviors, policies, and attitudes ranging from institutionalized murder to unwitting support of insensitive practices by the well-intentioned."[5] A second relates what she thinks of as "the dual discriminations of sexism and racism," explaining that "*Racism* refers to the ideological, structural, and behavioral systems in society which deny and limit opportunities for some groups because of their racial identity in order to create and maintain a racial hierarchy. *Sexism* refers to a system of control which maintains and legitimates a sexual hierarchy in which males are dominant."[6] Plainly, her intent is to draw on the detail provided in the understanding of racism she offers to elucidate that she provides for sexism. The "system of control" in the latter must comprise the society's "ideological, structural, and ideological systems" mentioned in the former, and the way in which this system "maintains and legitimates sexual hierarchy" is, presumably, by "deny[ing] and limit[ing] opportunities" for women, in the same manner that, she has explained, racism acts thereby to "create and maintain...racial hierarchy." Some even go on to rebut claims of "reverse sexism," mirroring responses to current complaints against race preferential affirmative action policies as 'reverse racism,' and to level charges of "institutionalized sexism," mirroring common talk of 'institutional racism.'[7]

Our examination also reveals that among these same writers, all of whom are sure that sexism structurally resembles racism, there is no agreement on just what sexism is. This is because they disagree about that in which the prior notion of racism itself consists. Some feminists understand racism and sexism as ways of thinking and talking about people; others see both as ways of treating people; one group maintains they lie within individuals, while a different one maintains they can be found only in institutions and social systems.[8] To understand sexism we should begin by analyzing racism, first to see what it is; second, to assess its suitability as a conceptual model for understanding sexism; and third, to consider in what sexism will consist if the term's originators were correct in seeing sexism as structurally, formally similar to racism.

My procedure here will be, in section 1, to investigate an influential analysis of racism, which promises application also to sexism. In section 2, I propose a different account of racism, in light of difficulties found in others. In section 3, I examine an important account of the nature of sexism, to see if the topic is better grasped by confronting it directly, rather than through the model of racism. In section 4, I sketch what sexism is if it really is structurally like racism. In section 5, I elaborate one element of this reconceptualization of sexism to deal with a salient form of sexism whose analogous form of racism has been little examined.

I. WASSERSTROM ON RACISM AND SEXISM

In an early, but oft-reprinted and still highly influential, article on racism and sexism, Richard Wasserstrom offers a promisingly unified picture of the two phenomena. He writes:

> "[R]acism and sexism consist in taking race and sex into account in a certain way, in the context of a specific set of institutional arrangements and a specific ideology, which together create [a system of unjust institutions and unwarranted beliefs and attitudes] and [which together] maintain a system of unjust institutions and unwarranted beliefs and attitudes. That system is and has been one in which political, economic, and social power are concentrated in the hands of those who are white and male."[9]

Wasserstrom allows that there are differences between racism and sexism, but stresses that "the mode of analysis I propose serves as well...for an analogous analysis of the sexism of the legal system.... In theory, the foregoing analysis can be applied as readily to the social realities of sexual oppression as to racism." Nonetheless, his more detailed explanation focuses on law's racism. Unfortunately, his promise of a unified account, in which the claimed structural similarity of racism and sexism is maintained and explained, remains unrealized on examination. His account of racism's nature tries but fails, for several reasons, to provide necessary conditions for racism. First, there may be racism in individuals' attitudes even if there are no surrounding racist institutional arrangements or general ideology. Consider the solitary old anti-Black bigot, alone in her room, raging within over the signs of Black advancement she sees on TV, reads about in magazines, witnesses even in the evident prosperity of some of the Black people she sees walking or driving along beneath her window. She is a racist, if anyone is, irrespective of the ideology and institutions that surround her. Indeed, it is grotesque to maintain she gets off the hook of racism, merely when and because, contrary to her heartfelt desires, all such embodiments of racism have been eliminated.[10] Second, racism can exist if the institutions and beliefs are maintained but only unsystematically—in a haphazard, disconnected, sporadic, hit-and-miss, discontinuous way. For example, a group of racists may succeed in getting the athletic office—but not the principal's—at public school #1 to discriminate, the promotions office—but not the hiring officer—in company #35, and so on. This would be institutionalized but, nonetheless, nonsystematic racism. Third, if the claims about racism's success-ful concentration of power at the end of Wasserstrom's account are meant to be part of the definition or essence of racism, then they constitute another unneces-sary condition, for racism also exists when the system tries but fails to concentrate power racially.[11]

Nor does Wasserstrom's account of the nature of racism provide sufficient con-ditions. Suppose that the causal connections he supposes exist, but are accidental, neither intended to harm nor born of callous disregard. Perhaps a group of insti-tutions and beliefs do work together to form a system and this system operates to maintain itself to the disadvantage of one racial group. Imagine, however, that this occurs by accident. In that case, I want to say, there is no racism, although there is an oppressive system. This hypothesis might seem so far-fetched it is not worth attending to. However, what I am imagining has serious consequences for the real world, consequences that attend any account of racism that makes something racist depending simply on what it happens to "create," "maintain," or "concentrate." Imagine Twin Earth, where some of the complaints that conservatives raise against "the new (self-) segregation," "reverse discrimination," etc., really hold true. On Twin Earth, these antiracist efforts really do work to undermine self-confidence and self-esteem among those in the oppressed racial group; really do perpetuate racial stereotypes and the belief that members of the group are unable to "make it" economically, or socially, or academically on their own; really do generate hostili-ty and resentment among those in the favored group; really do undermine self-confidence and the 'work ethic' among intended beneficiaries. Wasserstrom's account implies that on Twin Earth such measures, undertaken by those on the bottom socially and economically, are not only ill-advised and counter-productive, but are themselves racist, simply because, quite contrary to their purpose, they have the systematic effect of confirming unwarranted beliefs ("those people can't make it on their own"), promoting unwarranted attitudes ("I never feel comfortable about those people, they're so clique-ish"), perpetuating unjust institutions ("there's nothing wrong with our White Male's Party, segregated clubs, etc., if there's nothing wrong with their Women's Bank, Black Engineers' Association, etc."), and thus have the effect of further concentrating power in white male hands. Moreover, his account of what racism is unacceptably implies that, on Real Earth, we have to wait and see how things turn out before we know whether such self-help measures are counterproductive and therefore themselves racist!

Wasserstrom completes his account of racism by adding to his claims about its nature a discussion of three types: overt, such as Jim Crow laws; "covert but inten-tional," such as "grandfather clauses"; and institutional. Institutional racism resides either in "sub-institutions" with the law, such as mechanisms leading Black defen-dants to have disproportionately White juries, or consists in "conceptual institutional racism…[wherein,] often without [our] realizing it, the concepts used [in law] take for granted certain objectionable aspects of racist ideology."

Wasserstrom's account of the types and sub-types of racism is also problematic. First, what distinguishes "institutional racism" from "overt" and from "covert" racism within a legal system? Is not all state action *eo ipso* institutional? For that matter, is not any intentional (or unintentional) institutional racism necessarily either overt or covert?[12] *Tertium datur*? Second, the examples of institutional racism that Wasserstrom offers, e.g., selecting jurors from voting lists whose segregation leads to segregated juries, seem to consist in *not* taking race into account in cases where, Wasserstrom thinks, it should be. Suppose that this is a defect in these procedures and that it even makes them racist.[13] They still cannot count as racist by Wasserstrom's account. That account requires that racism consist in taking race into account in certain ways and contexts. It says nothing of things being racist because of the ways in which race is *not* taken into account.

I conclude that Wasserstrom's understanding of racism cannot provide us the philosophical understanding of racism we should need to vindicate the view—held by those who coined the term 'sexism'—that sexism is structurally similar to the social phenomena they identified in order to oppose. I shall suggest a different conceptualization.

II. RACISM RECONCEIVED

One of the many strengths of Wasserstrom's proposed account of racism and sexism is that it encompasses the principal types of phenomena with which people have identified racism and sexism: oppressive institutional practices and prejudiced individual beliefs. Oppressive institutional practices, however, turned out neither necessary nor sufficient for racism. What, then, of prejudiced beliefs? Again, someone may hold such a belief without properly incurring the charge of racism—for example, some *naif* hoodwinked by Plato's "noble lie" about the origins of the golden, silver, and bronze races.[14] Likewise, racism can characterize someone without her holding prejudiced beliefs—for example, when someone acts from or is filled with racial animosity neither derived from prior unfavorable beliefs about the hated race nor rationalized by later adoption of such beliefs.[15]

Some respond to these counterexamples to the sufficiency of prejudice for racism by conceding that it is not *what* a racist believes but *how* she believes it that makes her a racist. Kwame Anthony Appiah, for instance, maintains that a racist holds her prejudices in an ideological way, immunizing them from counter-argument. Lewis Gordon, legitimately worried that Appiah's account threatens to exculpate the racist by assigning her ugly beliefs to irrationality, insists that what characterizes the racist is that she self-deceptively chooses to hold her prejudiced beliefs as a matter of what existentialists call 'bad faith.'[16]

I think none of these efforts to defend the view that racism is a matter of what one believes and how she believes it succeeds.[17] However, they suggest a different

49

GARCIA

way of understanding racism. The person who holds to her 'anti-Black' (or anti-whatever) prejudices regardless of counterevidence, or who deceives herself into holding onto them, is committed to opposing the advancement of those whose race she makes her enemy. She wants, and thinks she needs, those of the targeted race to suffer, at least to suffer in comparison to her. That indicates that the core of her racism lies not in her beliefs, and still less in social systems, but in her desires, hopes, and goals. Similarly, common sense indicates that the most egregious racists are race-haters. Certainly, the paradigmatic racist is: the Nazi, the Klansman, the White-supremacist 'Skinhead,' the slave-driver. Hatred, I think, is not itself necessary; some lesser forms of racial disregard—contempt and callous indifference, for instance—suffice for racism. The fact remains that racism lies primarily in the heart, that is, in hopes, fears, joys, desires, and intentions. Of course, it need not remain there. Normally, racism gets out to infect the racist's behavior, and when the racist exercises institutional authority, or when racists design social practices, the racial disregard that constitutes racism can become institutionalized and corrupt the operations of social systems and practices as well.[18]

Understanding racism as race-based ill will (or a race-based deficiency in good-will) has advantages. It explains how racism, while having its primary occurrence in individuals' hearts, can also infect their beliefs and actions. Moreover, it explains how group and institutional behavior, policies, and practices can be racist. It correctly classifies such paradigms of racism as the Nazi and the Klansman. Unlike attempts to understand racism in terms of effects, however, it need not extend the charge to cover antiracist groups and undertakings simply because they prove counterproductive. Before we proceed to see how sexism would look if modeled on such an understanding of racism, however, we should examine how feminists have understood sexism. Since they do not agree on what sexism is, as with racism I will closely investigate one especially sophisticated, influential, and time-honored philosophical suggestion on how to conceptualize it.

III. FRYE ON SEXISM AND SEXISTS

In an article early in the career of the new academic feminism, and reprinted since, Marilyn Frye offers distinct and seemingly independent accounts of (1) some*thing*'s being sexist and of (2) some*one*'s being *a* sexist. About what makes a thing to be sexist, she writes, "The term 'sexist' in its core and perhaps most fundamental meaning is a term that characterizes anything that creates, constitutes, promotes, or exploits any irrelevant or impertinent marking of the distinctions between the sexes." She adds it "is commonly applied to specific acts or behavior or to certain institutional processes, laws, customs, and so forth."[19] About what it is for someone to be a sexist, she writes, "One would standardly characterize a person as a sexist in virtue of his sexist beliefs, opinions, convictions, and principles. A person might also be called a sexist in virtue of his acts and practices, but in general only if they are seen as associated with sexist beliefs.... Speaking quite generally, sexists are those who hold certain sorts of general beliefs about sexual differences and their consequences." These beliefs "would, for instance, support the view that physical differences between the sexes must always make for significant social and economic differences between them in any human society" and can be summed up in the "simple proposition: Males are innately superior to females."

Frye offers sophisticated accounts of what sexism is and of what a sexist is. Unfortunately, these accounts may not be consistent in their implications. The two accounts seem to lead to different and potentially inconsistent accounts of, at least, X's (i) being a sexist belief, (ii) being a sexist person, and (iii) being a sexist action. Should we say, for example, that a belief is a sexist belief when it "creates [or] promotes" irrelevant consideration of sex, as Frye's account of what makes a thing sexist implies? Or should we call it a sexist belief just when it can be "represented by the simple proposition: Males are innately superiority to females," as the account of what makes someone to be a sexist requires? In short, is a belief sexist because of what it *is* (that is, by the proposition that "represents" it) or because of what it *causes*? Frye winds up committed to both; but they are plainly different and open to inconsistent implications.[20]

Similar questions arise for her account of what makes people sexists. Let us assume that a person who is a sexist is a sexist person. Is someone a sexist person because of what she "promotes or creates"? Or is it what she believes that makes her a sexist? An affirmative answer to the former follows from Frye's account of what it is for something to be a sexist such-and-such, and an affirmative answer to the latter follows from her account of what it is for someone to be a sexist.

51

In addition to problems of inconsistency in her accounts of sexist belief and sexist persons, consider her view of sexist conduct. Frye says, "A person might also be called a sexist in virtue of his acts and practices, but in general only if they are seen as associated with sexist beliefs." But must not the actions on whose basis a person is properly called a sexist themselves be sexist actions? It seems so, and Frye herself at this point speaks of "sexist behavior" even in non-sexists (agents who are not sexists). However, if so, then our question arises again. Is my behavior sexist when it is duly associated with my sexist beliefs, as what she says here suggests? Or when it "promotes [or] creates" irrelevant marking of sex difference, as her general account of what makes things sexist commits her to?

Finally, notice, that Frye's account of sexism, like Wasserstrom's, implausibly allows that someone and her efforts can be sexist simply because of bad luck in their unintended and perhaps unforeseeable effects. Even feminists' antisexist measures (e.g., forming an all-women's support group or a pro-woman advocacy group) might counterproductively create or promote an irrelevant (marking of) sexual difference. That might make them ill-advised, but it does not mean that they are sexist, *pace* Frye. Whether a person and her conduct are sexist is never just a matter of bad luck.

GARCIA

IV. WHAT IS SEXISM, IF IT IS LIKE RACISM?

Alison Jaggar has suggested a more promising account of sexism. She writes that in addition to "institutional sexism [which] is a social disadvantage which attaches to individuals of one sex or the other as a result of a certain way of institutionalizing activity," there is also "individual sexism which occurs when a certain individual or group of individuals express hatred or contempt for an individual or group of (usually) the other sex by an act of hostility which may or may not be violent but which is not part of a socially stabilized pattern of discrimination."[21] We need not endorse Jaggar's view that individual sexism need, for some reason, exclude institutionalized sexism, nor with her assumption that sexism need be something that "occurs." What is appealing in Jaggar's view is her suggestion that sexism is necessarily connected to something like "hatred or contempt." However, I see no reason to follow her in thinking the attitude must be expressed for there to be sexism. Sexism, if it is like racism, exists in the attitudes of someone filled with hatred or contempt, whether or not she expresses it in acts of hostility. It is enough that she be hostile in a certain way.[22] If a man hates or disdains women as such, but never has opportunity to express this attitude in hostile acts towards them (perhaps he is part of an all-male ship's crew or prison population), this does not get him off the hook of *being* a sexist, even if he never treats women hostilely.

If sexism is like racism, then, it consists in sex-based disregard or ill will. Such an understanding of sexism has certain advantages. Feminists aim to improve the lot of women, and since they see sexism as their special enemy we can reasonably expect sexism to be a stance of opposition to women's welfare.[23] What is important for our purposes here is that it is only when so conceived that sexism is, as those who coined the term thought of it as being, a close structural relative of racism. That important fact highlights a second advantage to this sort of approach. When thought of as a certain kind of ill will (or, again like racism, as a deficit of goodwill), sexism is—like racism, xenophobia, and anti-Semitism—something that is obviously immoral. Appreciation of the central moral significance of such attitudes is one of the chief contributions of the recent revival of virtues-based moral theory. Since sexism was identified in order to condemn it and provide a clearer focus on what it is that demands censure, reform, and elimination, taking sexism as a vicious attitude helps the concept do its work.[24]

Thought of as hostility to women in the form of hatred or contempt, 'sexism' seems to be merely a new name for misogyny. This result, however, need not trouble us. Though the term 'sexism' is new, it is no part of feminist thought to insist that what the term refers to is itself new. Quite the contrary. However, there is a problem in that sexism appears to include phenomena not usually considered parts or types of misogyny. Some people count insensitivity to women's needs, feelings, etc., as forms of sexism; yet it seems excessively severe to characterize much of this as "hatred or contempt." These people may need reminding that much insensitivity has moral import only in that it is something the morally virtuous person will try to eliminate from her attitude as undesirable, not in the stronger sense that it is itself vicious. Moreover, sometimes the fault lies less in X's insensitivity than in Y's oversensitivity. Still, the term 'insensitivity' itself means a lack of feeling, and any adequate account of virtues and the moral life will sometimes fault people not only for how they do or do not think and act, but also for how they do or do not feel.

A related, but more complicated, problem is that sexism is also thought to include paternalistic attitudes towards women, attitudes of solicitude and even protection. Yet this is not the way we think of misogynists. (Nor racists.) As Laurence Thomas trenchantly reminds us, while the sexist may plausibly claim to be trying to protect women, to shield them from adult responsibilities, the White racist is not normally trying to protect Black people, even on her own (perhaps perverse) understanding of their interest.[25] So, we shall need briefly to examine the nature of sexist paternalism before we can say whether reconceiving sexism along the lines I have sketched really can adequately delineate the social phenomenon with which it is concerned or successfully model that phenomenon on racism.

V. PATERNALISM, DISRESPECT, AND SELF-DECEPTION IN SEXISM

The root idea of paternalism is that A treats B paternalistically when A treats B as if B were a child under A's authority, overriding B's preferences, making the principal decisions in B's life. (Not merely like A's (possibly full-grown) offspring, that is, but like A's child.) Paternalism is not always objectionable. Children need to be treated paternalistically by those responsible for them. It is easy to see why paternal treatment breeds frustration and resentment, but what makes it immoral? When B is a responsible adult and A treats her as if she were something less than that, then A may be violating B's dignity by degrading her. Then A's act violates the virtue of justice in its disrespect. However, A only violates justice by treating B paternalistically if A does or should see B's true stature. When A is innocently unaware of B's status as a responsible moral agent, then neither A nor her action is unjust, for there is no viciousness through mere accident, mistake, or error.

Paternalistic behavior, then, is sometimes unjust. It is when someone who treats a responsible adult paternalistically knows what she is doing or is morally at fault in not knowing it. How is this sort of injustice related to something like Jaggar's "hatred or contempt"? I think that, like them, it is a type of ill will. Hatred is the opposite of love. Since loving someone is devoting one's will, affection, and desires to her welfare—in short, goodwill—hating her is comparably devoting oneself to depriving her of goods—that is, ill will. On that basis, we can say that the kind of disrespect and degradation that characterizes such paternalism as that of Thomas' condescending, "protective" sexism is vicious insofar as it is rooted in disrespect, a failure to *regard* and to *treat* members of one sex, S1, as having the full rights and status that it is one of the marks of the virtuous to accord all people. Such lack of respect, as such, is a failure of goodwill and thus an offense against the moral virtue of benevolence, in that it manifests morally insufficient concern that S1s enjoy such

53

GARCIA

goods of status, deference, and opportunity. The paternalist sexist acts viciously insofar as she is uninterested in securing to those in one sex these autonomy goods, and this failure to will goods of a certain sort is a failure in (and offense against) that moral virtue we call goodwill or benevolence.

When paternalism is immoral, then, the paternalist aims to secure another some good by depriving her of others. It is goodwill pursued through willing evils: doing evil that good may come. This way of understanding the morality of paternalism does more than provide a conception of sexist paternalism that fits a wider account of sexism as modeled on racism. It also is preferable for theoretical reasons both to understanding immoral paternalism as pursuing benevolence by violating an independent principle of autonomy—a conception now common in medical ethics— and to understanding vicious paternalism as embodying an 'excess' of benevolence in violation of some quasi-Aristotelian mean. The former account, insofar as it leaves us with a conflict among basic principles, threatens to deprive us of rational ways of resolving the controversies surrounding paternalism. The latter account, inspired by Aristotle's doctrine of the mean, fails because benevolence itself is a moral virtue—not an Aristotelian one, of course, but a close relative of what Christians call charity—and thus not the sort of thing of which Aristotle said there could be a vicious excess.

This approach to sexism works well in explaining the immorality of failing to treat as an adult someone we know to be one. It threatens, however, to exculpate and even exonerate us in acting paternalistically toward those whose status as responsible, capable adults we do not recognize. What can be the *moral* fault in this mere *cognitive* lapse? Here, I think, some remarks of Frye's can help. We criticized her analysis of sexism above. However, she is at pains to distinguish sexism from a supposedly different phenomenon, which she initially calls 'male chauvinism.' "[T]he feminist" who used this (now somewhat dated) term, according to Frye, was "accusing the male chauvinist of...acting as though what really is *only* a group of human beings [viz., males] were all there is to the human race...." For reasons that need not concern us here, Frye prefers the term 'phallism' to the then-current 'male chauvinism.' She bluntly attributes to 'phallism' "a picture of humanity as consisting [only] of males."[26] She elucidates, "The phallist approaches females with a superiority and condescension that we all take more or less appropriate to encounters with members of other species.... The phallist does not treat women as persons."

While Frye thinks some phallists are simply malicious, "it is more common for a person to shrink from such blatant immorality, guarding his conscience with a protective membrane of self-deception. The phallist can arrange things so he does not experience females as persons...." After summarizing some strategies for so arranging things, Frye talks of "the phallist's *refusal* to experience women as persons." (Emphasis added.) This reference to a refusal to face the facts ties Frye's account of so-called 'phallism' to Gordon's account of racism as involving 'bad

54

faith,' which he sees as a way of hiding from oneself. Plainly, self-deception is an attractive way of hiding from truths whose recognition threatens our interests, as recognition of women as equals threatens the interests of those (of both sexes) who benefit in various ways from the degradation of women. This self-deception to which Frye and Gordon direct our attention, then, can be seen as rooted in the sexist's or the racist's perceived self-interest and, more important, mediated through the sexist's or racist's disregard for, and even hostility to, the competing interests of others. Such self-deception would secure the connection we needed between the sexist (or racist) paternalist's failure to see those of another sex (or race) as fully responsible and offenses against the moral virtue of benevolence.[27] If this is correct, such sexism can now be understood as immoral for the same reason other forms are: it is infected by vicious disregard for others, that is, by a form of ill will, such as hatred or contempt, where contempt includes that form of ill will or non-benevolence directed especially against someone's enjoying the goods of status and their requisite deference.

I have suggested that, once we properly understand racism as race-based ill will (or a racially-based deficit in goodwill), it follows that, if we are to vindicate the early feminists' view that sexism is structurally similar to racism, then sexism must also consist not in a social system, practice, or belief, but in sex-based contempt or other ill will. The good news in this is that the immorality of sexism is insured and clarified. It consists in vicious failures in the moral virtue of benevolence.

This understanding of sexism has implications for social discussion. If sexism, that is, misogyny, consists in having certain hostile feelings, desires, and intentions toward those of one of the sexes, then, while this may explain in some instances why this or that person believes a certain proposition about the differences between women and men and their proper social implications, by itself it generally does nothing to show the truth or falsity of these propositions. Of course, some such propositions—as that the rights of women are systematically less important than those of men—may seem plausible only to the vicious. Such theses aside, there remain many currently controversial claims about sex differences. That means that, as far as morality and sexism are concerned, the jury may still be out on the supposed complementarity of the sexes, on the special suitability of those of one or the other sex for certain roles, on the need of society or of individuals for sex-differentiation in how children are reared, directed, educated, and so on. There need be nothing on its face insulting or hostile to women in entertaining these ideas. On those matters of fact, we really are dealing with opinions—not vices—and we will need to hear various views with an unprejudiced mind. I think Dinesh D'Souza is wrong in thinking that racism (and, therefore, sexism, if it is like racism) is ultimately just an opinion.[28] However, he is right to insist that opinions are best combatted on their merits rather than through impugning, with charges of sexism or racism, the morality of those who may offer them. A given person S's holding a proposition p may be a matter of S's vicious self-deception. (Though normally S

55

is entitled to the benefit of the doubt.) Whether it is or is not, we will need to marshal epistemic reasons against (the truth of) *p* itself, if we are to feel secure in rejecting *p*, not just moral reasons against holding *p* true. To do otherwise is to prove the critics of 'political correctness' right when they complain that oversensitivity to sex (and race) stifles intellectual freedom and much-needed social inquiry.[29,30]

NOTES

1. Attributed to a 1965 comment of D.M. Leet's, in Jane Mills, *Womanwords: a Dictionary of Words about Women* (New York: Macmillan, 1989), *s.v.* "Sexism/Sexist," p. 214. On the analogy with racism, "[S]exism…[is a t]erm constructed by analogy with racism…" Lisa Tuttle, ed., *Encyclopedia of Feminism* (New York: Facts on File/Pletus, 1986), *s.v.* 'sexism,' p. 292. "[The term 'sexism' was] coined during the feminist renaissance of the sixties, probably by analogy with the term racism." Mary Anne Warren, *The Nature of Woman* (Inverness: Edgepress, 1980), p. 424. (I owe this quotation to Cheris Kramarae and Paula Treichler, eds., *A Feminist Dictionary* (Boston: Pandora, 1985), *s.v.* "sexism," p. 412.)

2. Many would nowadays prefer to say "gender" where I have said "sex." I will not get into the issues surrounding the supposed "social construction" of gender and its supposed difference from sex, and will use the terms interchangeably.

3. Mills, *Womanwords*, attributes the former quotation to S. Vanauken and the latter to C. Bird. Both remarks are dated 1968.

4. The former quotation is attributed to Ambalvaner Sivanandan in Robert Miles, *Racism* (London: Routledge, 1989), p. 53. David Theo Goldberg critically treats the widely held view that racism must be irrational because it consists in attending to race in cases where it should be clear that race is irrelevant, in Goldberg, *Racist Culture* (Cambridge: Blackwell, 1993).

5. Claudia Card, "On Race, Racism, and Ethnicity," in *Overcoming Racism and Sexism*, Linda Bell and David Blumenfeld, eds., (Lanham, MD: Rowman and Littlefield, 1994) pp. 141–152.

6. Deborah King, "Double Jeopardy," in Helen Tierney, ed., *Women's Studies Encyclopedia* vol. I (New York: Greenwood, 1989), pp. 111–113.

7. "Although men also claim to be victims of sexism, either in personal relationships or in regard to affirmative action programmes, this is more accurately known as 'inverse sexism' or 'reverse sexism,' and is actually a response to the institutionalized sexism which oppresses all women." Tuttle, *Encyclopedia*, p. 292.

On institutional racism, see Kwame Ture and Charles Hamilton, *Black Power* (New York: Vintage, 1992); reissue, with new Afterwards, of 1967 edition.

8. Thus, "sexism" is variously defined as, for example: (i) "Thought or practice…which assumes women's inferiority to men…." (Jennifer Hornsby, "Sexism," in Ted Honderich, ed., *Oxford Companion to Philosophy* (New York: Oxford University Press, 1995), p. 824); (ii) "[A]ttitudes or conditions that promote stereotyping of social roles based on gender; discrimination based on sex…." (Alan and Theresa Von Altendorf, *Isms: a Compendium of Concepts, Doctrines, Traits, and Beliefs* (Memphis: Mustang, 1991), *s.v.* "sexism," p. 278); (iii) "[D]iscrimination or bias against people because of their sex, particularly used to denote discrimination against women." (Michele Paludi, "Sexism," in Tierney, ed., *Women's Studies Encyclopedia*, p. 335); (iv) "A social relationship in which males have authority over females." (Attributed to Linda Phelps in Kramarae and Treichler, eds., *Feminist Dictionary*, p. 411); (v) "Behavior, policy, language, or other action of men or women which expresses the institutionalized, systematic, comprehensive, or consistent view that women are inferior." (Quoted without attribution in Kramarae and Treichler, eds., *Feminist Dictionary*, p. 411).

9. Richard Wasserstrom, "Racism, Sexism, and Preferential Treatment: an Approach to the Topics," *UCLA Law Review* (February, 1977), pp. 581–615. Reprinted, in part, as "Racism and Sexism," in Sharon Bishop and Marjorie Weinzweig, eds., *Philosophy and Women* (Belmont: Wadsworth, 1979), pp. 5–20. Page references are to this reprint.

10. It seems there may be racism in individuals' attitudes even when there are such institutional and ideological arrangements, should those arrangements fail in either their task of creating or that of maintaining such an institutional and ideological system (despite their being meant to do harm). Maybe the system fails to be self-perpetuating, as Wasserstrom requires, either because it passes away or because it is maintained only by external forces operating independently of the system of beliefs and institutions itself.

11. In any case, these remarks about power would need to be generalized before they were acceptable, so that, in another possible world, at least, racism might work to concentrate power in the hands of white females, or black males, or black females.

12. Wasserstrom defines "overt racism" so that it "assign[s] benefits and burdens in such a way as to bestow an unjust benefit upon a member or members of the racially dominant group or an unjustified burden upon members of the racial groups that are oppressed." This seems to exclude any *possibility* of state racism against the disadvantaged group. So-called "reverse discrimination," then, *cannot* be racist in principle and of necessity. To see the moral absurdity of restricting racism to the powerful, consider Dinesh D'Souza's nice point that such a restriction immediately exonerates Klansmen and "skinheads" (who are unlikely nowadays to serve, say, as CEOs, DAs, etc., less likely, at least, than are African Americans) from the charge of racism. Dinesh D'Souza, *The End of Racism* (New York: Free Press, 1995), p. 410.

13. Jesse Jackson certainly agrees with him. He told the University of California regents, as they debated eliminating affirmative action programs in admissions, hiring, and contracts, "To ignore race and sex is racist and sexist." B. Drummond Ayres, "California Board Ends Preferences in College System," *New York Times*, July 21, 1995, pp. A1, A14.

14. See Plato, *The Republic*, 415.

15. For additional discussion of this, see the more developed argument in J.L.A. Garcia, "Current Conceptions of Racism," *Journal of Social Philosophy*, 1997 forthcoming.

16. See Kwame Anthony Appiah, "Racisms," in David Theo Goldberg, ed., *Anatomy of Racism* (Minneapolis: University of Minnesota Press, 1990), pp. 3–17; Kwame Anthony Appiah, *In My Father's House* (New York: Oxford University Press, 1992); and Lewis Gordon, Jr., *Bad Faith and Antiblack Racism* (Atlantic Highlands: Humanities, 1995).

17. Appiah's view of racism and its types commits him to the implausible claim that efforts among oppressed races to advance racial solidarity or promote racial loyalty are not just ill-advised or troublesome but themselves racist, even if they encourage no racial hostility and avoid claims of racial superiority. (See my critique in "Current Conceptions of Racism," *op. cit.*) Lewis Gordon confusedly identifies racism both with a certain kind of choice and with a certain kind of belief. Moreover, his claim that the racist believes either "that one's own race is the only race qualified to be considered human or…is superior to other races," if taken (as the context suggests) as a commitment to the superiority of one's race to *all* other races, seems, implausibly, both: (i) to exonerate from racism a race-hater who sees her race as superior to some others but not to all, and (ii) to exclude any possibility that someone might internalize ambient racism to the extent of becoming a racist against her own group.

18. I develop such an account of racism and tie it to the moral virtues and virtues-based moral theory in Garcia, "The Heart of Racism," *Journal of Social Philosophy* 27, 1996: 5–45, and in Leonard Harris, ed., *Racism* (New York: Humanities, forthcoming).

19. Marilyn Frye, "Male Chauvinism: a Conceptual Analysis," in Robert Baker and Frederick Elliston, eds., *Philosophy and Sex* (Buffalo: Prometheus, 1975). Reprinted in Bishop and Weinzweig, eds., *Philosophy and Women*, pp. 26–33.

20. By the way, is the "support" that Frye here claims sexist beliefs must lend views about how to shape society meant to be: (a) causal influence, or (b) epistemic/probative endorsement, or (c) moral justification? Perhaps (a) jibes reasonably well with her claim that what makes something sexist is what it "promotes" (p. 26); but (b) and (c) do not, again raising the specter of inconsistent implications. Of course, it is true that (a) seems to work principally only through (b) or (c). After all, how does one's holding such a belief about the nature of the sexes influence her social views except either by confirming her confidence in them or by offering moral rationalization for acting from them, i.e., removing moral qualms about mistreating women? The difficulty is that the epistemic or moral support [(b) and (c)] that a sexist belief, *p*, can lend beliefs about social organization appears to be just as important for determining whether *p* is sexist. This raises perhaps the most troubling question for this part of Frye's account. Why should whether a belief counts as sexist depend at all on its relationships to other beliefs or to actions? Why is that not determined by, for example, its relationship to a preference that some people suffer because of their sex?

21. Alison Jaggar, "On Sexual Equality," *Ethics* 84 (1974); reprinted in Bishop and Weinzweig, eds., *Philosophy and Women*, pp. 77–87.

22. Jaggar presumably means that, in sexism, this interpersonal hostility is sex-based. She does not say that, but without that assumption her stated position commits her to the overly broad view that any expression of hatred or contempt for someone (of the opposite sex, at least) is sexist.

I should point out that throughout I use feminine pronouns in a gender-neutral way and continue to do so when talking here of sexists. Even if most sexists are male, that fact no more requires using male pronouns for sexists in general than the fact that most physicians are male mandates use of male pronouns for physicians in general.

23. Thus, Jaggar, for example, writes, "[A]ll feminists, by definition, agree that sexism should be eliminated." *A Feminist Dictionary*, Kramarae and Treichler, eds., attributes to Liz Stanley and Sue Wise the claim that sexism "Is the name of the problem addressed by feminism." (*s.v.* "sexism," p. 412) *The Encyclopedia of Feminism*, Tuttle, ed., says that "all feminists are agreed that sexism is the evil that feminism exists to fight." (p. 293) "Feminism," in turn is typically said to "refer…to belief in and commitment to equal rights and opportunities for women." (Tierney, ed., *Women's Studies Encyclopedia, s.v.* "feminism," p. 139).

24. It is important that sexism be something that is in itself immoral. Conceiving of it merely as an opinion about the sexes invites a response analogous to that D'Souza makes to his own insistence that racism is an opinion about the (inequality of the) races: if it is an opinion, then it is not a sin and it needs to be combatted with counter-arguments, not moral preachments. But whatever sexism is, it is morally vicious. The U.S. National Conference of Catholic Bishops, whom not all would expect to be especially sensitive to sexism, are quite clear about this. They define sexism as "unjust discrimination against women" and consider it a sin. *Strengthening the Bonds of Peace: a Pastoral Reflection on Women in the Church and in Society* (NCCB, 1995).

25. Laurence Thomas, "Sexism and Racism: Some Conceptual Differences," *Ethics* 90 (1980), pp. 239–250.

26. Frye, "Male Chauvinism." Frye's grounds for preferring the term 'phallism' to 'male chauvinism' are complex. She begins by: (1) defining a chauvinism as an excessive identification with one's country (or religion, etc.); (2) claiming that one can identify only with what is a person or "pseudo-person"; and (3) taking the abilities to act as a unit, to relate in a person-like way to other comparable beings, and to stand subject to moral assessment as marks of pseudo-personhood. She then reasons that, since (4) the male segment of humanity does not have these characteristics and thus (5) is not a "pseudo-person" (6) one cannot

really identify with it and *a fortiori* cannot identify with it excessively. Hence, (7) the phenomenon called "male chauvinism" "is not a chauvinism," and so would be better designated by another name. Whatever the merits of the other premises (#2, 3 and 4), chauvinism is better understood if we follow a standard dictionary in taking it to consist in excessive favoritism for one's country (etc.). (Notice that identification only matters at all here insofar as we are specially devoted to what we identify with.) There is no reason to think we can favor or excessively favor only "pseudo-persons," so I see no parallel argument to #7, once we replace #1 with a better definition of chauvinism (such as that from a dictionary). If we should drop talk of 'male chauvinism,' it is because the term is dated and murky, and, pace Frye, the phenomenon it picks out is better understood as merely a type or aspect of sexism.

27. Self-deception is a problematic concept. For discussion of some difficulties, see Brian McLaughlin, "Exploring the Possibility of Self-Deception in Belief," in Brian McLaughlin and Amelie Rorty, eds., *Perspectives on Self-Deception* (Berkeley: University of California Press, 1988), pp. 29–62.

28. O'Sousa, *End of Racism*, pp. 525–556.

29. See Glenn Loury, "Self-Censorship in Public Discourse," in Glenn Loury, *One By One, From the Inside Out*, (New York: Free Press, 1995) chap. 8, pp. 145–182.

30. I am grateful to Catherine McKeen for bibliographic information; and to George Rudebusch for discussion of these topics, especially his suggestions about, and objections to, my understanding of paternalism.

59

GARCIA

RACISM AND SEXISM:

The Common Ground

James P. Sterba

chapter 4

ADVOCATES OF feminist justice seek to remedy the injustice of sexism, while advocates of racial justice seek to remedy the injustice of racism. In this paper, I will argue that it would be a mistake to pursue either of these forms of justice alone, given that they are both theoretically and practically connected. What is required, I argue, is their joint realization. In the longer work from which this paper is drawn, I go on to argue that for similar reasons both homosexual justice and multicultural justice should be pursued together with feminist justice and racial justice as well.

THE THEORETICAL CONNECTION

As it turns out, both the sexism opposed by advocates of feminist justice and the racism opposed by advocates of racial justice are supported by similar theoretical arguments. The more blatant argument begins by noting certain differences between either individuals or groups. It then claims that these differences are grounds for regarding some individuals or groups as superior to other individuals or groups. This superiority is then claimed to legitimate the domination of some individuals or groups by other individuals or groups.[1] In each case, the theoretical argument moves from a claim of difference to a claim of superiority and then to a claim of domination. In the case of sexism, the biological differences between men and women, or other differences that are claimed to be linked to these biological differences, are said to be grounds for regarding men as superior to women. This superiority is then claimed to legitimate the domination of women by men. In the case of racism, specifically the principal form of racism in the United States,[2] the biological differences between whites and blacks, or other differences that are claimed to be linked to these biological differences, are said to be grounds for regarding whites as superior to blacks. This superiority is then claimed to legitimate the domination of blacks by whites. In response, feminist justice and racial justice claim that neither of these forms of domination can be justified.

Sometimes, however, the theoretical argument for sexism or racism takes a less blatant form. This argument begins by renouncing forms of domination used in the past as unjustified. Simply to deny people equal opportunity on the basis of their sex or race is claimed to be wrong by this version of the argument. But the argument further claims that people now, for the most part, are no longer denied equal opportunity on the basis of sex or race. Accordingly, it is claimed that the ways that men are still favored over women or whites over blacks must either be grounded in a legitimate superiority of one over the other or be a residue of past injustices which cannot be removed without doing additional injustice. Of course, those who employ this form of argument do not usually think of themselves as supporting sexism or racism, but, as I shall show, they are nonetheless.

There is no denying that under current societal structures, men are still favored over women and whites over blacks. In the case of women in the United States, forty-six percent of women are either subjected to rape or attempted rape at some point during their lives, between a quarter and a third of women are battered in their homes by husbands and lovers, fifty percent of women in the workplace say they have been sexually harassed, and thirty-eight percent of little girls are sexually molested inside or outside the family.[3] Women employed full time still earn only $.70 for every dollar men earn. In the world at large, women are responsible for 66% of all work done (paid and unpaid), yet they receive only 10% of the salaries.[4] Men own 99% of all the property in the world, and women only 1%. All of this shows that men are clearly favored over women.

In the case of blacks in the United States, almost half of all black children live in poverty. Black unemployment is twice that of whites. The infant mortality rate in many black communities is twice that of whites. Blacks are twice as likely as whites to be robbed, seven times more likely to be murdered or to die of tuberculosis. A male living in New York's Harlem is less likely to reach 65 than a resident of Bangladesh. Blacks are 50% of the maids and garbage collectors but only 4% of the managers and 3% of the physicians and lawyers.[5] While one study of the nation's ten largest cities showed that blacks and whites rarely interact outside the workplace, another study showed that about 86% of available jobs do not appear in the classified advertisements and 80% of executives find their jobs through networking, thus showing the importance for employment of contacts outside the workplace.[6] According to another study, black children adopted by white middle class families score significantly better on the Wechsler Intelligence Scale than black children adopted by black middle class families, and the scoring difference is of the magnitude typically found between the average scores of black and white children.[7] Thus, there is plenty of evidence to show that, at least in the United States, whites are significantly favored over blacks.

Of course, whether the more blatant or less blatant argument for sexism or racism is employed depends on how plausible it is to claim that people now are no longer denied equal opportunity by one or another of these forms of domination, but sometimes this claim is made about men and women and about whites and blacks. Only then is the less blatant argument for sexism and racism employed, maintaining as it does that the ways that men are still favored over women, and whites over blacks, must either be grounded in a legitimate superiority of one over the other or be a residue of past injustices which cannot be removed without doing additional injustice. Still, it is difficult to defend this argument because data like we noted above makes it difficult to maintain that equal opportunity currently exists either between men and women or between whites and blacks. As a consequence, those who employ this form of the argument usually try to show that most of the inequality that does exist is a residue of past injustices which cannot be removed without doing additional injustice. Specifically, they attack both affirmative action and comparable worth as attempts to correct for past injustices that produce additional injustice.

AFFIRMATIVE ACTION

Now affirmative action with respect to women and minorities is a policy of preferring qualified women and minority candidates who have been disadvantaged by past injustices over equally or more qualified white male candidates who have not been similarly disadvantaged. In fact, it is generally the case that the white male candidates who are passed over by a policy of affirmative action have themselves benefited from past injustices suffered by women and minority candidates (e.g., unequal educational opportunities). To be justified, however, such a policy of affirmative action must favor only candidates whose qualifications are such that when their selection or appointment is combined with a suitably designed educational enhancement program, they will normally turn out, within a reasonably short time, to be as qualified as, or even more qualified than, their peers. Such candidates have the potential to be as qualified as or more qualified than their peers, but that potential has not yet been actualized because of past injustices. Affirmative action with its suitably designed educational enhancement program purports to actualize just that potential. In this way, persons who receive affirmative action are like runners in a race who, for a time, are forced to compete at a disadvantage with other runners, e.g., by having weights tied to their legs, but then, later, are allowed to compete against those other runners by first removing the weights and then receiving some special assistance for an appropriate period of time so that the results of the race will now turn out to be fair. Affirmative action, therefore, is a policy that is directed at only those women and minority candidates who are highly qualified yet because of past discrimination and prejudice are less qualified than they would otherwise be; it seeks to provide such candidates with a benefit that will nullify the effects of past injustices by enabling them to become as qualified as or more qualified than their peers.

Now affirmative action is said to lead to injustice for the following reasons:

(1) it harms those who receive it.
(2) it is directed at the wrong people.
(3) it is not directed at all of those who deserve it.
(4) it is unfair to the white males that it discriminates against.

In support of the first objection, Charles Murray claims that affirmative action harms those who receive it by putting women and minorities into positions for which they are not qualified.[8] Murray cites examples from his personal experiences and the personal experiences of others of women and minorities who were harmed in this way. In one example, a black woman is put into a position for which she lacks the qualifications; as a result, her responsibilities are reduced, rendering her job a dead-end position. Yet, according to our earlier account, when affirmative action has such an effect, it is not justified. To be justified, affirmative action must be directed at candidates whose qualifications are such that when their selection or appointment is combined with a suitable designed educational enhancement program, they will normally turn out, within a reasonably short time, to be as qualified as or even more qualified than their peers. So if affirmative action is properly carried out, it would not harm those who receive it.[9]

In support of the second objection, James Fishkin claims that affirmative action benefits the most qualified, who are actually the least deserving because they are the least discriminated against.[10] Yet the most qualified who benefit from affirmative action may not have been subjected to less discrimination; they may simply have resisted discrimination more vigorously. And even supposing the most qualified were subject to less discrimination in the past, why wouldn't affirmative action be the correct response to the degree of discrimination to which they were subjected? If we assume that affirmative action is provided only to those candidates whose qualifications are such that when their selection or appointment is actually combined with a suitably designed educational enhancement program, they will normally turn out, within a reasonably short time, to be as qualified as or even more qualified than their peers, then affirmative action does seem to be appropriately directed at the most qualified candidates of those who have suffered from past discrimination. Other forms of discrimination whose effects upon a person's qualifications and potential are even more detrimental would require correctives other than affirmative action, such as remedial education and job-training programs.

In support of the third objection that affirmative action is not directed at all those who deserve it, Carl Cohen claims:

> Compensatory affirmative action, if undertaken at all, must be undertaken for every person who qualifies on some reasonably objective standard, a standard free of racial (or sexual) orientation.[11]

Robert Simon agrees, maintaining that there are candidates besides women and minorities who have suffered from discrimination and prejudice or from simply being economically disadvantaged.[12] Cohen mentions Appalachian whites and impoverished Finns from upper Michigan as additional candidates for affirmative action.[13] Why should affirmative action not be directed at these candidates as well as at women and minorities?

Why not indeed! Surely if other individuals have suffered comparable hardships from discrimination and prejudice or from simply being economically disadvantaged, some remedy would be appropriate. So Cohen's and Simon's objection is not an objection to affirmative action *per se*, but rather an objection to affirmative action as a narrowly conceived rather than a broadly conceived program. So, in fact, Cohen's and Simon's analyses point to the need for a more broadly conceived affirmative action program.

It should be noted, however, that if affirmative action is to be extended in this way to deal with other injustices in society, it must become a larger program. The few positions that have been targeted for affirmative action candidates have been created with the idea of simply remedying injustices suffered by women and minorities. If we now wish to remedy other comparable injustices in society as well, we will need to create many more positions to deal with the increased scope of affirmative action. Properly understood, Cohen's and Simon's analyses point to the need for just such an expansion of affirmative action.

Nevertheless, there might be good moral grounds for using the law to correct for sexual and racial discrimination but not for discrimination against Appalachian whites and impoverished Finns from upper Michigan given that sexual and racial discrimination are two of the deepest and most pervasive forms of discrimination in our society. The law, it may be argued, should not be thought to be the instrument for correcting every injustice, but only for the deepest and most pervasive injustices.

In support of the fourth objection, Barry Gross claims that affirmative action is unfair to white males because it deprives them of equal opportunity by selecting or appointing women or minority candidates over more qualified white male candidates. To help fix ideas, consider the following two programs. Program A first hires women and minorities candidates who are qualified over equally or more qualified white male candidates and then puts them through a six-month training program, after which it lets go any trainees who are not as qualified as or more qualified than anyone else in the hiring pool. Program B first admits certain highly qualified women and minority candidates into a six-month training program for which white male candidates are not eligible, and then hires just those women and minority candidates who, after completing the program, are equally qualified with, or more qualified than, anyone else in the hiring pool. I take it that Gross would object to Program A because it involves hiring women and minority candidates who are less qualified, but he need not object to program B because he need not object to every attempt to compensate women and minorities for past discrimination, but only to programs, like Program A, which he believes to be unfair because they involve hiring woman and minority candidates who are less qualified over more qualified white male candidates.

In response, Bernard Boxill denies that affirmative action is unfair to white males who are passed over for affirmative action candidates. After all, although these white males may not actually have discriminated against women and minorities themselves, Boxill argues that they have benefited from the discrimination of others, for example, through unequal educational opportunities. Hence, women and minorities do deserve compensation for this unjust discrimination, and, moreover, affirmative action seems to be an appropriate form of compensation. It also is difficult to understand how the opponent of affirmative action could object to attempts to remedy past discrimination like Program A while accepting attempts like Program B given that they are so similar.

Of course, there are white males holding desirable positions in society who have benefited more from past discrimination than have the white males who would lose out to women or minority affirmative action candidates. So ideally an affirmative action program should be demanding sacrifices from these well-positioned white males as well. This could be done by requiring them to retire early, or by reducing their workweek in order to avoid having to lay off affirmative action hires, or by allowing affirmative action considerations to take precedence over seniority rules when actual layoffs become necessary.[14] Maybe we could target, among others, white male college professors who have taught for more than twenty years. Yet while it would be morally preferable to place the burdens of affirmative action on those who have benefited most from past discrimination, when the political power to do so is lacking it would still be morally permissible to place the burden primarily on white males who are competing for jobs and positions with affirmative action candidates, given that they still have benefited from past discrimination, although not as much as others.

COMPARABLE WORTH

While affirmative action is a policy of preferring qualified women and minority candidates who have been disadvantaged by past injustices, comparable worth is the policy of correcting for existing wage discrimination by providing equal pay for comparable work. Its implementation would require significant changes in existing income distributions. In the United States, only a few jobs are substantially integrated by sex. Of the 503 occupations listed in the U.S. census only 87 are integrated by sex, that is, are 30 to 50% female.[15] In addition, men in male-dominated occupations are usually paid more than women in female-dominated occupations. According to one study, men employed as stockroom attendants made much more than women employed as dental hygienists. In another study, women employed as school librarians were paid less than men employed as groundskeepers. While in each of these cases the women earned at least 20% less than the men, the women's jobs when evaluated in terms of skill, responsibility, effort, and working conditions were given equal or higher scores than the men's jobs with which they were compared. Nor are these isolated examples. In fact, it would be difficult to come up with a single example of a male job paying less than a comparable female job.[16] There is also evidence that racial as well as sex discrimination exists with respect to comparable jobs. In San Francisco, for example, job evaluations revealed that janitors, mostly minority males, received 97 evaluation points and $18,000 in pay, while truck drivers, mostly white males, had 98 evaluation points, but $27,000 in pay.[17] Consequently, paying women and minorities the same as white men earn in comparable jobs would involve a significant shift of income from men to women and from whites to blacks and other racial minorities.

Now comparable worth is objected to on grounds of justice for the following reasons:

(1) it undermines the free market.
(2) it eliminates nondiscriminatory wage gaps.
(3) it purports to compare jobs that cannot be compared.

In support of the first objection, Clifford Hackett argues that comparable worth would destroy the link between work and marketplace evaluation.[18] In the private sector, Hackett claims that this link is vital to keeping a company competitive. In government, he claims paying employees without regard to their cost in the local job market destroys confidence in government's ability to match the efficiency of business. Moreover, it could be argued that a free market itself eliminates discrimination, because if some employers discriminate against women, any other employer can save money by hiring women in men's jobs for less than they currently pay men in such jobs. Presumably, some profit-maximizing employers will do this, and when enough of them do it, the discrimination against women will cease. This tendency of a free market to undermine discrimination is minimized, however, due to the fact that many companies have internal labor markets that keep those outside the company from effectively competing for the higher paying jobs within the company. For such companies, the only impact a free market has is on entry-level positions. Thus, even if a free market were to function optimally with respect to these entry-level positions, it would take a very long time for the market to eliminate discrimination in employment all the way up the employment ladder.[19] In addition, as Elaine Sorensen points out, it took new laws and court rulings to eliminate some of the most blatant discriminatory practices that prevailed in the U.S. labor market in the past.[20] So here too with regard to equal pay for comparable work, we will need to constrain the free market in order to produce that result within a reasonable length of time.

With respect to the second objection to comparable worth, Solomon Polachek argues that much of the wage gap between women and men is due to nondiscriminatory factors for which no corrective is needed.[21] Some of the gap, it is claimed, is due to women's roles as wives and mothers which affect their pay by reducing their years of employment experience.[22] As evidence of this, it is pointed out that the gap between never-married men and never-married women is considerably smaller than the overall wage gap between women and men.[23] Advocates of comparable worth, however, argue that studies show that less than half of the wage gap between women and men can be accounted for by nondiscriminatory factors such as years of employment and willingness to choose a lower paying job if it provides more flexible working hours.[24] In addition, the smaller wage gap between never-married women and never-married men can be accounted for by the higher income potential of never-married women compared to never-married men.[25] So this still leaves a significant wage gap between women and men that can only be accounted for by discrimination.

In support of the third objection, Ellen Paul argues that job evaluations are inherently subjective, like comparing apples and oranges.[26] In response, it should be pointed out that companies already do compare people working at different jobs. In fact, two-thirds of American workers have their salaries set by job evaluations.[27] Hence, all that comparable worth requires is that the same job evaluation procedures currently used by management be used for different purposes, that is, to compare the work done by women and men in different jobs.

Moreover, comparable worth is a policy that has been put into practice. Twenty states have begun to pay comparable worth adjustments, and twenty-two other states and Washington, DC, have conducted or are conducting studies to determine if their wage-setting systems require comparable worth adjustments.[28] Other countries have made even greater strides through comparable worth programs. For example, in Australia women now earn more than $.80 for every dollar men earn, and in Sweden women now earn more than $.90 for every dollar men earn.[29]

Conceivably, people who raise these flimsy objections to affirmative action or comparable worth, all the while remaining culpably ignorant of the gross inequalities of opportunities that favor whites over blacks[30] or men over women do not think of themselves as racists or sexists, but I think that the unreasonableness of the stances they take convicts them of racism or sexism nonetheless. This is because one can be a racist and a sexist not only by unjustifiably intending harm to blacks and women but also by unjustifiably denying them important benefits that they should have, like affirmative action and comparable worth.

THE PRACTICAL CONNECTION

I have argued for a theoretical connection between feminist justice and racial justice. To achieve each of these forms of justice, we need to expose either a blatant argument that moves from a claim of difference to a claim of superiority and then to a claim of domination, or a less blatant argument that renounces past domination as unjustified but then claims that people are no longer denied equal opportunity on the basis of sex or race, so that whatever inequalities remain must either be grounded in a legitimate superiority or constitute a residue of past injustices which cannot be removed without doing additional injustice. In view of this theoretical connection between feminist justice and racial justice, the practical connection between the pursuit of these forms of justice is quite straightforward. It is that these forms of justice should be pursued together, as much as possible. This is because given the theoretical connection between these forms of justice, failure to pursue them together will be looked upon with suspicion and distrust by anyone whose cause is excluded. In fact, this has already happened. Failure to pursue racial justice along with feminist justice has left some black feminists, like Audre Lorde and bell hooks, wondering about the commitments of at least some advocates of feminist justice.[31] Suspicion and distrust can be aroused in the opposite direction as well. Advocates of racial justice may not express a commitment to feminist justice, thereby arousing doubts among feminists about the commitments of these advocates. There are also other reasons for recognizing a practical connection between these forms of justice: most obviously, the fact that 50% of those who need racial justice also need feminist justice as well.

Of course, it can be difficult to pursue both these forms of justice together. To build a political movement strong enough to effect the necessary changes, it may be necessary to focus attention on the pursuit of just one of these forms of justice. Yet even when this is necessary, it is possible to recognize the need for the other form of justice while still focusing attention primarily on only one form of justice. For example, advocates of feminist justice can recognize the need to achieve racial justice as well as feminist justice and vice versa. Thus, being as inclusive as possible, particularly given the theoretical connection between these forms of justice, can

69

serve to bring people together, and also to signal to supporters and nonsupporters alike the uncompromising justice of one's cause.

NOTES

1. For a discussion of this form of argument, see Karen Warren, "The Power and Promise of EcoFeminism," *Environmental Ethics* (1990).

2. Although I will normally be focusing on racism directed at African Americans, the argument I will be developing applies to all forms of racism.

3. Catherine MacKinnon, *Feminism Unmodified* (Cambridge: Harvard University Press, 1987).

4. Report on the World Conference of the United Nations Decade for Women, Copenhagen, July 14–30, 1981.

5. *New York Times*, July 12, 1994; Gerald Jaynes and Robin Williams, eds., *A Common Destiny* (Washington, DC: National Academy Press, 1989), p. 23; Andrew Hacker, *Two Nations* (New York: Ballantine Books, 1992) pp. 46, 231; Gertrude Ezorsky, *Racism and Justice* (Ithaca: Cornell University Press, 1991), p. 27.

6. For a discussion of these studies, see Ezorsky, pp. 14–18.

7. Ezorsky, p. 20. See also *New York Times*, October 19,1994. It also turns out that the I.Q. gap between Protestants and Catholics in Northern Ireland is the same as the gap between whites and blacks in the U.S. See *New York Times*, October 26, 1994.

8. Charles Murray, "Affirmative Racism," *The New Republic*, December 31, 1984.

9. In the example cited from Murray, the black woman appears to lack the qualifications so that even "a suitably designed educational enhancement program" would not have resulted in her becoming, within a reasonably short time, as qualified as or even more qualified than her peers. For that reason, affirmative action was not justified in this case.

10. James Fishkin, *Justice, Equal Opportunity, and the Family* (New Haven: Yale University Press, 1983), pp. 88, 89, 105.

11. Carl Cohen, *Against Racial Preference* (Lanham: Rowman and Littlefield, 1995), p. 40.

12. Robert Simon, "Affirmative Action and Faculty Appointments," in Steven Cahn, ed., *Affirmative Action and the University* (Philadelphia: Temple University Press, 1993), pp. 93–121.

13. Cohen also suggests, however, that the inclusiveness of such an affirmative action program might lead to its abandonment. He writes:

> If the complications grow excessive we may think it well to avoid the artificial inequalities likely to flow from inadequate data, or flaws in the compensatory calculation by refraining altogether from those calculations and again treating all applicants on the same footing.

But if this is Cohen's view, it would have the effect of simply freezing in place the effects of past injustices.

14. For a discussion of this issue, see Gertrude Ezorsky, *Racism and Justice*; Michel Rosenfeld, *Affirmative Action and Justice* (New Haven: Yale University Press, 1991); and Jeffrey Rosen, "Is Affirmative Action Doomed?" *The New Republic*, October 17, 1994.

15. Paula England, *Comparable Worth* (New York: Aldine De Gruyter, 1992), Chapter 1.

16. Ibid.

17. Julianne Malveaux, "Comparable Worth and Its Impact on Black Women," in Margarette Simms and Julianne Malveaux, eds., *Slipping Through the Cracks* (New Brunswick: Transaction Books, 1986), p. 56.

70

STERBA

18. Clifford Hackett, "Comparable Worth: Better From a Distance," *Commonweal*, May 31, 1985.

19. England, Chapter 2.

20. Elaine Sorenson, "The Comparable Worth Debate," in Robert Cherry, ed., *The Imperiled Economy, Book II* (New York: Union of Radical Political Economics, 1991).

21. Robert Williams and Lorence Kessler, *A Closer Look at Comparable Worth* (Washington, DC: National Foundation for the Study of Equal Employment Policy, 1984).

22. Of course, it is far from clear that these roles as they presently exist are not fashioned at least in part by discriminatory practices, but for the sake of argument here let us assume that they are not.

23. Solomon Polachek, "Women in the Economy," in *Comparable Worth: Issues for the 80s* (Washington, DC: U.S. Commission on Civil Rights, 1984), pp. 34–53.

24. For example, see Elaine Sorenson and Paula English, notes 19 and 20. Again, let us assume for the sake of argument that these are truly nondiscriminatory factors.

25. Ronnie Steinberg, "The Debate on Comparable Worth," *New Politics*, 1986, pp. 108–126.

26. For example, Ellen Paul, *Equity and Gender* (New Brunswick: Transaction Books, 1989), pp. 46, 51.

27. National Committee on Pay Equity, "The Wage Gap: Myths and Facts," in Paula Rothenberg, ed., *Race, Class and Gender*, 2nd ed. (New York: St. Martin's Press, 1992), p. 134.

28. Ibid.

29. Steven Willborn, *A Comparable Worth Primer* (Lexington: Lexington Books, 1986), p. 94.

30. In one survey over 60% of Americans claim that blacks already have equal opportunity, and presumably an even greater percentage think that women already have equal opportunity. See *New York Times*, July 12, 1994. According to a ABC Nightline poll done in the fall of 1994, 70% of whites believe that blacks have achieved equality with whites while 70% of blacks do not believe that they have achieved equality with whites.

31. Audre Lorde, "The Master's Tools Will Never Dismantle the Master's House," in *Sister Outsider* (Trumansburg, NY: The Crossing Press, 1984), pp. 110–114; bell hooks, "Sisterhood: Political Solidarity between Women," in Janet Kourany, James Sterba and Rosemarie Tong, eds., *Feminist Philosophies* (Englewood Cliffs: Prentice-Hall, 1992).

71

COMPARISON

"BUT WOULD THAT STILL BE ME?":

Notes on Gender, "Race," Ethnicity, As Sources of "Identity"

Anthony Appiah

IF YOU had asked most Anglo-American philosophers 25 years ago what conditions someone had to meet in order to be (identical with) me, they would, no doubt, have taken this (correctly) to be a conceptual question, and (incorrectly) inferred that it was to be answered a priori by reflection on the properties whose presence would have lead them to *say* that an imagined entity was Anthony Appiah. Since there are hardly any properties of persons whose absence we cannot intelligibly imagine, it was tempting to conclude that there was something odd about the very question.

In these enlightened post-Kripkean times, we think we know that it was the way of trying to answer the question that was odd. For we now think that the question whether (as we are likely to put it) some individual in a possible world is AA is an a posteriori question about a real essence. Some believe not only that this is a question about real essences, but that we know its answer:

that the real essence of a person is the chromosomal structure produced by the coition of their actual parents, a thesis that is the biological fleshing out of the metaphysical doctrine of the necessity of origins.

These are important issues in the semantics, metaphysics, and logic of identity, and they are centrally concerned with the identification of individuals across (metaphysically) possible worlds. But it seems to me that there is an equally important set of questions that recent theorizing has left to one side, a set of questions that can also be raised by asking, about a possible individual, "But would that still be me?" I want to argue that there is a sense of this question that is best answered in the "old-fashioned" conceptual way: and to get at what I have in mind, nothing could provide a better starting point than questions about "race," ethnicity, gender, and sex.

Consider, for the purposes of an initial example, the possibility that I might have been born a girl. Someone convinced of the chromosomal account of individual identity, and convinced, too, that what it is to be biologically female or male is to have the appropriate chromosomal structure, will argue that this is only an apparent possibility.[1] A female person could have been born to my parents when I was, if a different sperm and egg had met: but she would not have been me. It will be false, in this view, that I could have been born a woman.

I am prepared to concede all this for the purposes of argument; but there is a different question I might want to consider about a different possibility. Might I not, without any genetic modification, have been raised as a girl? This sort of thing certainly can happen; as when, for example, surgeons engaged in male circumcision remove the whole penis in error: rather than face a child with what—in our society—is bound to be the trauma of growing into a man without a penis, surgeons will often, in such circumstances, remove the testes from the abdomen, construct a facsimile of the female external genitalia, and ask the parents to bring the child back for hormone therapy in time to manage a facsimile of female puberty. If the good doctor who circumcised me had made such a mistake, couldn't I—this very metaphysical individual here—have been raised with a feminine (social) gender even though, on the chromosomal essentialist view, I was still of the male (biological) sex?[2]

My claim in this paper is that, while there may be a sense of the question "Would that have been me?" under which the answer to this question is "yes," there is another, intelligible reading under which it could, surely, be "no."

To get at that reading, consider the—admittedly, very different—possibility that I might seek to have a sex change, prior to which I could consider our guiding question about the possible future social female this metaphysical individual would then become. "Would that still be me?" I could ask. Now it seems to me that I can give either of two answers here, and that which answer I should give depends in large part on how central my being-a-man—my social masculinity and, perhaps, my possession of the biological appurtenances of maleness—is, as we would ordinarily say, to my identity. And it is in exploring this sense of the term 'identity' that we can come to learn why it is that there is a sense to this question——I shall call it the ethical sense—in which I may chose to answer it in the negative.

To say that I may choose, is to speak loosely. The issue is not really a matter of choice. What answer I should give to the question understood this way depends on how central my being a man is to my identity, not on how central I choose to make it. Transsexuals will surely answer in the affirmative; they often say that they were always of the "other" sex all along. For the chromosomal essentialist, this will be false. But a transsexual might (after reading Kripke) come to conclude that what he or she really had in mind was the different thought that their real identity, in the sense of the term I am now trying to explore, was that of the sex into which they were not born. And if I were a transsexual convinced of this I would say, contemplating the feminine person that I might become, "Yes, that would be me; in fact it would be the real me, the one I have always really been all along."

But what I am actually inclined to say is "No. A sex-change operation would make of this (metaphysical) person a different (ethical) person." And so there is a sense in which she would not be me.

As many people think of them, sex—female and male, the biological statuses—and gender—masculine and feminine, the social roles—provide the sharpest models for a distinction between the metaphysical notion of identity that goes with Kripkean theorizing and the notion of identity—the ethical notion—that I am seeking to explore. I say "as many people think of them" because the real world is full of complications. Not every human being is **XX** or **XY**. And there are people who are **XY** in whom the indifferent gonad was not prompted to form the characteristic male external genitalia; people whom it seems to me odd to regard as "really" biological males. Just as it would be odd to treat an **XX** person with male external genitalia, produced as the result of a burst of testosterone from a maternal tumor, as "really" biologically female. Once you have an inkling of how messy the real world of the biology of the reproductive organs is, you are likely, if you are wise, to give up the idea that there are just two biological sexes into which all human beings must fall. And this is important because most people do not make the distinctions (or know the facts) necessary to appreciate this, and thus have thoughts about what it is to be a man or a woman that involve concepts that essentially presuppose falsehoods about how people biologically are. Before someone has made a sex-gender conceptual distinction we cannot always say whether what these thoughts were about was one or the other: there are, so to speak, thoughts that no one who *had* made these distinctions could have.

But the general point can be made in cases far from the biological hard cases: if you consider a straightforward case of an **XY** biological infant, born with standard male internal and external genitalia, who is assigned a feminine gender as the result of early loss of his gonads, it is clear that such a person can agree to a Kripkean "metaphysical" identification as a biological male and insist on the centrality to her of her feminine gender identity, on being, so to speak, ethically a woman. But before I say more about what this means, it will help to have a couple of rather different cases before us.

Take next, then, so-called "racial" identity. Here the biological situation is much worse than in the case of sex. No coherent system of biological classification of people—no classification, that is, that serves explanatory purposes central to biological theory—corresponds to the folk-theoretical classifications of people into Caucasian, Negro, and such. This is not, of course, to deny that there are differences in morphology among humans: people's skins do differ in color. But these sorts of distinctions are not—as those who believe in races apparently suppose—markers of deeper biologically-based racial essences, correlating closely with most (or even many) important biological (let alone nonbiological) properties. I announce this rather than arguing for it, because it is hardly a piece of biological news, being part of a mainstream consensus in human biology. This means that here we cannot make use of an analog of the systematic sex-gender distinction: the underlying biology does not deliver something that we can use, like the sex chromosomes, as a biological essence for the Caucasian or the Negro.

But this does not mean that people cannot have ethical identities tied up with being, say, Euro- or African- or Asian-American; what it does mean, given that such identities often presuppose falsehoods about the underlying biology, is that, once the facts are in, a different theoretical account of those identities is required. From an external point of view, we can construct an account of what it is that people take to be grounds for assigning people to these racial categories. We can note that they are supposed to be asymmetrically based on descent: that "whites" in America are supposed to have no non-"white" ancestry, but that "blacks" and Asians may have non-"black" and non-Asian ancestry. But from the point of view of someone whose ethical identity is at stake, it is not going to be enough to remark simply how others classify them. And to see this we can return to our guiding question.

Let us suppose[3] that an American of African descent could be offered the possibility of losing all the morphological markers that are associated in this society with that descent. Her skin is lightened, her hair straightened, her lips thinned: she has, in short, all the services of Michael Jackson's cosmetic surgeon and more. Surely, in contemplating this possibility, she could ask herself whether, once these changes had occurred, the resulting ethical person "would still be me." And, so far as I can see, almost everyone who does contemplate this question in our society is likely to judge that, whether or not these changes are desirable, the answer here must be yes.

I am asserting here, therefore, a contrast between our attitudes to (ethical) gender and (ethical) "race." I suggest that we standardly hold it open to someone to believe that the replacement of the characteristic morphology of their sex with a (facsimile) of that of the other (major) one would produce someone other than themselves, a new ethical person; while the replacement of the characteristic morphology of their ethical "race" by that of another would not leave them free to disclaim the new person. "Racial" ethical identities are for us—and that means something like, us in the modern West—apparently less conceptually central to who one is than gender ethical identities.

That this is so does not entail that being an African American cannot be an *important* ethical identity: it is a reflection, rather, of the fact that that ethical identity is not a matter of morphology, that skin and hair and so on are simply signs for it. Such an identity is as we ordinarily understand it exactly a matter of descent: and nothing you do to change your appearance or behavior can change the past fact that your ancestors were of some particular origin. Nevertheless, even for those for whom being African American is an important aspect of their ethical identity, what matters to them is almost always not the unqualified fact of that descent, but rather something that they suppose to go with it: the experience of a life as a member of a group of people who experience themselves as—and are held by others to be—a community in virtue of their mutual recognition—and their recognition by others—as people of a common descent.

It is a reasonable question how such "racial" identities differ from those we call "ethnic." What matters about the identity of, say, Irish Americans—which was conceived of racially in the nineteenth century in North America—is that it, like an African-American identity, involves experiences of community in virtue of a mutual recognition of a common descent. What differentiates Irish-American from African-American identity, as understood in these United States, is that it is largely recognized nowadays that what flows from this common descent is a matter of a shared culture. People of Irish-American descent adopted and raised outside Irish-American culture are still, perhaps, to be thought of as Irish Americans: but they have a choice about whether this fact, once they are aware of it, should be central to their ethical identities, and their taking it as central would involve them in adopting certain cultural practices. Someone who refuses to do anything with the fact of their Irish-American descent—who fails to acknowledge it in any of their projects—is not generally held to be inauthentic, is not held to be being unfaithful to something about him or herself to which they ought to respond. So far as I can see, by contrast, African Americans who respond in this way fall into two categories, depending on whether or not their visible morphology permits them to "pass," permits them, that is, to act in society without their African ancestries being noticed.

If they cannot pass, they will often be thought of as inauthentic, as refusing to acknowledge something about themselves that they ought to acknowledge, though they will not be thought to be dishonest, since their morphology reveals the fact that is being denied. If they can pass, they will be thought of by many as being not merely inauthentic but dishonest. And while they may have prudential reasons for concealing the fact of their (partial) African descent, this will be held by many to amount to inauthenticity, especially if they adopt cultural styles associated with "white" people.

Now, so far as I can see, these differences between the identities that we think of as "racial" and those that we think of as "ethnic" cannot be made intelligible without adverting to certain (false) beliefs. Someone who conceals the fact of an African ancestry in their social life quite generally is held to be inauthentic, because there is still around in the culture the idea that being (partially) descended from black people makes you "really" black—in ways that have ethical consequences— while being descended from Irish stock merely correlates roughly with a certain cultural identity. If "races" were biologically real, this would, perhaps, begin to be a possible distinction, though it would require further argument to persuade me that ethical consequences flowed from membership in races. But since they are not, this distinction seems, as I say, to require a distinction that someone apprised of the facts should just give up.[4]

That "race" and gender have interestingly different relations to metaphysical identity should not obscure the fact that as ethical identities they have a central importance for us. What this means is, presumably, something like this: that for us, in our society, being of a certain gender and being of a certain race are for many people facts that are centrally implicated in the construction of life plans. To ignore one's race and one's gender in thinking about the ethical project of composing a life for oneself requires, in many minds, a kind of ignoring of social reality that amounts to attempting to fool oneself; and that is part of what is involved in the thought that passing for the "wrong" gender or race involves a certain inauthenticity.

We construct ethical identities—woman, man, African American, "white"—in ways that depend crucially on false beliefs about metaphysical identities; something like each of them could be reconstructed out of other materials. But if we were to live in a society that did not institutionalize those false metaphysical beliefs, it is unclear that the project of reconstruction would be an attractive one. In a truly non-sexist, nonracist society, gender, the ethical identity constructed on the base of sexual differences, would at least be radically differently configured, and might, like "race," entirely wither away; ethnic identities, by contrast—and this is something an African-American identity could become—seem likely to persist so long as there are human cultures and subcultures, which is likely to mean as long as people are raised in families.

NOTES

1. Given the underlying biology, this is too simple a view: I assume it in this paper as a first approximation.

2. I'll use male and female for biological identities (sex) and feminine and masculine for social identities (gender). See the remarks on the topic of **XX** and **XY** genotypes below.

3. As George Schuyler actually did in his engaging moral fantasy *Black No More* (New York: Negro Universities Press, 1931).

4. Like race-ethnicity, sexuality provides an interesting contrast case to sex-gender. It would be interesting to explore, for the sake of further contrast, the ways in which the notion of a "gay" identity requires assumptions about whether sexuality is and is not a matter of acculturation.

PARALLELS OF ETHNICITY AND GENDER

J. Angelo Corlett

chapter 6

I. INTRODUCTION

THE LANGUAGES of ethnicity[1] and gender are, in some respects, not unlike the emperor's new clothes. Words such as "African-American," "European-American," "Asian," "Hispanic," "man," and "woman" are used without much thought as to whether or not such categories are, in the end, meaningful or admit of definition beyond mere convention. Popular theories of "race" and "sex" purport to classify human individuals into a few distinct groups based on genetic analyses: "Negroid," "Mongoloid," "Caucasoid," "male," and "female." So persuasive have been such genetic analyses of "race" and "sex" that they have become part of the folk construal of how people are to be classified. What is needed is a more holistic understanding and clarification of the nature of humans. To accomplish this, the primitive (purely genetic) conceptions of "race" and "sex" must be abandoned in favor of a more precise categorization of humans into *ethnic* and *gender* groups, one which takes into consideration *both genetic and experiential* features of human life. Do ethnic groups share common properties? Do gender groups share common properties? If so, then what are they?

In this chapter, I argue that ethnicity and gender are not natural kinds, and sketch a new analysis of the concept of ethnicity, and of gender. This is a genetic-experiential analysis that rejects "primitive race theories" which categorize peoples into different "races" based solely on certain genetic traits possessed by members of each putative racial group. Likewise, the analysis rejects "primitive sex theories" which categorize peoples into different "sexes" based purely on certain genetic traits possessed by members of each putative sex group. In order to distance itself from these primitive theories of "race" and "sex" in the minds of readers, the genetic-experiential analysis categorizes persons into groups of ethnicity and gender (rather than the primitive race and sex categories), respectively. This categorization in no way supposes, however, any distinctions between ethnic or gender groups such that one might be thought to be "better" or qualitatively superior to another, at least no such differences based on mere genetics. If any such distinctions of quality do exist, it is because, on average, one group or another has out-performed others in certain ways, perhaps due to its having greater social advantages or opportunities than other groups, or perhaps because it exists in an environment more congenial to its own flourishing than other groups in the same or different environments.

84

II. PRIMITIVE "RACE" AND "SEX" THEORIES

It is helpful to clear the way for a new philosophical analysis of ethnicity and gender by explaining why primitive "race" and "sex" theories are inadequate.[2] Among the difficulties with primitive race and sex theories are that of their *arbitrariness in the selection of which traits are definitive of racial and sex groups*, their *fundamental incompleteness in accounting for the notions of race and sex*, and their *apparent lack of significance*. I shall refer to these as "the genetic arbitrariness objection," "the incompleteness objection," and "the insignificance objection," respectively.

The Arbitrariness Objection

First, there seems to be an arbitrariness in the ways in which primitive race and sex theorists have selected which genetic traits become decisive in distinguishing "racial" and "sex" groups. Let us assume that there are n traits which geneticists have identified as those which distinguish "Negroids" from "Caucasoids," and that there is one distinguishing genetic trait, m, separating human males from human females (namely, that human males are XY and human females are XX). One difficulty, however, is whether or not each member of, say, the "Negroid" group possesses each of the n features which distinguishes "Negroids" from "Caucasoids." Even if this is true, a deeper analysis of genetic traits might very well reveal that there are $n+1$ or more traits which would distinguish several—even hundreds—more such human groups. Surely it is plausible that the evolution of peoples results in the development of additional distinguishing traits between groups. If so, then there is a degree of arbitrariness concerning the selection of genetic traits which are said to categorize peoples into a mere few "racial" groups. Similar concerns might be raised about what is said to distinguish "sex" groups. Is it not arbitrary that the mere possession of XY or XX chromosomes "makes" one (or qualifies one as) either a human male or a human female? Why would not differences in psychology, if they do exist, also distinguish men from women? If there turns out to be a regress of such groups over time in that of the evolution of various and additional distinguishing genetic traits, then primitive race and sex theories are in need of rethinking. How does the primitive race or sex theorist know which and how many genetic properties count as sufficient for distinguishing between groups to warrant the claim that there exist different *"races"* and *"sexes,"* respectively?[3]

One can imagine a somewhat less primitive race/sex theorist revising her position in light of this concern, arguing that the genetic arbitrariness objection is evaded by her openness to the evolution of additional distinguishing genetic traits and, in turn, additional "racial" and "sex" groups. But if this line is taken by the less primitive race/sex theorist, she admits that primitive race/sex theories are in need of revision in a rather crucial way. The genetic-experiential analysis of ethnicity and gender, then, requires that we go beyond mere genetics in differentiating ethnic and gender groups.

The Incompleteness Objection

However, even the less primitive race/sex theorist faces the obstacle of the "incompleteness objection." For if the genetic categorization of "races" is nonarbitrary, it is implausible to suppose that a mere genetic analysis of human differences suffices as the conceptual means by which to properly differentiate humans. Is there not more to a "race" than mere genetic characteristics? Is there not a history, a culture, a certain life-form or experience? If so, then primitive race theory needs to provide an account of what *else*, besides genetics, suffices to categorize peoples into "races." However, once it accomplishes this in any important measure, it ceases to be *primitive* race theory, conceding that the very feature which makes itself "primitive" is theoretically inadequate. The genetic-experiential analysis of ethnicity and gender, then, requires that we go beyond mere genetics in differentiating ethnic and gender groups.

The Insignificance Objection

Finally, primitive race theories face "the insignificance objection." Even if it can be shown that the distinguishing of peoples into "races" is not arbitrary, and even if primitive race theory admits that it is incomplete and seeks only to provide a purely genetic analysis of commonalities and differences amongst humans, it is not obvious what significance the theory has beyond its giving an account of genetic similarities and differences among humans. It would still not warrant the categorization of humans into distinct "races," unless by "races" it is meant merely that there are some genetic differences between "breeds" of humans as members of certain groups. But then it remains unclear as to whether such differences are significantly more interesting than the differences between biological traits between persons *within* "races." If genes are what give some people, say, kinky hair and dark colored skin and others neither of these traits, what makes such a genetic difference of sufficient importance to categorize persons according to different "races?" Here the genetic arbitrariness objection comes back to haunt primitive race theory.

Similar concerns arise for primitive sex theories. Briefly, although there are some differences, genetically speaking, between human males and human females, this is hardly sufficient to show that such mere genetic differences between them alone justifies our categorizing some humans as men and others as women. There are an array of experiential (psychological, sociological, etc.) factors which comprise a person's being, and gender categories require that such factors be taken into consideration when categorizations of gender are made. In any case, the categorization of persons into ethnic and gender groups should be sensitive to the fact that a person's belonging to this or that group is a *matter of degree*. Thus, for example, one might be more or less a Latino, based on factors concerning one's family heritage(s), culture(s), language(s), etc. Or, one might be more or less a man or a woman (as the case may be), based on an array of factors, including genetics.[4]

86

Given the plausibility of the genetic arbitrariness objection, the incompleteness objection, and/or the insignificance objection, the genetic-experiential analysis adopts the categories of ethnicity and gender rather than of race and sex. For these categories do not presuppose that there are distinct groups of people based on purely genetic traits. Nor do they assume that specific traits of ethnic or gender groups are fixed. For they may evolve over time. They are not, moreover, natural kinds.[5]

III. THE GENETIC-EXPERIENTIAL ANALYSIS OF ETHNICITY

Is it plausible to argue that there exist conditions of ethnicity and gender, respectively? Are there ethnic and gender essences? Naomi Zack argues that no such conditions and essences exist for race.[6] But consider the following analysis of the nature of ethnicity: A person, S, belongs to an ethnic group, G, *to the extent that S* is:

(1) a genetic descendant of G.

This analysis, which I shall refer to as the "naïve conception of ethnicity," seems to capture what is both necessary and sufficient for one's being in an ethnic group. However, it is unclear whether or not (1) is sufficient for ethnic group membership. The reason for this is because (1) is ambiguous. For the question arises as to which ethnic group one belongs if one is of mixed ethnicity. This poses particular problems for primitive conceptions of race according to which there are clear genetic markers between Caucasoid, Mongoloid and Negroid persons. Instances of mixed race where the mix is equal, genetically speaking, seem not to admit of answers to the question, "Of which race is X?" Less primitive conceptions of ethnicity might argue that such cases of mixed race demonstrate that ethnicity is a matter of degree. Even so, the less primitive conceptions of ethnicity still do not provide a complete picture of ethnicity. There is more to ethnicity than mere genetic history. In an effort to bolster the naïve conception of ethnicity, biological views of ethnicity might add:

> (2) distinguished by (visible or apparent) features of her ethnic group members (e.g., hair texture, facial features, etc.)

to complete the analysis. But (2) poses certain troubles if it is construed as a necessary condition of ethnicity. For it raises questions of ethnic identity not unlike some problems of personal identity.[7] Consider the African American who, at t_1, possesses what are considered to be full African-American features, biologically speaking, but who, for whatever reason(s), has those features surgically removed at t_2 such that he is no longer distinguishable from, say, one of "pure" European descent. For example, this person has his skin color changed from a dark black to a pale color, has his nose and lips reworked such that they resemble the typical European features. The question is whether or not the surgical alterations have actually changed this person's ethnicity. If so, then (2) is a necessary condition of one's being an African American. But there is reason to think that the person in question has not, in having the deemed African-American biological features altered, effected a change in ethnic identity. The reason for this is because there may be more to ethnicity than mere biology or genetics. It might be the case that this person shares a significant sense of self-pride in being an African American, including having a pride of a certain culture which he still deems as his own. Perhaps he even participates in cultural activities which are identified as African-American, including the use of a recognizable African-American dialect. Indeed, for these and other reasons, he considers himself to be an African American despite what some other African Americans might think of his having certain of his biological features altered. Here we assume that the reasons for the changes in physical appearance did not include self-deception or an attempt to opt out of the group of African Americans. Now to say that this person is no longer an African American seems to beg the question concerning the nature of African-American as an ethnic category. Yet there seems to be no non-question-begging way for one to insist that this person has lost his ethnicity as an African American due to the change in biology. It follows that (2) is *not* a necessary condition of one's ethnicity, and it follows that

87

(1)-(2) is not an unproblematic analysis of the nature of ethnicity. It is of interest to note that similar difficulties arise for attempts to complete the analysis in terms of psychological, political or linguistic factors of persons. There are no psychological, political or linguistic features shared by all members of an ethnic group. For instance, the psychological trait of, say, being conscious of one's own ethnicity is shared by some African Americans, but not by all. The political standpoints of African Americans also differ widely. While many are of a Democratic bent, a growing number are aligning themselves with the Republican agendas. Furthermore, while many African Americans speak some dialect of "black English," others refrain from speaking in that way. In any case, such factors do not seem to figure into the analysis of ethnicity. Rather, they appear to be present as properties which, if possessed, identify a person as being more or less of a certain ethnic group, or being a certain type within the group.

Now it might be argued that the analysis be modified in order to properly define "ethnicity." To (1) might be added:

(3) has an *intentionally shared experience* with the members of G.

(1) and (3) evades the above mentioned ambiguity with (1). In addition to its stipulating degrees of ethnic group membership based on shared genetic traits among members of G, (1) and (3) also admit of degrees of ethnicity as shared experience among ethnic group members is a matter of degree. For one might share the experience of being an African American with most but not all African Americans. Or, one might share such an experience with relatively few such persons. In the former case, we might say that the person in question is an African American in a stronger sense than is the person in the latter instance. Anthony Appiah argues that ethnicity involves a shared culture among a group of people,[8] one which they can call their own. I would argue that a shared culture is part of what is meant by "shared experience" in (3). I would add that it is not just a matter of genetic ties between persons in a group that makes them part of the same ethnic group, but also a matter of one's having a sense of shared values, language, and a life-form with others of a certain group. Moreover, one might argue that binding in-group members of the ethnic group is a common myth or culture established by convention and sustained from one generation of group members to the next. One might refer to this as an *ethnic heritage*.

Note that the experience shared in (3) must be intentional. This means that whatever ethnic experience there is cannot be shared by accident or coercion. It must result from the intentional and free action of humans. The language shared by members of G, the shared culture among G's members, the manners in which members of G experience the world and are perceived by out-group members, etc., are not the result of moral good or bad luck, but are the consequence of intentional choices by members of G.

It is this set of factors which primitive race theories ignore when they attempt to provide understandings of the idea of the nature of ethnic groups. The importance of this analysis, if it goes through, is that it provides an analysis of ethnicity which states that ethnic groups must involve existential connections, as well as genetic ties between members of the groups. In this way, genetic and existential ties become the essences of ethnic groups. Therefore, it is not conceptually absurd to imagine a nonhierarchical ethnic essentialism which evades the difficulties posed to race essentialism by Zack.[9]

Thus whether the question is one of African American, Latino, Asian, Irish, or another ethnic group, (1) and (3) captures what is essential for ethnicity. But is such an analysis a plausible account of gender categories? What is needed here is an analogous, nonarbitrary way of defining the nature of men and women, of human males and human females. Is this possible?

IV. THE GENETIC–EXPERIENTIAL ANALYSIS OF GENDER

Consider the following analysis of the nature of gender: S is a member of a gender group, G, *to the extent that*:

(4) S has a human chromosome structure (XX, XY) of G; and
(5) S has standard internal and external genitalia of the members of G.

This *seems* to be a simple and accurate understanding of sex. In fact, it amounts to the primitive sex theory, e.g., of what is sufficient to categorize humans into groups of men and women, respectively. However, (5) is not a necessary condition of *gender* or a more complete account of what humans are as men and women, respectively. For just as ethnicity can be retained while removing all external physical traits of one's ethnicity, so can one retain gender after having one's genitalia surgically removed. Moreover, (4) seems inadequate except as a mere genetic understanding of gender. To insist that (4) is sufficient to capture what it means to be a member of a gender group would be to ignore other basic features of such persons, namely, that of a *shared experience* as a member of a certain gender. This shared experience relates human males to one another, just as a shared gender experience ties human females to one another, whether or not such experience amounts to sociological bonding between members of the gender. To (4), then, must be added the following criterion of gender:

(6) S has an *intentionally shared experience* with the members of G.

(4) and (6), then, comprise the genetic-experiential analysis of gender. This analysis evades the objection to (4)-(5), and more narrowly construes gender beyond mere genetic analyses. Just as with the previous analysis of ethnicity, the shared experience of each member of G must be intentional, uncontrived, unforced, etc.

89

V. OBJECTIONS TO THE GENETIC-EXPERIENTIAL ANALYSIS OF ETHNICITY AND GENDER, AND REPLIES.

There are a number of important objections which must be faced by the genetic-experiential analyses of ethnicity and gender. Let us consider them in turn in order to test the plausibility of these analyses. For even should primitive race and sex theories fail, it does not follow that the genetic-experiential analyses of ethnicity and gender are either theoretically adequate or plausible.

Against the proposed analyses of ethnicity and gender, one might argue that a family resemblance view of ethnicity is plausible, one which states that even though there are no essential features of, say, African Americans, that there exist a cluster of features which are shared by various members of the group. In-group members are identified by themselves and out-group members by the extent to which they share some of these features.

Zack argues that such a view of race is problematic because "it does not preserve the *intention* behind American racial designations."[10] This objection can also be applied to family resemblance views of ethnicity and gender. However, a speaker's intention is not always decisive in determinations of linguistic meaning. I can use "good" in reference to a crooked politician, intending "good" to mean "evil" in reference to her. Likewise, I can refer to a good politician as "evil," intending that "evil" carry the same informational content as "good." The point is that the intentional use of language does not tell the entire story of language usage. For one can use a term in a confused or incorrect way. So that Americans do not intend to use ethnic terms in a family resemblance fashion does not count decisively against it as a normative view of language use.

But there is a more convincing objection to the family resemblance theory of ethnicity and gender. What is in dispute for purposes of this project is whether or not there are conditions shared by members of an ethnic group, not whether or not such groups really exist. Thus a family resemblance objection to (1) and (3) confuses two different questions related to ethnicity. One is the question of which features, if possessed by persons, make one a member of an ethnic group. The other is the question of whether or not there are, objectively speaking, distinct ethnic groups that satisfy those conditions. If the family resemblance theory of ethnicity seeks to provide an answer to the latter question, it seems plausible. But to the extent that it wants to give an answer to the former question, it is found wanting. The plausibility of the family resemblance notions of ethnicity and gender is contingent on the logical impossibility of there being adequate analyses of ethnicity and gender. To the extent that the genetic-experiential analyses of ethnicity and gender set forth herein are plausible, family resemblance views are unnecessary. Thus it is important to consider additional objections to (1) and (3), and to (4) and (6), respectively, in order to discern the plausibility of the genetic-experiential analyses of ethnicity and gender.

90

CORLETT

Another objection to genetic-experiential analyses of ethnicity and gender is that the experiential condition is not a necessary condition of either ethnicity or gender. Suppose, the objection goes, that S is born of parents X and Y, but that just after birth S is transferred to an island where S is alienated from any social interaction for the remainder of S's life. Under such conditions, it is not possible for S to acquire or share a language, a culture, or any other experience with those to whom S is genetically tied. Yet it would be incorrect to hold that S has no membership in some ethnic group, and equally incorrect to say that S belongs to the ethnic group to which X and Y belong. The requirement of having a shared experience is not possible in S's case. How, then, do the genetic-experiential analyses classify the ethnicity and gender of S?

Although the genetic-experiential analyses of ethnicity and gender admit of degrees to which one belongs to an ethnic or gender group, the concept of degrees of group membership do not assist in evading this criticism. However, it is open to the genetic-experiential analyst to reply in the following way: There is nothing inherent in the genetic-experiential analyses which requires that all humans belong to both (or either) an ethnic and (or) a gender group. In the case of S, it might be said that S has no opportunity to qualify as either an ethnic or a gender group member. For S cannot, because of circumstance, intentionally share an ethnic or gender experience with others. That there is no conceptual absurdity in this reply enables the genetic-experiential analyses of ethnicity and gender to evade the objection of isolated humans and the challenge to intentionally shared experience as a necessary condition of ethnicity or gender.

A general objection to the genetic-experiential analyses of ethnicity and gender is that it falls prey to the above objections to primitive race and sex theories discussed above: such analyses, it might be argued, are arbitrary, incomplete, and insignificant. More specifically, the same genetic method which is used to identify "races" and "sexes" in an arbitrary manner is used by genetic-experiential analyses of ethnicity and gender. That is, it is unclear, the objection goes, precisely how genetic arbitrariness is avoided in the case of genetic-experiential analyses.

There is a sense in which the genetic arbitrariness objection is faced by all theories of race, sex, ethnicity and gender. But in the case of genetic-experiential analyses of ethnicity, and gender, the problem is not as acute as it is with primitive race and sex theories. For the former admit from the outset that there can be any number of ethnic and gender groups determined in part by genetic traits. They also admit that there are different levels of genetic and experiential analyses. This is significant in that the numbers of groups identified might differ between levels of, say, genetic analysis. At one level, there might be three discernible groups, genetically speaking, while at another level, there might be dozens, even hundreds, of such groups. But in no case do the genetic-experiential analyses hold that genetics can tell us the entire story of human groups. Thus while the choice of distinguishing genetic traits between ethnic and gender groups is somewhat arbitrary, it is not as grossly arbitrary as is the case with primitive race and sex theories. Whatever arbitrariness exists in genetic-experiential analyses of ethnicity and gender (insofar as what distinguishes such groups is concerned) is less true of genetic-experiential analyses than it is of any other analysis or theory pertaining to the classification of humans into groups. Thus it appears that the charge of arbitrariness does not pose a special problem for genetic-experiential analyses of ethnicity and gender.

VI. CONCLUSION

In sum, I have raised objections to primitive theories of race and sex, ones which call into question the very basis of folk conceptions of humans as categorized beings. Following this, I set forth a genetic-experiential analysis of ethnicity, and one of gender. I then defended these analyses against criticism. If the arguments of this paper go through, then a new paradigm of how humans ought to be categorized, if they are to be categorized at all, emerges. It evades the problems of primitive race and sex theories, and provides a more holistic conception of humans as evolving and complex beings.[11]

NOTES

1. Following Ashley Montague [*Man's Most Dangerous Myth: The Fallacy of Race* (Cleveland: World, 1965); and *Race, Science, and Humanity* (New York: Van Nostrand Reinhold, 1963)], I use "ethnicity" instead of "race" in that of the primitive nature of the latter. Strictly speaking, there are no races of people in the sense that there is no purely biological or genetic basis for traditional racial classifications (as found in primitive race theories). There is only one human race, including various ethnicities. In the spirit of Montague's critique of the concept of race, I use "gender" instead of "sex" for similar reasons. The use of "ethnicity" and "gender" are meant to signify the belief that whatever differences exist between humans along the lines of ethnicity and gender, the differences are matters of degree and in no way point toward some fundamental distinction between levels or kinds of humanity, qualitatively speaking.

2. For a discussion of some problems related to a species of primitive race theory (called the "ordinary concept of race"), see Naomi Zack, *Race and Mixed Race* (Philadelphia: Temple University Press, 1993), Chapter 2.

3. As Appiah argues, "This is not, of course, to deny that there are differences in morphology among humans: people's skins do differ in color. But these sorts of distinctions are not—as those who believe in races apparently suppose—markers of deeper biologically-based racial essences, correlating closely with most (or even many) important biological (let alone nonbiological) properties." (Anthony Appiah, "But Would That Still Be Me? Notes on Gender, 'Race,' Ethnicity, as Sources of 'Identity,'" *The Journal of Philosophy*, LXXXVII (1990), p. 496.) [See this volume, pp. 71–8—Ed.]

4. More needs to be said, admittedly, about the precise extent to which certain factors are necessary/sufficient for one's belonging to a certain ethic or gender group.

5. Zack, *Race and Mixed Race*, p. 17. For discussions of natural kinds and natural kind terms, see Saul Kripke, *Naming and Necessity* (Cambridge: Harvard University Press, 1972), pp. 116–144; W.V. Quine, "Natural Kinds," in Stephen P. Schwartz, ed., *Naming, Necessity, and Natural Kinds* (Ithaca: Cornell University Press, 1977), pp. 155–175.

92

CORLETT

6. Zack, *Race and Mixed Race*, Chapter 2; Naomi Zack, "Race and Philosophical Meaning," *APA Newsletter on Philosophy and the Black Experience* 94, no. 1 (Fall 1994), p. 14. [See this volume, pp. 29–30—Ed.]

7. Important discussions of personal identity include those found in A.J. Ayer, *The Problem of Knowledge* (New York: Penguin, 1956), Chapter 5; G.F. Macdonald, ed., *Perception and Identity: Essays Presented to A.J. Ayer With His Replies* (Ithaca: Cornell University Press, 1979); Robert Nozick, *Philosophical Investigations* (Cambridge: Harvard University Press, 1981), Chapter 1; Derek Parfit, *Reasons and Persons* (Oxford: Oxford University Press, 1984); and Sidney Shoemaker, *Self-Knowledge and Self-Identity* (Ithaca: Cornell University Press, 1963).

8. Appiah, p. 498.

9. Zack, *Race and Mixed Race*, pp. 15–17; Zack, "Race and Philosophical Meaning," pp. 14–15. [See this volume, pp. 29–31—Ed.]

10. Zack, "Race and Philosophical Meaning," p. 16. [See this volume, pp. 33–5—Ed.]

11. I wish to express my gratitude to Nathan Salmon and Naomi Zack for their helpful comments on the topics of race, sex, ethnicity and gender.

RACE, GENDER, AND HUMAN NATURE[1]

Nancy Holmstrom

JUST AS the differentiation of human beings from other species has tradition-ally been thought to be based on some common essence or nature, so has the division of humankind into certain groups, in particular, men and women and races, been thought to be based on their distinct natures. For all three, the tra-ditional idea was that there were fixed, natural essences determining the cog-nitive, moral, and emotional traits and abilities of the group in question. Some theorists have applied the idea to different social classes as well. I will call this view essentialism, and note that it is compatible with various metaphysical analyses.[2] These essences have been used to explain and also, explicitly or implicitly, to justify existing hierarchical social relations of class, sex, and race. In the past century, the "naturalness" of these essences has been understood to consist in their being biologically determined. Because of the political use to which the idea of essences or essential natures[3] has been put, most social critics have taken an anti-essentialist position on all three concepts, though some have embraced essentialism and tried to use it for liberatory ends. Oftentimes, political debates have been fought on this terrain without much analysis or clarity regarding the basic concepts.[4]

What I will argue in this paper is that despite the similarities in how they have been used and also in the debates surrounding them, there are important and interesting differences in the usefulness of these concepts. Specifically: while essentialist accounts of race and gender have to be rejected both for scientific and political reasons, the concept of human nature is not open to the same objections. Not only is it intellectually defensible, but it is politically important for feminists and antiracists.

I. RACE

Of the three concepts, "race" shows most clearly the fallacies of an essentialist approach. As the term is usually used today, only a small number of races, usually three, would be differentiated among the human species, most particularly so-called whites and blacks. Many people, including most of the scientific community until quite recently,[5] still accept the essentialist view that each race is constituted by certain heritable traits, including cognitive and moral traits, and tendencies that all and only members of that race share. Many more believe this to be true on average though not universally. But biologistic accounts of race were challenged almost seventy years ago by progressive sociologists and anthropologists, most notably Franz Boas, and the mainstream scientific view of race came to diverge from the popular view about fifty years ago. When the groups conventionally considered races, the populations of Africa and Europe and their descendants, are compared for genetic variation, it turns out that, except for the obvious morphological features of skin, hair, and bone, there is as much genetic variation within what is conventionally considered a race as between races. So it turns out that there really are no races in the scientific sense.[6]

But probably most people believe that the division of the species into races (usually three) is a natural or biological one because they believe people can be so classified simply on the basis of "how they look," i.e., the gross morphological features of skin color, hair type, and facial features and they cannot understand why anyone would deny this (except for political reasons). But when one denies the scientificity of the category "race," one is not denying visible physical differences between individuals and groups that are conventionally called racial, nor that people *can* be so divided along these lines. However, it does not follow that such a division is a natural or scientific one. Human beings could also be divided into two races or forty (as Marvin Harris reports they are in Brazil)[7] or 110, but so *could* they be divided into various numbers of size/shape groups. The arbitrariness is less obvious to us when based on color primarily because we are used to it, i.e., because this is a racist culture. Since we now know that differences in skin color no more reflect genetic differentiation between the groups defined on this basis than do differences in height or weight, "any use of racial categories must take its justification from some other source than biology."[8]

And that justification has always been political. In the United States, anyone with some minimum of (sub-Saharan) African ancestry is classified as black; 1/32 was often sufficient for state laws that enslaved or denied full rights of citizenship to "blacks." As some historians have shown, whiteness was constructed along with blackness in the early days of the American colonies. Divided and conflicted ethnic groups, some very subordinated and even "racialized" like the Irish, forged a new identity as free *white* men against blacks.[9] (Women were never fully part of this identity, but that is another story.) Much the same basis of classification still exists informally, with those designated black having shorter life expectancies and suffering astronomical rates of poverty (almost one out of two black children lives below the poverty line) and incarceration (one out of three black men are "connected to" to the criminal "justice" system).

These appalling facts give ample justification for organizing around issues of race. Racism, in short, has created the group that needs to struggle against it. But while essentialist notions are tempting because they can help to create and sustain solidarity among the oppressed as well as oppressors, essentialism is an illusion and a dangerous one. Moreover, they obscure class, sex, and other differences within the group and commonalities with members of other groups. Thus, so long as racism exists, "race" cannot be ignored, but it must be radically reconceived.

II. SEX/GENDER

Ideas of women's nature or essence have functioned in the same way as racialist ideas, viz., to explain and to justify their subordination. Although allegedly rooted in their distinct biology and frequently conflated with it, the idea of a distinct women's nature cannot be simply identified with their biology because otherwise, since women are by definition different biologically from men, to say that women have a distinct nature from men would be tautologous. To put in clear contemporary terms the assumption operating throughout the centuries: biological differences between the sexes lead to psychological differences, which lead to behavioral differences, and these are the bases of hierarchical social roles based on sex. The concept of women's nature or essence is best interpreted as referring to these distinctive psychological traits.

Feminists deny that women's and men's "natures" account for the hierarchical relations between them and usually deny the existence of any such essences. Feminists introduced the concept of gender, as distinct from sex, to clarify such facts as that, in our society, a woman can fail to be "a real woman," even if she is the mother of several children. Gender is usually understood to have several aspects: (a) norms about how a person of a given sex is supposed to behave, think, and feel, (b) institutions and relations within institutions, structured along sex lines, most broadly, the sexual division of labor within society, and c)characteristic psychological and behavioral differences between men and women that both result from and reinforce the other aspects. There is no necessary connection between sex and gender, nor between sex, gender, and sexuality. Nor should the sex/gender distinction be understood as pure biology versus pure culture. No aspect of human existence is entirely separable from culture. Even facts about our reproductive capacities, e.g., when puberty and menopause occur, are historically and socially quite variable. And certainly how men and women understand and experience their bodies is socially and culturally variable. Thus gender is analogous to race and eliminable in a non-sexist society.

This position, at one time almost universal among feminists, is rejected by two very different groups of feminists. One group finds a social account of gender hard to swallow, while the other extends it to sex as well as gender. The latter, most prominently, Andrea Dworkin and Monique Wittig,[10] argue that the enormous physical variations among infants and adults, the several aspects of sex identity that do not always fit together, show that it is not the physical similarities and differences by themselves that are determining of the division into males and females, but rather it is the interests of a sexist and heterosexist society. Sex, then, is analogous to race; (hetero)sexism creates the group that needs to struggle against it.

While I agree that the division of all humans into two discrete biological sexes cannot be justified scientifically,[11] it does not follow that sex is simply a socially constructed category. Social elements (including biases) enter into decision-making in *all* sciences, and classifications are not so neat in other areas of biology. Given that the sex difference is what allows for physical reproduction of most kinds of things, and that the difference between things that reproduce sexually and asexually is a very important one in biology, the division into two sexes has great importance for biological theory. Why then should the sexual division not be considered a natural or biological one, taking the concept "natural" and "biological" to mean something like "the subject of biological theory." Moreover, the political importance of the revelation that supposedly natural categories like race or gender are actually social in origin is greatly reduced if *everything* turns out to be social. So let us assume that there would still be two sexes that most people fell into, even in a society free of sexism and heterosexism.

In contrast to this extreme social constructionist position, some feminists are unhappy with the account given above of gender because they feel it underestimates the importance of biology. Given the biological differences, it seems commonsensical to suppose that there would always be some psychological sex differences, specifically regarding sex and reproduction, and that these would play an important determining role in behavior. Hence, unlike race, gender is ineliminable, even if any *particular* gender differences might be otherwise.[12] The most important objection, however, to all biologistic explanations of gender differences is this: in order to know that there are biological factors pushing in the same direction as the social, we would have to find some way to tease out the biological factors from all the others and determine their relative contribution, a feat quite beyond scientific capability now and in the foreseeable future. Unless some reason is given to discount the different social and environmental influences on men and women, the principle of methodological simplicity bids us to reject the biological account.[13]

Moreover, the real question is the importance—theoretically and politically—of any such differences. Why should we suppose that psychological sex differences, *if* they should turn out to exist, would inevitably lead to a whole host of other psychological and behavioral differences, and, further, that there would be social roles based on these differences? The crucial point is that gender involves a number of systematically related differences between the sexes that have some structured social importance. There simply are not good reasons to think that this can all be accounted for by biological differences between the sexes.

A more basic criticism of gender essentialism is that there may not even be the two genders these theories presuppose. In my judgment, the *most* the research on psychological sex differences shows is that with respect to certain qualities relevant to gender roles, there are statistically significant differences between the sexes. It is not clear whether these facts would justify speaking of two genders.[14] But there are problems even with this modest conclusion, viz., that most of the findings are based on research in white middle-class college towns in the United States. On what grounds can we assume that what is true of these women is true of all women? In fact, what little research has been done on the issue shows that gender is inseparable from other categories like race and class.[15]

Are there, then, no (nonphysical) differences between the sexes that cut across these lines? Do the categories "men" and "women" dissolve, except as biological categories? This would be too hasty a conclusion, in my opinion. It is plausible to suppose that the differences in the lives of boys and girls and men and women, of whatever race and class, particularly having to do with women's role taking care of children and others, would produce statistically significant psychological differences between the sexes.[16] What we might find is a common core of psychological traits related to gender roles found more often among women than men—and others more common to men—but women of different (sub)cultures have different (sub)sets of these traits. If such sex differences exist, then we could speak of two genders, i.e., sex-differentiated psychological traits which are explanatory of gender roles. On the other hand, if there are useful psychological generalizations differentiating men and women only within other groups, then we could not usefully speak of two genders *simpliciter*. Whether there are two genders, then, is partly an empirical question and partly a theoretical one, in that we need a theoretical context to evaluate the importance of whatever generalizations we come up with. In my opinion, that there are two genders, with class and race variations, is a very plausible hypothesis.[17] However, that is all it is at this point.

An important impetus to essentialism among feminists may be the worry that unless there is something universal to all women—whether it be their biology or their shared oppression, then there is no basis for feminism. I think this is mistaken. Regardless of whether and how gender is manifested in the psyches of men and women, gender is organized socially, particularly in a division of labor that gives women fewer choices, more work, and less power and money than men. A United Nations Report in 1988 found that women constitute half the world's population, perform nearly two-thirds of its work hours, receive one-tenth of the world's income, and own less than one-hundredth of the world's property. This creates a common interest in equal pay for equal and comparable work, and, most radically, an end to the sexual division of labor, even though these interests will manifest themselves differently in different groups and for each individual woman. And women's biological commonality creates crucial common interests too. Whatever their race, creed, or national origin—or their gender or sexuality—all women share an interest in preventing sexual violence and in having birth control and abortion available. But having abortion available simply means having it legal if one is middle class; if one is poor, it also means having it publicly funded. Thus women have differences as well as commonalities, and a desire for unity should not lead to the sacrifice of the interests of some. But while rejecting essentialism (based either on biology or experience), neither should we overlook the real—overlapping, crisscrossing, clustering—commonalities of women.

III. HUMAN NATURE

Throughout the history of human thought, philosophers, scientists, and ordinary people have puzzled over what human nature is like, what difference it makes, and whether there is any such thing at all. Many of the same arguments I have offered against essentialism in the case of race and gender have been urged against the concept of human nature. I will argue that they do not have the same weight in this context, at least not against all theories of human nature. I have chosen to examine the controversy regarding human nature in and around the Marxist field, both because I believe a theory roughly like Marx's can withstand objections better than most others,[18] and also because advocates of a cooperative and egalitarian society, like Marx, have always been met with objections based on a view of human nature as egoistic, competitive, and aggressive, characteristics supposedly fixed and biologically determined. This Hobbesian view has found support in various scientific theories, most notably Social Darwinism and today's Sociobiology, by which I mean A.O. Wilson's thesis that "all human behaviors, social relationships, and organization are genetically encoded adaptations."[19] Marx and Engels subjected the Hobbesian view of human nature to withering criticism as not only reactionary but circular, since it projected onto nature features of capitalist society which it then claimed were justified because they were natural. Much the same arguments have been given against Sociobiology by scientists and philosophers in exacting detail, so I will not repeat these critiques here.[20] Nevertheless, biological deter-

100

HOLMSTROM

minist theories of human nature have enjoyed a considerable revival in the past thirty years and are probably hegemonic today.

While some interpreters have denied that Marx had a theory of human nature in his mature as well as his early work, it is now pretty well settled that he did.[21] More important, however, and equally debated, is the question whether Marx should have accepted a theory of human nature: Is it consistent with his theory? Is it a useful concept? (And, of course, exactly what does the concept consist in?) This debate has pretty much the same people lining up on the same sides, with Louis Althusser the most influential exponent in the Marxist camp of what has been called an antihumanist view of history and society,[22] and Norman Geras, the British political theorist, providing the most articulate defense on the left of the concept of human nature.[23] Recently, Post-Structuralism has entered the debate regarding humanism with a fundamental rejection of both sides as totalistic.

The arguments against the concept of human nature are typically a blend of the metaphysical, methodological, and political. In brief, the charge is that a concept of human nature—invariant, transhistorical, decontextualized—is simply too abstract to be meaningful because people always come embedded in a mode of production, a culture, a class, etc. The idea of a real essence underlying all of that is seen as idealist. If this underlying essence is supposed to be biological, the problem is that human beings have always lived in society and everything characteristically human has been acquired in social interaction. So how could we know what was "underlying" all forms of social life? And why would we want to anyway? Instead, writers who deny human nature stress the changing nature of human beings due to changing social relations. While some writers will simultaneously affirm invariant biological needs and capacities, they are reluctant to use the word "human nature" because of its conservative political associations, but also because the biological has, for humans, no existence apart from the social. Furthermore, they hold that whatever constants there are are unimportant for understanding history and society. What is important, in this view, are the variations, the changes, and the social relations that transform and explain them; for example, what, how, and why different human beings eat what they do, rather than that we all must eat. Some rejections of human nature are so nuanced they may be merely terminological.[24] Moreover, many of these critics argue, this supposedly neutral view of human beings *as such* actually incorporates characteristics of the dominant culture, gender, class, etc., as, for example, in Hobbes. In the name of a universal, it denies all particularities but one. The abstract individual of liberal theory is actually the white bourgeois male.

Marxists who defend the importance of a concept of human nature accept the truth and the importance of a great deal of what the critics say, but they reject the conclusion. While agreeing that theories of human nature have usually played a conservative political role, they deny that this is inevitable. Nor, they argue, need the idea of invariant features of human beings be idealist or abstract in some objectionable sense, even if they usually have been. Certainly the concept is an abstrac-

101

tion, but so is the concept of the environment or social change, which critics of human nature are happy to use. To be a useful concept does not at all require that what it is a concept of be ontologically distinct from everything else, whatever exactly that would be. Marx used the concepts of religion and government, although he explicitly denied they had an independent existence. Nor need the concept of invariant human needs and capacities be understood as excluding or necessarily underemphasizing the specific forms they take due to changing social conditions and relations. Indeed, Marx is most plausibly understood as offering a theory integrating the two. To avoid confusion, I will use the terms "human nature" to designate (relatively) invariant features of human beings and "the nature of human beings" in a broader sense to include both variant and invariant features.

Not only are human beings always embedded in variable social relations, as critics of the concept of human nature emphasize, but they are always embodied. They are biological beings and, simultaneously and essentially, social beings in that their biological needs and capacities bind them into relations with others. Certainly scientists need to abstract and focus on that aspect of human beings appropriate to their study, but to understand the beings from which it has been abstracted, much less to understand the importance for human beings of what is being studied, these aspects must be integrated into a coherent conception of the human being. Marx stressed the social and economic, as opposed to politics and ideas, and, on the other hand, the biological, for two reasons. First of all, the social and economic had been omitted entirely in the dominant idealist or physical reductionist theories, respectively, and so he bent over backwards in the opposite direction. Secondly, Marx was interested in explaining history and social change, to which he believed changing social and economic conditions were key. But he did not deny other factors any explanatory role. Indeed, the biological is foundational to Marx's theory. This, however, does not mean the biological has epistemological primacy or greater explanatory power. Radical scientists and scientifically minded philosophers, almost all of whom reject reductionism, have discussed various alternative ways of conceptualizing the relations between the biological (and physical/chemical) and the social, one of the most popular being to understand them as nonhierarchical levels of explanation.[25]

But however precisely relations between the different aspects of human history are best understood, Marx made clear that what he called "the first premise" of his view of history is the existence of living individuals with a certain physical constitution, that is, certain invariant needs and capacities. While the theory of historical materialism is, in part, about how human beings change given changes in their social relations of production brought about by their own labor[26] and develop new needs, nevertheless he stressed the fundamental material needs to eat, have shelter, and the like, as the basis of history. Despite all the variations in what individuals eat and why (a function both of their society and their particular place in it), people need a certain minimum number of calories per day or they will die or suffer ill health. That minimum will vary due to factors such as physical condition, labor, and climate, but when the power relations of a society enter into this determination, as they do, for example, in the belief in many parts of the world that women need less food than men do, this is simply refuted by women's higher rates of malnutrition and death due to starvation.

Moreover, even for those needs that developed only given certain productive forces and relations, "the very fact," as Geras says, "that [human beings] entertain this sort of relations, the fact that they produce and have a history, [Marx] explains in turn by their general and constant, intrinsic, constitutional characteristics; in short, by their human nature. The concept is therefore indispensable to his historical theory."[27] Within this integrated (some call it dialectical) conception of human beings, context and human purposes (what we want to explain and what we want to do about it) should determine which aspect should be emphasized when.

Humans share many capacities with nonhumans, eating and procreating, for example, but these can take distinctly human forms, and increasingly do so with the development of the environment and humans' relations to it. Even the senses undergo this sort of transformation. In Marx's words, "Man's musical ear is only awakened by music.... The cultivation of the five senses is the work of all previous history."[28] Of all the distinctly human capacities, the capacity to labor in a purposive way,[29] not only from necessity, is particularly important to Marx. He singles out this particular capacity as central to human nature because it is key to historical, cultural development, and it is this that increasingly differentiates human beings from other animals.[30] The kind of labor that makes this possible would find its fullest expression in a society of freely associated producers, first of all because more individuals would be able to engage in free, purposive activity than in any other society. But, secondly, because in such a society labor would be purposive on a collective basis as well: the producers organize social production according to a democratic and rational plan instead of a market, over which they have no control. So the nature of human beings changes to become, as Marx sees it, more distinctly human. This is not because the human essence is finally freed from repression or because it is the telos of human history, as critics have claimed (correctly so with respect to some Marxist humanist writers), but, rather, just because it is the most developed expression of what is distinctly human.

Now this social/historical development is dependent on—but not determined by—a particular feature of human biology: the brain. As Stephen Jay Gould explains, "Human uniqueness resides primarily in our brains...and in the flexibility of what our brains can do. It is expressed in the culture built upon our intelligence and the power it gives us to manipulate the world."[31] Thus there is no inconsistency between emphasizing social change and variability and rooting this in a relatively invariant biological constitution. On the contrary, it is our particular biological constitution, that is, our human nature, that makes possible the changed nature of human beings.

103

HOLMSTROM

Turning to the moral/political aspect of the controversy, it is clear that for Marx this transformation of the nature of human beings through the development of their distinctive capacities is an achievement, and an achievement with a high moral value. He refers to the full development of human creative powers as "an end in itself," which he also calls the "true realm of freedom," and he refers to the conditions under which the associated producers organize conditions as "most worthy of their human nature." Despite its utopian elements, Marx's conception of self-realization is, minimally, a plausible basis for a conception of the good life for human beings, as something each individual can aim for and many can at least partially achieve.[32]

But Marx also used the concept of human nature for a more direct and simple normative purpose: to critique modes of production which do not satisfy human needs, which include both things necessary for survival and things necessary for satisfaction, such as varied and satisfying work. (This is not a distinction between biological and nonbiological needs; sex is not necessary for survival at the level of individuals.) If it were impossible to speak of invariant human needs, i.e., human nature, if all needs were socially determined, then how could one make sense of a society's not meeting human needs? Even if some of the needs frustrated by capitalism are the product of capitalism, such, perhaps, as the need for creative work, the most fundamental criticism Marxists make of capitalism is that even the most elementary needs for food and shelter are not met for much of the population of even the most developed capitalist societies, as we can see on the streets of our major cities. So although certain views of human nature function to support conservative political values, other conceptions provide a foundation for radical political critiques.

Returning to racism and sexism, it is clear that ideas of human rights, based on a conception of human nature, have often provided important inspiration for feminist and antiracist struggles, even when the proponents of these rights had no intention of including women or nonwhite men in their domain. Consider C.L.R. James' account in *The Black Jacobins* of the impact of the French Revolution on antislavery struggles in Santo Domingo (Haiti), or Mary Wollstonecraft's appropriation of such ideas for women, or the importance feminists are finding today in defining many sexist practices as violations of human rights. The point is that although universalistic concepts can incorporate false and biased views, this is not inevitable; instead, a universalist politics (when combined with due recognition of differences) can justify the release of each individual from ideas and social arrangements that prevent self-determination.[33]

Thus while rejecting conservative views of human nature I also reject the arguments of many left thinkers that there is no such thing as human nature. Versus those leftists, there is and it's biologically based. Versus conservatives, it does not have the content—egoistic and so forth—they usually give it. Nor does it explain as much as they try to make it explain. This is because biological determinism is

false: the biological aspects of human beings are always intrinsically interconnected with the social. Another fallacy of biological determinist theories, Stephen Jay
Gould explains, is that they are theories of limits rather than potentials. As discussed
earlier, the flexibility of the human brain allows human beings to adapt to different circumstances; most importantly, to both create and adapt to different sets of
social relations, being more egoistic in some, more cooperative in others. The overall nature of human beings changes in different social conditions just *because*, not *in
spite of*, a biologically based human nature. Thus critics of hierarchical societies do
not need to fear the idea of a biologically based human nature, but rather those
who have controlled that idea. Rather than human nature precluding cooperative
and egalitarian relations between people, it is human biology, on the contrary, that
creates the possibility of human liberation. Actually achieving it, of course, depends
on other things.

NOTES

1. This is a shorter version of a paper entitled "Humankind(s)" that appeared in *Biology,
Behavior, and Society*, *Canadian Journal of Philosophy*, *Supplementary Volume 20*, pp. 69–105.

2. For example, one could oppose metaphysical essentialism, but accept essences in this
sense, as David Hume did. See his "Of National Characters," in David Fate Horton and
Richard Popkin, eds., *David Hume: Philosophical Historical Historian* (Indianapolis: Library of
Liberal Arts, 1965), p. 47. "I am apt to suspect the Negroes to be naturally inferior to the
Whites." Indeed some have argued that the empiricism of Locke and Hume helped to justify racism, while the essentialism of Cartesian dualism makes it more difficult conceptually. See Harry Bracken, "Essence, Accident, and Race," *Hermathena*, 116 (winter 1973), pp.
81–96, and "Philosophy and Racism," *Philosophia*, 8, no. 2 (November 1978), pp. 241–260;
Noam Chomsky, *For Reasons of State* (New York: Vintage, 1973), ch. 7.

3. The words "natures" and "natural" are extraordinarily slippery and sloppy. In this context, however, it is usually used synonymously with essences.

4. See Jane Roland Martin's "Methodological Essentialism, False Difference, and Other
Dangerous Traps," *Signs* 19, no. 3 (1994), pp. 630–657, regarding feminist debates and Kate
Soper's *Humanism and Anti-Humanism* (LaSalle, IL: Open Court, 1986), regarding debates
around human nature.

5. The shameful history of science's role in propagating racism (not entirely a fact of the
past) is documented, among other places, in Stephen Jay Gould's *The Mismeasure of Man*
(New York: Norton, 1981); Nancy Stepan, *The Idea of Race in Science: Great Britain,
1800–1950* (London: Archon Books, 1982); Martin Barker, *The New Racism* (London:
Junction Books, 1981).

6. Cf. R.C. Lewontin, Steven Rose, and Leon J. Kamin, *Not in Our Genes* (New York:
Pantheon Books, 1984).

7. "Race," in International Encyclopedia of the Social Sciences.

8. Lewontin, Rose, and Kamin, *Not in Our Genes*, p. 127

9. See George P. Rawick, From Sundown to Sunup: The Making of the Black
Community (Westport, CT: Greenwood, 1977), for the early period; see David R.
Roediger, The Wages of Whiteness: Race and the Making of the American Working Class
(London: Verso, 1992) for the nineteenth century.

10. Andrea Dworkin, *Woman-Hating* (New York: Dutton, 1974); Monique Wittig, "One is Not Born a Woman," *Feminist Issues 1* (1981), pp. 47–54, "The Category of Sex," *Feminist Issues 2* (1982), pp. 63–8.

11. See Ann Fausto-Sterling, *Myths of Gender* (New York: Basic Books, 1985).

12. Some feminists, known as cultural feminists, assume the biological differences determine more specific traits, (ironically, the same traits assumed by conservatives), but they reverse the valuation given by conservatives.

13. I take John Stuart Mill to be offering this sort of argument in *The Subjection of Women* (Cambridge, MA: MIT Press, 1970), p. 22, when he says, "I deny that anyone knows, or can know, the nature of the two sexes, as long as they have only been seen in their present relation to one another," although he can also be interpreted as taking an agnostic position.

14. Perhaps it should depend on how important the specific differences are. This, however, can only be determined within a theoretical framework. For more of these explorations and a somewhat different point of view, see my "Do Women Have a Distinct Nature?" *The Philosophical Forum* 14, no. 1 (Fall 1982), pp. 25–42; reprinted in Marjorie Pearsall, ed., *Women and Values: Readings in Recent Feminist Philosophy* (Belmont, CA: Wadsworth, 1986).

15. For example, P. Weston and M. Mednick, "Race, Social Class, and the Motive to Avoid Success in Women," *Journal of Cross-Cultural Psychology* 1 (1970), pp. 284–91.

16. Certainly many feminist and other psychoanalytic theorists have thought so. See Nancy Chodorow, *The Reproduction of Mothering* (Berkeley: University of California, 1978); Dorothy Dinnerstein, *The Mermaid and the Minotaur* (New York: Harper Collophon, 1976); and the vast literature, both critical and supportive, their work has spawned.

17. As Jerry Fodor wrote recently in a very different context, "Good taxonomy is about *not* missing generalizations." *Journal of Philosophy* 88, no. 1, p. 25.

18. Marx's theory is like that of Aristotle, whom he greatly admired, in a number of important respects, but Marx's theory is more inclusive, more explicitly sensitive to social and historical variations, and, of course, explicitly tied to a vision of liberation for the whole of the human species. Among those who have noted the similarity are G.E.M. de Sainte Croix, in *The Class Struggle in the Ancient World* (London: Verso, 1981); Alan Gilbert, *Democratic Individuality*, (Cambridge: Cambridge University Press, 1990); Martha Nussbaum, "Nature, Function, and Capability: Aristotle on Political Distribution," in George E. McCarthy, ed., *Marx and Aristotle* (Savage, MD: Rowman and Littlefield, 1992).

19. Ruth Bleier, *Science and Gender*, (Pergamon, New York 1984). Bleier uses a capital "S" for the Wilsonian version to distinguish it from the general study of the social behavior of animals.

20. See, among others, Stephen Jay Gould, *Ever Since Darwin* (New York: Norton, 1977); Arthur Caplan, ed., *The Sociobiology Debate* (New York: Harper and Row, 1978); Lewontin, Rose, and Kamin, *Not in Our Genes*.

21. Louis Althusser claimed there was an "epistemological break" between Marx's earlier humanistic, philosophical writings and his mature scientific work, noting the absence of "humanistic" language in *Capital*. This view lost all credibility with the publication in English of the notebooks for *Capital*, known as *The Grundrisse*, in which all the early language reappears.

22. Some of those taking this position are: Louis Althusser, *For Marx*, (London: Pantheon, 1969); Vernon Venable, *Human Nature: The Marxian View* (Cleveland: World, 1966); Sidney Hook, *From Hegel to Marx* (Ann Arbor: University of Michigan, 1962); Lucien Seve, *Man in Marxist Theory and the Psychology of Personality*, (Brighton: Harvester, 1978).

23. Norman Geras, *Marx and Human Nature: Refutation of a Legend*, (London: Verso, 1983). Some others who take this position are: Andrew Collier, "Materialism and Explanation in the Human Sciences," in John Mepham and David Hillel Ruben, eds., *Issues in Marxist*

Philosophy 2, *Materialism* (Brighton: Harvester, 1979); G.A. Cohen, *Karl Marx's Theory of History: A Defense* (Oxford: Oxford University Press, 1978); Agnes Heller, *The Theory of Need in Marx* (London: Alison and Busby, 1976); Bertell Ollman, *Alienation: Marx's Concept of Man in Capitalist Society*, (Cambridge: Cambridge University Press, 1971); and Soper, *Humanism and Anti-Humanism*; although they do not all agree about the precise content or its role in Marx's theories, G.A. Cohen, for example, giving it a larger explanatory role in historical materialism than some others.

24. Consider the following remarks by the distinguished biologists Richard Levins and R.L. Lewontin, who also happen to be Marxists: "If ideas of human nature have any value, they must be able to cope with such biologically basic functions as eating.... Eating is obviously related to nutrition, but in humans this physiological necessity is embedded in a complex matrix: *within which* what is eaten, whom you eat with, how often you eat, who prepares the food, which foods are necessary for a sense of well-being, who goes hungry, and who overeats have all been torn loose from the requirements of nutrition or the availability of food.... A study of the physical act itself, its biological preconditions, its evolution, its similarity to that behavior in other animals, or the regions of brain that influence it will simply be irrelevant to the human phenomenon." *The Dialectical Biologist* (Cambridge, MA: Harvard University Press, 1985), pp. 260–263.

25. See Steven Rose, "From Causation to Translation: a Dialectical Solution to a Reductionist Dilemma," in Steven Rose, ed., *Bressanone Papers* (London: New Left Books, 1981). An alternative is given by Martin Barker in "Human Biology and the Possibility of Socialism," in John Mepham and David Hillel Ruben, eds., *Issues in Marxist Philosophy* 4 (Brighton: Harvester, 1979). See also Sebastiano Timpanaro, *On Materialism* (London: New Left Books, 1970), on the importance of biology for Marxism.

26. He says in *Capital,* "By...acting on the external world and changing it, [man] at the same time changes his own nature," p. 177. Engels suggested labor was key not only to the development *of* human beings, but also to the development *to* human beings. (New York: International, 1967). See Frederich Engels, "The Part Played by Labor in the Transition from Ape to Man," in Karl Marx and Frederich Engels, *Selected Works* (New York: International, 1968).

27. Geras, Marx and Human Nature, p. 67.

28. "Economic and Philosophical Manuscripts," in Richard C. Tucker, ed., *The Marx-Engels Reader* (New York: Norton, 1964), p. 88–89.

29. This characterization of human labor comes from *Capital I* (New York: International, 1972), p. 178.

30. Marx says, "Men can be distinguished from animals by consciousness, by religion, or anything else you like. *They themselves begin to distinguish themselves from animals* (my emphasis) as soon as they begin to *produce* their means of subsistence, a step which is conditioned by their physical organization." *The German Ideology*, in R. Tucker, ed., *The Marx-Engels Reader* (New York: , 1978), p. 150.

31. Gould, *Mismeasure*, pp. 326, 331.

32. See Karl Marx, *Grundrisse*, (Baltimore: Penguin, 1973), p. 611; also Jon Elster, "Self-Realisation in Work and Politics: the Marxist Conception of the Good Life," in Jon Elster and Karl Ove Moene, eds., *Alternatives to Capitalism* (Cambridge: Cambridge University Press, 1989).

33. See Sabina Lovibond, "Feminism and Pragmatism: A Reply to Richard Rorty," *New Left Review* 178 (1989), pp. 5–28.

THE INFLUENCE OF GENDER AND RACE STATUS ON SELF-ESTEEM DURING CHILDHOOD AND ADOLESCENCE

Helena Jia Hershel

chapter 8

INTRODUCTION

SEX AND race status influence self-esteem and notably the developmental tasks faced during critical junctures in a person's life. As discussed in this chapter, the child develops in reference to both the socializing gaze of parents and community. The "gaze" refers to how the child is seen in the eyes of others. The gaze encompasses the respect and consideration, or lack of such respect and consideration, shown the child by people the child considers significant. This gaze includes the attitudes and feelings conveyed and perceived by the child through sight, sound, and touch. The parental gaze in childhood focuses on gender socialization and plays a significant role as part of early identity formation. The "societal gaze" plays a more significant role in adolescent identity formation and is focused to a greater extent on race.

Sex and race are significant indicators of social status. As contributors to status, "gender and ethnicity are undoubtedly the most permanent, most noticeable, and have the most established attributional systems to accompany them."[1] The valences of sex and race status are variable. Race plays an equal, if not more important, role in forming identity than does gender at certain life stages. At times being female is more salient to identity than being of color; at other times being of color matters more. A third variable is the combined effect of ethnicity and gender, which has been referred to as "ethgender."[2] The effect of race and gender on self-esteem (or self-concept) has been distinguished into two classes of self-esteem; these classes include a core self-concept and a public self-concept.[3]

The core self-concept relates to the central personal feeling of self-esteem. For example, among dominant-group children and minority children there is little difference in what is referred to as core or global self-esteem. Both race and social class are not considered significant factors in core self-esteem among young children.[4] Yet the core self-esteem of female children and adolescents is lower than of male children and adolescents in general.[5]

Public self-concept, on the other hand, is the way an individual perceives and internalizes how he or she is regarded by others. Public self-concept reverses everything because here race more than sex becomes a deciding factor in lower self-esteem. In terms of gender, female adolescents have a higher public self-esteem and a lower core self-esteem while male adolescents have the reverse: a higher core self-esteem and lower public self-esteem.[6]

As noted in the studies cited above, gender status, race status or ethgender status, significantly affect a child's senses of well-being and self-esteem. Self-esteem is not just feeling confident or worthy; it is a measure of internal self-cohesiveness that underlies the ability to function with ease in the world.

The core self-esteem of females is more at risk than their public self-esteem.[7] In order to understand this phenomena, the family and the family's relationship to gender status offers some insight on how this occurs.

I. THE PARENTAL GAZE AND GENDER

Self-esteem begins early with the gaze of the parent. Yet what is overlooked is that this particular gaze often begins even before birth. It is not uncommon for parents to know or surmise a child's sex during pregnancy. The effects of this knowledge may be the first recognizable sign of the unborn baby's identity. Parents will announce the gender of the gestating fetus; concomitantly sex role expectations and gender typing begin with the exchange of folklore on how boys are different from girls even as they are carried in the belly.[8]

During infancy, the parental gaze bestows a sense of well-being and security. Issues of trust and mistrust begin with the parental bond and are based on the child's ability to deal with object constancy (the ability to hold and internalize the image of a person and the feelings associated with that person cognitively). The child begins to form an internalized image of the parent so that when the parent is gone the child does not necessarily feel abandoned by the parent but can trust that the significant parent will remain.[9] The child in this way internalizes into his or her psyche the image of the parent. The world of the infant is primarily the infant-parent bond. So object constancy means the parent is constant and consistent, and this is reassuring, giving the infant a sense of trust in his or her world.

The gaze of the parent on the child gives the child the feeling that it is in unity with the world. A warm accepting gaze suggests to the infant that the world is OK. The child senses being held and comforted and seen. Being seen is tantamount to being understood. The infant is merged with the parent: "I am okay because you are okay. We are one and the same."

However, parents relay gender messages even at this tender age. In many cultures the female baby diminishes the status of the mother or father; consequently, the child's sex becomes a symbol of disappointment.[10] It is in the gaze expressed verbally or nonverbally that the gender status is communicated. The gaze of the parent is the locus of this approval and disapproval. The infant child is attuned to the nonverbal cues of the parent and registers this approval even prior to acquisition of language. She knows she is well cared for by being held, fed, and kept comfortable. She also learns to read distress in the parent's face and picks up disapproval, not just "you disapprove of me," but also "my world is in danger."

Girls tend to be very aware of relationships and of the emotional cues of others. How this sensitivity to both verbal and especially nonverbal cues arises is subject to speculation.[11] Perhaps the gaze of the parents demands this awareness, perhaps this awareness comes with subordinate status. This awareness, in part, may account for why females in general are more relational than males and more in tune with the context and the relationship of themselves to others.

Parental nurture brings a sense of security that is progressively built upon through the child's experimentation with his or her abilities, including testing the environment. Challenges arise for the child and continue to add to the child's sense of achievement, only if the challenges are not insurmountable, overwhelming, or intensely frustrating. The child's merger with the parent is gradually replaced by a growing sense of will. Two- and three-year-olds demonstrate this will by repeatedly saying "no," wanting to do things by themselves without aid, and occasionally trying to run away from the parents. Emerging is a sense of core self and testing of self boundaries with the parent. If this development of will is impeded, the child may become self-doubting and show a lack of initiative later in life and an unindividuated self may result.[12] Self-esteem takes hold as the child simultaneously feels the acceptance of the parent along with a growing sense of independence and achievement. Security, parental bonding, and the knowledge that the world is manageable and consistent is at the root of self-esteem and the emergence of the core self.

Recognition of a "core gender identity" is thought to start at one and a half years as a product of cognitive abilities, gender labeling, and parental attitudes.[13] By age three, gender preferences are noted in choice of different toys and preference to play with same-sex peers.[14] To aid in making the world a known place, the three-year-old distinguishes people by sex and race. Children at this age recognize physiological differences and are able to categorize people with the use of language. Racial differences can become an important distinction if reinforced culturally. When racial awareness occurs at this age, race like gender may also be given a value judgment. The internalized gaze of the parent is the locus of this approval and disapproval. By three years old a primitive morality encompasses most aspects of a child's life. Moral judgments such as good and bad are internalized. Sometimes at this age good and bad are qualifiers to many things, including sex and race: some girls want to be boys, and some children of color want to be white.[15]

The child's trust is intimately allied with parental expectations. As parental expectations are met by the child, the child assumes a trusting position, not only to her caretaker, but to her inner world and nascent world view. When these expectations are gender-coded with inferiority or subordination, the female child is co-opted into colluding with her own gender oppression. Gender-coded parental expectations may inhibit the development of self-esteem and give rise to a sense of inferiority. Inferiority is also the way the child defends against negative feelings toward the parent. Rather than risk devaluing the critical parent and threatening the relationship, the child devalues herself. In this way, the child can continue to idealize the parent. The parent remains good and the child becomes bad and blameworthy. But the child is not just bad, instead, she or he is "a bad girl" or "a bad boy." Because the parental bond is crucial to survival of the child, negative messages are internalized deep in the emerging core self.[16]

While the parental gaze may contribute to our understanding of why the core self is affected, it is only a part of the socialization of the female. Female children are kept in a bond with the mother longer than their male counterparts. On the other hand, boys are more often socialized away from the mother and brought into a male world often by the father.[17]

Sexism also originates in the family structure. Where preferences for male children are the norm, an often-desired birth order pattern is firstborn male child and secondborn female child. This pattern reinforces the higher male status over female status. Here age and sex work in combination. This familial pattern is conventionally replicated in adult marriages with older male status and younger female status, again conferring superiority to gender and age simultaneously. The sex of a child also may have economic implications; in communities where children serve as labor, males have been more desirable. Clearly, the impact of a child's sex interplays forcefully with many factors such as economics and patrilineal kinship systems.[18]

The acknowledgment of gender, and to a lesser degree race, begins in early life, as part of the growth process of learning. But how these statuses are valued is also tied to the cultural values of the child's community. As the child matures, the gaze of the parent is extended to the gaze of the community, and the child's well-being and self-esteem interact with and are mirrored by the community. The child now must find security and trust in the world that is away from the family, most notably upon the encounter with the larger community that begins with public school.

II. THE SOCIETAL GAZE TOWARD GENDER AND RACE

Sex is a prime determinant at the beginning of life because gender expectations are, for the most part, conveyed and socialized in the family. Race can be an aspect of early socialization in the family, but racism is most often encountered outside the family. However, it should be noted that in certain circumstance race may become an internal family issue. This is most likely to occur if the racial self-hatred of the parent is conveyed to the child; or if the child's race is put into question due to the lack of acceptance by extended family, as is the case for some mixed race children; or if determination of how light- or dark-skinned the child is a factor.[19] Familial ambivalence about race or color can be transmitted to the child at this earliest age.

As the child leaves the homogeneity of the family for a racially diverse society, the child encounters strangers to herself and feels the strangeness of herself as well. For example, the child becomes aware of a world outside of the family that does not resemble the previously taken-for-granted world that provided security. In seeing that which is different from herself the child begins to define the limits of and the context in which she lives. Self-awareness comes from being able to objectify oneself in this manner. The diverse community mirrors differences and in so doing offers a chance for self-evaluation. This is an important juncture in a child's life to recognize herself and others that are different from her racially and culturally. It is an opportunity for expanding her horizon.[20] The positive nature of self-awareness and objectification can turn into alienation if this self-awareness is prompted by the negative gaze of the community.

Adolescence is when many children begin having extensive independent contact with the social world. If the community conveys the message "we are okay, but you are not okay," then the child attempts to find some defensive strategy to ward off this gaze and the ensuing alienation: "Perhaps I'll change the way I look; perhaps I'll distance myself from my parents; perhaps I'll become defiant and angry; perhaps I'll withdraw; perhaps I'll give up; perhaps I'll show them." These attitudes are common to most adolescents. Many white suburban adolescents work at becoming self-conscious and invoke the alienation of their community as a way to begin to define an independent identity, that is, one individuated from their family of origin.[21] However, the alienation of the adolescent of color is not elective alienation. The community's reflection back to them defines even more readily the issue of race privilege or nonprivilege. The realities of opportunities, advancement, and one's future are dependent on finding a way to thrive in a society that has a

113

negative gaze. The negative gaze is seemingly more focused toward males of color than females of color; at this point males of color are viewed as a greater threat.

Adolescence is a time of reworking early childhood issues of rapprochement once again.[22] The issue of rapprochement exemplifies the development of a core identity. The child leaves the vicinity of the parent to explore, and then comes back for reassurance. The positive regard of the parent to this exploration allows a nascent self to emerge that is differentiated from the parent. If the parent demands the child's obedience in the service of the parent then the child's development of an independent self is arrested or delayed, and trust is broken between parent and child.

In adolescence, the child again moves to and from the parents in an attempt to define himself, in preparation for the final departure from home and launching into the larger community. The ability to move into the community is tempered by the quality of gender and racial acceptance. The gaze of the community, when different from the parental gaze, challenges the core self and reflects back a public self. The core self and the public self may be at odds. Or, the gaze of the community may be inconsistent, sending a mixed message to the adolescent.

The adolescent must find a way through the socialization of the parents and the community to achieve an identity that is suitable. As an adolescent, limitations of social status within the community become apparent. While females are most at risk due to the socializing gaze of the family, males of color are adversely affected by public self-esteem since race is a greater indicator of social status than gender in our communities.

III. CONCLUSION

A person's gender and race influences their sense of self-esteem and identity throughout the lifespan. This chapter only begins to explore the significance of the parental and community gaze as it applies to childhood; the effects are discernible in general patterns throughout successive stages of life. Though the effects of gender and race vary with each person, self-esteem is a continual process always effected either in the family or through society by the gaze of others.

Marginality as a social status is bestowed by those who have the power to define the relevance of gender and race. This power initially resides with parents through their transmittal of their culture, values, and prejudices and later through the community in which the adolescent seeks adulthood. Self-esteem is built upon security and trust, which in turn allows for challenge and mastery. Trust in the world is vital to a person's psychological survival. With trust there is resilience, without trust there is immense fragility.

NOTES

1. Pamela Trotman Reid and Lillian Comas Diaz, "Gender and Ethnicity: Perspectives on Dual Status," *Sex Roles: A Journal of Research* 22, nos. 7/8 (April 1990), p. 397.

2. Background on the development of the idea of "ethgender" is discussed in Ruben Martinez and Richard L. Dukes, "Ethnic and Gender Differences in Self-Esteem," *Youth & Society* 22, no. 3 (March 1991), p. 320–321. Martinez and Dukes' study of ethgender with junior and high school students concluded that "racism and sexism appear to grind female minority group members down as they move from junior to senior high school, reflecting, perhaps, cumulative effects." (Ibid., p. 330.) However, this grinding down is not uniform. Asian and white females measured lower on self-perceived self-esteem than other ethnic groups, with Asian females rating the most dissatisfaction with themselves in this study. And yet, the combined status of being black and female has shown higher self-perceived self-esteem than other race/females in this and other studies. Self-perceived self-esteem has much to do with levels of self-expectation and the ability to meet them, whether high or low. This differs from self-esteem as used in this chapter which is comparative across gender and race and not self-perceived. See for example, J. Heiss and S. Owens, "Self-Evaluations of Blacks and Whites," *American Journal of Sociology* 78 (1972), pp. 360–370; C.B. Turner and B.T. Turner, "Gender, Race, Social Class, and Self-Evaluations Among College Students," *The Sociological Quarterly* 23 (1982), pp. 491–507; Carlton T. Pyant and Barbara J. Yanico, "Relationship of Racial Identity and Gender-Role Attitudes to Black Women's Psychological Well-Being," *Journal of Counseling Psychology* 38, no. 3 (1991), pp. 315–322. A comparison of white and black children demonstrated how gender stereotypic behavior is less pervasive among pre-adolescent black children. See Reid and Diaz, "Gender and Ethnicity," pp. 397–407.

3. See Turner and Turner, "Gender, Race," pp. 491–507; P. Hines and L. Berg-Cross, "Racial Differences in Global Self-Esteem," *The Journal of Social Psychology* 113 (1981), pp. 271–281; H.W. Marsh and R. Shavelson, "Self-Concept: Its Multifaceted Hierarchical Structure," *Educational Psychologist* 20, pp. 107–123; and Richard L. Dukes and Ruben Martinez, "The Impact of Ethgender Among Adolescents," *Adolescence* 29, no. 113 (Spring 1994), pp. 105–108.

115

4. See Aaron M. Pallas, Doris R. Entwisle, and Karl L. Alexander, "Social Structure and the Development of Self-Esteem in Young Children," *Social Psychology Quarterly* 53, no. 4 (December 1990), pp. 302–315.

5. "…[W]e find large, early differences between boys and girls in levels of self-esteem and clear indications that these disparities increase with time." Pallas, Entwisle, and Alexander, "Social Structure," p. 314. See also Maykel Verkuyten, "Impact of Ethnic and Sex Differences on Global Self-Esteem Among Adolescents in the Netherlands," *Psychological Reports* 59 (1986), p. 446; Dukes and Martinez, "The Impact," pp. 105–108.

6. Dukes and Martinez, "The Impact," p. 113.

7. Ibid.

8. Speculation about gender has created a lot of folklore as a prediction of the gender of the newborn. For example, Italian-American folklore suggests that boys are carried up front in the belly while girls are carried back on the ass.

9. The game of peek-a-boo is a training as well as an exercise in the accomplishment of this task. The child's joy at refinding the person who temporarily disappears from view to reappear causing some anxiety, followed by a sudden startle at the reappearance and then reassurance.

10. A lament of mothers in traditional societies where boys are more highly valued is: "If only I had a boy I would be more valued in my household." Also, if the mother's status is inferior to her husband the female child is given this same birthright of low status.

11. Much work has been done in this area of "self in relation" theories by the Stone Center in Massachusetts. See Judith V. Jordan, Alexandra G. Kaplan, Jean Baker Miller, Irene P. Stiver, and Janet L. Surrey, eds., *Women's Growth in Connection: Writings from the Stone Center* (New York: The Guilford Press, 1991).

12. Willfulness is more easily tolerated in males than females. The tolerances for being a bad girl are less than the tolerances for being a bad boy. Boys are given more latitude: as the saying goes, "boys will be boys." This difference gives boys more space to define themselves away from the parental bond. Girls on the other hand often grow into women not knowing who they are independent of the relationships they are in. It is in this sense that they are unindividuated. Gilligan refers to this as "The fusion of identity and intimacy" [Carol Gilligan, *In a Different Voice: Psychological Theory and Women's Development* (Cambridge, Mass.: Harvard University Press, 1982), p. 159]. This is also manifested in the struggle of women to be in a relationship but not lose their identity which can be precarious depending on earlier socialization. Women often struggle with dependency and autonomy and conflict arises in trying to discern the difference between intimacy and dependency and the difference between isolation and autonomy.

13. See the discussion of R. J. Stoller, "The Sense of Femaleness," *Psychoanalytic Quarterly*, 37 (1968), pp. 42–55, in Irene P. Stiver, "Beyond the Oedipal Complex: Mothers and Daughters," itself in Jordan, Kaplan, Miller, Stiver, and Surrey, eds., *Women's Growth*, p. 103.

14. Henry Gleitman, *Psychology*, 2nd ed. (New York: W. W. Norton & Company, Inc., 1986), p. 548.

15. Lillian Comas-Diaz explores these dualities of good/bad female/color in what she calls the metaphor of colonization, whereby a woman must resist "her dualistic and dichotomous mode of thinking...[and]...confront her internalized negative self image." See Lillian Comas-Diaz, "An Integrative Approach," in *Women of Color: Integrating Ethnic and Gender Identities in Psychotherapy*, Lillian Comas-Diaz and Beverly Greene, eds. (New York: The Guilford Press, 1994), p. 290.

116

16. The survival of female children is of grave concern in China where the single child policy and desire to have a male child to take care of the older generation and pass the family name on has renewed the ancient practice of female infanticide. Sex choice as a factor in abortions brings this practice closer to home.

17. See Alexandra G. Kaplan, "Women's Self-Development in Late Adolescence," in Jordan, Kaplan, Miller, Stiver, and Surrey, eds., *Women's Growth*, pp. 122–142.

18. For example, less valued is female labor. An exception to this is the large farm family with many children and the older female running the house so as to free up the labor of husband and wife. Primogeniture and patrilineal kinship systems secure rights to males in traditional societies. The economic rights of firstborn male still play out in many societies where the father's business is passed on to a male child.

19. Helena J. Hershel, "Therapeutic Perspectives on Biracial Formation and Internalized Oppression," in Naomi Zack, ed., *American Mixed Race: The Culture of Microdiversity* (Lanham, Maryland: Rowman and Littlefield, 1995), pp. 169–184.

20. This encounter happens for people at various ages. In some insular and xenophobic communities, the individual may not encounter this until adulthood or never. For others, college or high school may present the first opportunity to develop self-awareness in reference to race awareness.

21. Suburban parents react with consternation when they discover how their kids adopt urban black culture in dress, music, and attitudes. Part of the move to the suburbs is to distance themselves from this influence.

22. See Peter Blos, "The Second Individuation Process of Adolescence," *Psychoanalytic Study of the Child*, 22 (1967), pp. 162–186.

PHENOMENOLOGY

RACE, SEX, AND MATRICES OF DESIRE IN AN ANTIBLACK WORLD:

An Essay in Phenomenology and Social Role

Lewis R. Gordon

In appearance too a boy is like a woman, and the woman is as it were an infertile male; for the female exists in virtue of a particular incapacity, in being unable to concoct seed out of the nutriment in its last stage (which is either blood or the analogous part in the bloodless animals) owing to the coldness of her nature.

—Aristotle

We are accustomed to say that every human being displays both male and female instinctual impulses, needs and attributes; but though anatomy, it is true, can point out the characteristics of maleness and femaleness, psychology cannot. For psychology the contrast between the sexes fades away into one between activity and passivity, in which we far too readily identify activity with maleness and passivity with femaleness, a view which is by no means universally confirmed in the animal kingdom.

—Freud

…the Negrophobe is a repressed homosexual…. Is the lynching of the Negro not a sexual revenge? We know how much of sexuality there is in all cruelties, tortures, beatings. One has only to reread some pages of the Marquis de Sade and one will easily be convinced. Is the sexual superiority of the Negro real? Everyone knows that it is not. But that does not matter. The prelogical thought of the phobic has decided that such is the case.

—Fanon

OUR EPIGRAPHS are two classic statements on sexuality and one classic, provocative statement on its intersection with race.[1] In Aristotle's world, where the hierarchies of a mythology are writ large and are at the core of a rational ordering of the universe, we find that the question of gender is colored by an indirect reference to the cold and consequently the dark. In that world, where the biological is linked to the reproductive, woman is worse than a derivative of man; she is also a derivative of the human being. For whereas male stands as the formal constitution of human reality, female is treated as an undeveloped male and consequently an undeveloped human being, a less-than-human being. To be is to be both form and a mover, which Aristotle linked to fertility. The male was a fertile mover who brought form into matter (female) and hence the concrete reality of the human species. In that world, then, one does not see female as a gender at all, another constituent of the human species. One sees simply males/human beings and less-developed-males/less-developed-human beings—that is, *one* gender.[2]

By the time of Freud, we witness a schism between reproductive capacities and gender, where male and female refer to realities that are fertile, in spite of the etymological link between *gender* and Greek words like *gênesis* (birth) and *genos* (kind). For Freud, the psychological constructions of sexual identity need not be linked to the markers male and female. In Freud's world, then, a female can be what psychologists regard as masculine and a male can be what psychologists regard as feminine.[3]

Separating the gender-sex link does not entail, however, a schism between the acts signified by the previous relationship. Thus, the masculine performance of a female can restructure her relation to a feminine male. This coding is made particularly multivalent when we add, as does Fanon, racial significations to the context. If we make as our model the context that I have coined elsewhere[4] as an *antiblack world*, we can see immediately how Fanon's remarks come into focus. For if a group is structured in a phobogenic, overdetermined way to signify hot/active/masculine/white and another group is constructed as cold/passive/feminine/black, then relationships between males and females in such a world may be skewed with subtexts of transformed sexual meanings: white males and black males may relate to each other in homoerotic ways that may be more genital than social; on the social level, the relation may be heterosexual and misogynous.

In chapters 14 and 17 of my book, *Bad Faith and Antiblack Racism*, I explored the significance of intersections between sexual relationships and race through Sartrean conceptions of desire and provided an analysis of black and white bodies in bad faith. My discussions of sexuality there were cursory, however, since they were situated only as considerations along the road of a phenomenological ontology.[5] In this essay, I would like to provide a discussion of racial and sexual matrices and their significance for the understanding of phenomenological treatments of social role. It is my aim to show how the false reality created by such bad-faith forms of desire ironically provides a clue for richer understanding of desire and, consequently, racial and sexual roles.

I begin by articulating a few key concepts. I have noticed in Freud's and Fanon's descriptions indirect references to the constructability of human identity formations. An implication of this conception of identity is the view that human identity is made or lived; it is not a "natural" feature of the world. Where it is made or treated as constituted by an already existing social order, we may call it a social identity or a social role. Where it is lived, we can simply call it an existential identity or existential reality.

Existential realities are transphenomenal realities. What this means is that how they are lived always surpasses how they are understood. Their existence precedes their essence or conceptualization, as it were. When the order is reversed, and the essence is treated or lived as preceding existence, we shall refer to that circumstance or attitude as *bad faith*. Bad faith closes human reality into an essential reality that precedes existence or lived reality.

A key feature of all social realities is that they are constituted realities. What that means is that they are *Geist*-realms or spirit-realms. They add nothing physical to the world, although they are positive, meaningful additions to reality. Two human beings standing side by side in love are no different from two human beings standing side by side in lust or hate from a physical point of view. But from what may be called the point of view of intentionality, the point of view of realities conditioned by meaning-contexts, there are worlds of difference. In bad faith, the difference is played upon and an effort at evasion emerges where social realities are either treated as consequences of nature and hence not constituted by human beings, or fictionalized and hence treated as nonexistent by virtue of being nonphysical. At the heart of bad faith, then, is a denial of agency in the human condition and a denial of the relationship between such agency and the constitution of meaning.

We find, then, in the advancement of bad faith as an index of human possibilities, a principle of positive contingency and agency: that although the human world may be contingently constituted (neither by necessity nor fate nor destiny) it is never accidental. It is a world of responsibility and the irony of limited choices. By limited choices are here meant decisions on the basis of options available. Options are what are available *in* the world; choices are what we make on the basis of those options, including how we may interpret the options themselves.

In order to articulate options, choices, and meanings, our inquiry must make an appeal to context. For options are not conditions etched in stone. They are simply wherever we happen to find ourselves or whatever is most relevant for our inquiry at hand. (Irrelevance has, as Schopenhauer would say, no principle of individuation.)

To decode matrices of race and sex requires contexts premised upon racial and sexual identities. The context that we shall here focus upon is the context of the

121

antiblack world. We shall focus on the antiblack world primarily because of its unique relation to the Western world. The Western world, as we see in Aristotle's depiction but can also see in many other sources, is conditioned by a binary logos of opposition. What this means is that the system functions contextually by always placing any two terms as far from each other as possible on the basis of that which supposedly differentiates them. Since the Western valuative system has historically placed positivity and its self-identity on the value of the white, that means that its primary opposition is structured on the level of the black. To speak of racial opposition, then, is to speak of white and black.

Now although this may make it seem that one can immediately speak of race and gender simply by placing the opposition in respective lines, that would be an error. For although an antiblack world is fundamentally a misogynous world, a misogynous world is not necessarily an antiblack one. For instance, in Aristotle's world, there was simply one gender: male. What we call female was in that world simply not-male. Race, in that world, was simply meant in the form of genus. Only males were considered to be really part of the human *race*. Women, as women are envisaged in contemporary Western society, were not *seen* in Aristotle's world. On the other hand, in an antiblack world race is only designated by those who signify racial-identification. A clue to that identification is in the notion of being "colored." Not being colored signifies being white, and as a consequence, being raceless, whereas being colored signifies being a race. Thus, although the human race is centered as being white, racialized human beings, in other words, a subspecies of humanity, are nonwhite. The negation is the supposedly opposite term—in a word, the black. In effect, then, in the antiblack world there is but one race, and that race is black. Thus, to be racialized is to be pushed "down" toward blackness, and to be deracialized is to be pushed "up" toward whiteness. So, we have

> *Aristotle's world*: to be gendered and to avoid being non-gendered—that is, female (not-male-enough).

> *The antiblack world*: to be raceless and to avoid being racialized—that is, being black (being never-white-enough).

It is ironic that today when we say "gender studies" we invariably mean discourses on women. A lot has changed since Aristotle's time. The centered significance of gender has been pushed to a racial paradigm, where gender has begun to function like race. As a consequence, the genderless designation has become a goal similar to the racial designation. How can this be possible without a shift in the binaries by way of a third term?

Let us call this third term *power*. What thus emerges is the following:

The antigender world: to be genderless and to avoid being gendered—that is, determined, powerless, defined by others, feminine.

The antiblack world: to be raceless and to avoid being racialized—that is, determined, powerless, defined by others, black.

The third term of power: to be neutral, genderless, raceless—that is, self-determined, powerful, self-defined, neither feminine nor black, which amounts to being masculine and white.

There are obvious breakdowns of logic in this triad. Take the third. If to have the power of self-determination means to be white, what can be made of determinations not to be white? Although the determinations may be lived as raceless and genderless, the social meanings are clearly skewed, since the "meaning" of being white in an antiblack–infected social sphere equates whiteness with such neutrality. Clearly, then, all three worlds are bad-faith worlds. To analyze the world that is conditioned by all three, which is the focus of this essay, requires multiple levels of analyses that correlate with the evasive nature of bad faith: one must, in other words, analyze a world lived as a world encountered; a world of contingency without accident.

How does desire correlate with sexual identities in such a world?

Desire is normatively constituted as avoiding *being* the black and feminized. What this means is that in such a world it is considered best to be the white and masculine. But since white and masculine are treated as positive variables, there is a short step in reasoning to white *or* masculine to white *as* masculine to white *equals* masculine and masculine equals white.

We find, in this logic, a complex framework of identity and desire premised upon the context itself as fundamentally *antiblack*. If white equals masculine and masculine equals white, then blackness and femininity become coextensive realities in an antiblack world. Such a world becomes diadic, with "mixture," if you will, being indexed by two polar realities as follows:

(Supposed) *Highest Nonmixture*: white/masculine. The claim to this position, in an antiblack world, is the white man. (We do not say white male since we have already problematized the relationship between masculinity and maleness, although we concede, as did Freud, that the tendency of masculinity to manifest itself in males must be acknowledged.)

(Supposed) *Lowest Nonmixture*: black/feminine. The claim to this position, in an antiblack world, is the black woman. (We do not say black female for the same reasons that we did not say white male.)

Mixture is now left for structures that cross the color-gender convergence. Thus

> *Mixture α*: white and mixed with feminine. The claim to this position in an antiblack world is not always clear. For now, we shall simply designate this α-mixture as white woman by virtue of the order of the pairs white and feminine. (We do not say white female since the significance of color/gender designation is already conditioned by the context itself—an *antiblack world*. A white female is not necessarily a mixture, since masculinity can attach to males and females; whereas a white woman is necessarily a mixture.)

> *Mixture β*: masculine and black. The claim to this position in an antiblack world is similarly problematized. (We do not say the black male for similar reasons as in the α-mixture.)

Now, what should be apparent is that the highest nonmixture functions as what Fanon calls a governing fiction over the mixed categories. And in fact, since the mixed categories do not stand as "pure" and therefore extremes, then we should have a proper hierarchical articulation in an antiblack world as follows:

> *Highest nonmixture* → α *mixture* α → *mixture* β → *lowest nonmixture.*

The reason for this schema is that the antiblack world is conditioned by what we can here describe as two principles of value:

> (1) It is best to be white but (2) above all, it is worst to be black.

When one fails to achieve principle (1), it becomes vital to avoid embodying the group designated by principle (2). We can reformulate our two principles thus:

> (1★) "be white!" but (2★) "don't be black!"

Mixture in this world is therefore conditioned by principles (2) and (2★) more than by principles (1) and (1★). The impact on sex-race constructions thus follows from the extent to which the sex-gender relationship serves as a leitmotif for the identities. For the extent to which sex is separated from gender will make all the difference between certain coextensive realities being homoerotic and homophobic on the one hand, or heteroerotic and misogynous on the other.

Our concerns are problematized even more by the constructivity dimension of color itself. For it should be obvious that 'black' and 'white' are not here meant to refer to colors in any ordinary sense but to the valuative expectations placed upon people who are meant to exemplify those colors. One doesn't "see" white and black people ordinarily but instead sees pink, brown, and a host of other shades of people, shades that may not correlate with the color designation—as we see so well in cases of brown caucasians and pink, in a word, *Negroes*.[6]

The constructivity of color designation has led some critical race theorists to reject race itself on the basis of its social constructivity and natural scientific invalidity.[7] A problem with the appeal to scientific invalidity, however, is that it is of no consequence in any other world but that of scientific positivism, for in effect it centers natural science as a model of assessment. But scientific positivism, as Edmund Husserl,[8] Alain Locke,[9] and Maurice Merleau-Ponty[10] have shown, is incapable of critical and admittedly *valuative* assessments of its own assumptions without contradiction. On the interpretive level, the basis of scientific meaning and value itself is at stake. To get to these questions requires metascientific considerations. We can see how the problem of a neopositivist and social constructivist approach to race plays itself out when we choose supposedly preferred descriptions like "human being" and "person." To define the human being in biophysical terms is one thing but to define what it means to "be" human is another. For assessments of the basis of adjudicating philosophical anthropological claims, more radical articulations of human "science" may be needed. Such radical articulations also demand interrogations of appeals to even the social constructivity of science itself. Our discussion suggests that the framework of the social is itself conditioned by intentional features which situate it on the level of constructivity as well. Thus, social constructivity amounts to asserting, redundantly, constructed constructivity.[11] To get at the heart of the matter requires, then, realization of both the active and passive components of social phenomena, that human communities maintain phenomena that are lived as pre-given phenomena. This pre-given dimension of phenomena carries reality principles and meaningful features that make them accessible to phenomenological reflection at disparate periods of time. It is in this regard that phenomena such as language and humanity, albeit constructed, are not fictional realities; they are dimensions of social reality.

Now, in worlds where social reality has been skewed, where it has become aim-inhibited, where it has become fundamentally antisocial, antihuman, anticommunicative, there are rigid, underlying themes of subverted recognition. What this means is that although there may be human beings in such a world, the sociohistorical features of that world may be such that ordinary expectations of human contact are inhibited. In an ordinary human environment, for instance, human phenomena are accessible to all human beings and as such have an anonymous dimension to their meaning; they become, in a word, *typical*. In a skewed context, however, the typical has been transformed in such a way that the atypical becomes normative. As a consequence, relationships are skewed in such a world, and what counts as typical of certain groups hides, in effect, rather atypical realities. For example, in an antiblack world, to be a typical black is to be an abnormal human being. Thus, normativity is indexed by its distance from blackness. As a consequence, the most the black can hope for is to be a black who is typically white, which in effect is to be atypically white. To be black in that world is therefore to be trapped in an obversion of normative reality: to be an extraordinary black is to be an ordinary person; to be an ordinary black is to be an extraordinary person. "Normal blackness," as Fanon has shown in *Peau noire, masques blancs*, is to be locked in the absurdity of everyday or banal pathology. The implications of this absurdity become stark when we return to our matrices of value and consider them with the added element of desire.

Desire can be constructed along matrices of (a) *most desired*, (b) *desired*, (c) *less desired*, and (d) *least desired*. Context will dictate what ideal types fall along each category. Since our context is an antiblack world, it should be obvious that on the level of color, to be white has its conclusion in (a) and to be black has its conclusion in (d). When gender is colorized and treated as coded forms of color, we find ourselves facing a world with a number of social enigmas.

On the one hand, there are two groups: the white and the black. Whoever lays claim to being "in between" does so only as a matter of distance from the black or closeness to the white, which is, for the white, still too close to the black for comfort. Since mixture is ultimately a function of colored gender configurations, the notion of "white woman" carries within it a positive element of whiteness and a negative element of blackness. Now, although most day-to-day activities carry an air of anonymity, where typically women and men pass by, in an antiblack world blacks and whites do not typically pass by. For to pass by typically means to be situated as a limited place of epistemic clarity: one simply doesn't know much about the typical Other beyond her or his typicality. In an antiblack world, however, to see black is to see a typicality that is epistemologically conclusive. What this means is that to see black is to see all that needs to be seen. It is to see a superfluous existent, a plenitude. To see the whiteness of white woman, then, calls for an act of epistemic closure on her blackness, to the point of closing off the color-coded dimension of her femininity—to, that is, not see her femininity. With such a seeing, she will have become "purified." "She" will become desire. "She" will be a point at which more needs to be known. "She" will be an informant into her subjective reality, realities that, if known, will be of objective value since they will be realities onto which and from which action will be encouraged. If, however, the closure is not possible and the feminine dimension, her blackness, is acknowledged, then she becomes a form of tainted whiteness. Her power in an antiblack world becomes a denial of her femininity. The conclusion? Her phallic order, power, becomes linked, fundamentally, to her skin, to her epidermal schema. In an antiblack world, the phallus is white skin.[12]

One may wonder what type of situation it is that emerges when the white (woman) is declared rapable, for as we know, there is a rich history around the avowed protection of whites from rapacious blacks in antiblack worlds. The obvious conclusion is that the history has nearly nothing to do with white *women* at all. In *Peau noire, masques blancs*, Fanon has observed that white male's aggression toward black males is saturated with homoerotic content. In his discussion, "Le Nègre et la Psycopathologie," he points out that the black is a phobogenic object, a stimulus to anxiety, in negrophobic people.[13] For the negrophobe, the black is not a symbol of certain negative realities. The black *is* those negative realities. Thus, if femininity is regarded as a negative characteristic of that world, the black will "be" femininity. The white concern with rape in such a world is conditioned by the extrication of the feminine dimension of woman in white woman. Rape in such a world is thus premised upon violating whiteness.

Since whiteness has been fundamentally structured as masculine, the violation becomes a violation of masculinity. The rape of white women—translated into this schema simply as "whites"—becomes to white men ultimately the rape of white men. The violent response that has been the history of lynching in the name of redressing the offense of rape in the U.S. antiblack world is therefore indicative of the form of bad faith manifested in homophobia: public violence locates the masculine identity's *rejection* of homosexual desire. But as is well known, there is a twist to this affair, for the lynched black body was often mutilated in a ritual of surgical restructuring; genitals were often removed and holes gauged into the bodies to eradicate vestiges of claimed masculinity. The sexual dimension of lynching, in other words, had to be restructured into a heterosexual framework. The black body becomes woman in toto. Woman, as the body of clay on which any form can be forced, becomes the motif of lynching. As a result, we find the history of mutilation, a history of literally cutting away all protruding and active bodily appendages, in the lynching of blacks of all sexes and ages.

Rape, as a form of violation, depends upon human agency for its existence. In our portrait of the conditions for rapability in an antiblack world, the place of subjectivity, and as a consequence consent and dissent, was the highest point on the hierarchical scale: whiteness/masculinity. For the phenomenon to appear as a violation of an agent and hence have standing before law requires that it embodies the phallic order in that world, that it be white. Where agency is denied, so, too, is violation. As a consequence, our matrices can be restructured as a portrait of rapability to "unrapability." In such a world, it would seem, black women (a redundant reality) are literally not rapable, for they lack the ability to dissent. A portrait of desire is implied by this conclusion.

Recall our two principles, that (1) it is best to be white and (2) it is worst to be black. We can add two correlates to these:

(1**) desire white and (2**) reject black.

Since the values of an antiblack world are existentially serious values—that is, values that are treated as material features of the beings who comprise that world[14]—we find ourselves encountering two more correlates:

127

GORDON

(1★★★) whiteness is the desired desire and (2★★★) blackness is the rejected existent.

As the desired desire, the white man's relation to the black woman becomes obvious in such a world: he is incapable of raping her because she is incapable of not desiring him. He is constructed as her desired desire, whereas he is constructed as not having desired her in the first place. In effect, she would be constructed as having violated *him* if physical contact occurred.[15]

Since the white female can only be recognized as rapable through suspending her womanness to the point of simply becoming "the white," then we find a similar derivation; "she" *must not have desired* the black and the black *must have desired* "her."

We find also that these considerations affect even avowed homosexual and lesbian structures in such a world. For white men in sexual relations with white men become the homosexual paradigm, whereas black women with black women become the lesbian paradigm. White female liaisons are restructured where whiteness becomes the operative dimension of gendered identity; the relationship becomes, in a word, masculine and therefore homosexual—unless, of course, womanness is the operative dimension of the specific instance of that relationship. Likewise, black male liaisons are restructured where blackness becomes the operative dimension of gendered identity; the relationship becomes feminine and hence a lesbian relation. We find even more twists in interracial relations, for the white female with a black female, given these matrices, becomes a "heterosexual" liaison; and so, too, becomes the white male with black male liaison.

Destruction of the link between the penis and the phallus and advancing an alternative configuration like white skin may, however, raise the following objection: but aren't black men nevertheless men by virtue of their chromosomal make up and their extended urethra, their penis? What about the extensive literature on the reduction of black males to their penis? On penis size?

Our analysis suggests that the significance of penis "color" must be brought into consideration in an antiblack world. Two penises of equal length are not of equal significance when they are of different "color." For, in an antiblack world, a black penis, whatever its size, represents a threat. Given our discussion of the black signifying the feminine, the underlying nature of the threat should be obvious: the black penis is feared for the same reason that a woman with a penis is feared. She represents a form of revenge. Literally, the very notion of a black *penis*, a demand *for* masculinity, spells danger. The rationale for lynching returns with an added dimension of prevention. In lynching and other forms of "castration" and bodily reconfiguration, the objective is to prevent the black from doing not what the black supposedly has done, but what the black *must want to do.* The black "penis" is phobogenically not a penis at all. It is a vagina bent upon revenge.

Now the reader should bear some obvious facts in mind, given our discussion thus far. The first, and most obvious, is that our stated existential commitments entail that the portrait presented here is limited to realities that are conditioned by its context. As Fanon has cautioned all of us who tread along the critical race terrain, not everyone will find her or himself in such texts.[16] The antiblack world is what phenomenological sociologists refer to as an *ideal type*.[17] An ideal type is a subjunctive reality. It is a world with a strict logic and strict rationality. It is a world that is governed by a specific ontology where the human being collapses under the weight of existence. Although in such a world there is only one perspective, the *critical* theorist who attempts a hermeneutic of such a world has the triple task of interpreting the two poles as perspectives and interpreting her or his own relation as a critical relation to such a world. By positing perspectivity to the bottom-pole of such a world, the theorist raises the question that Fanon raised in 1952: What is "the lived-experience of the black"? The theorist will then find two directional poles of theocratic values.

> *The white*: It is desirable to be a human being, but it is undesirable to be black. Whites are human beings but they are not gods, since to be gods would mean to be a desired desire, to be, in other words, better than human. Blacks, on the other hand, although human-like, are less than whites and therefore less human—or at least not the type of beings to desire to be.

> *The black*: Whites are the desired desire. They are therefore better than human. They are gods.[18]

129

Although the theorist ascribes perspectivity to both poles and to her or himself, in order not to slip into being the white, the theorist must be properly critical. What this means is that the theorist must not construct the theorist's position as a desired desire, or even a desirable position. Whether this is possible requires another discussion, but suffice it to say that a value-neutral theorist, even if desirable, is susceptible to our concerns about ideal typification and existence. As Merleau-Ponty cautions us in *Phénoménologie de la perception*, we should not lose existence for the sake of validity.[19]

So, what does our analysis offer for an understanding of social role?

The first and obvious conclusion is that context is a complex existential affair. Although we have been speaking of an ideal type, an antiblack world, the existential significance of bad faith enables us to understand how the ideality of the types are concealed by how they are *lived*.[20]

Next, although it may be common knowledge that some identities are more basic than others, as is the general view toward sex and gender, the phenomenological critique of the mundane permits the extraordinary dimensions of the ordinary to make themselves manifest. In the case of social role, the logic of gender in

GORDON

an antiblack world can be demonstrated to converge with the logic of race in ways that question the very meaning of sex.

Thus, third, the significance of social role emerges through the significance of context itself. The antiblack world is one context among many, but even in its case the extratextual consideration of gender comes into play. Isolated meanings, although useful for modeling and assessments premised upon formulating paradigm cases, will never achieve *social* significance without exhausting themselves.

Finally, as we saw in our discussion of desire, identities can be structured by multiple matrices of value. These matrices take multivalent forms of sexual, political, and theological economies of expression premised upon centers of power. In the intersection of sex and race, we found not only white people and people of color, men and women, but we found also prosthetic gods and a dark continent of effeminate existent—a world, that is, of spirit and nature conditioned by identities that transform themselves along grids of institutional power.

Where do we go from here?

Our project was primarily interpretative. The obvious methodological consideration is that theorizing sex, gender, and race in an antiblack world calls for understanding of ideal typifications of lived realities. It demands an existential sociology.

On the question of the antiblack/misogynous world itself, our existential concern, committed to preceding essence, beseeches us to admit what we see as we attempt, in the spirit of an eleventh thesis of a century ago, to change our world.

130 **NOTES**

I would like to thank Lisa Anderson, Lisa Gordon, Joy Ann James, T. Denean Sharpley-Whiting, and Naomi Zack for comments on early drafts of this work. This essay is dedicated to all those women and men who have suffered through the lived-nightmare of silent screams.

1. Epigraph citation: Aristotle, Aristotle's "De Partibus Animalium I" and "De Generatione Animalium I" (with Passages from II. 1–3), D.M. Balme, ed. (Oxford: Clarendon, 1972), 728a17–21; Sigmund Freud, Civilization and Its Discontents, trans. and ed. by James Strachey, Standard Edition (New York: W.W. Norton & Company, 1961), pp. 58–9; Franz Fanon, Peau noire, masques blancs (Paris: Éditions de Seuil, 1952), pp. 127, 129; the translation is mine. The standard English edition of Peau noire is Black Skin, White Masks, trans. Charles Lam Markmann (New York: Grove 1967), and the relevant passages are pp. 156, 159.

2. Cf. Judith Butler, *Bodies that Matter: On the Discursive Limits of "Sex"* (New York and London: Routledge, 1993).

3. Teresa Brennan has argued that it is this disjunction of sex and gender that led to the Freudian riddle of femininity: "Why is [femininity] found in men?" (*The Interpretation of the Flesh: Freud and Femininity* (London and New York: Routledge, 1992), p. 8.) We also find an existential psychoanalytical dimension of this question in Simone de Beauvoir's restructuring womanhood away from birth and into the realm of project and historicity; see her classic *Le deuxième sexe* (Paris: Gallimard, 1949).

4. Lewis R. Gordon, *Bad Faith and Antiblack Racism* (Atlantic Highlands, NJ: Humanities Press, 1995).

GORDON

5. For discussion and critique of that work, see Paget Henry, "African and Afro-Caribbean Existential Philosophies," in Lewis R. Gordon, ed., *Existence in Black: An Anthology of Black Existential Philosophy* (New York and London: Routledge, 1996) and Patricia Huntington, "White Gods, Raw Desire, Misogyny: A Feminist Conversation with Gordon's *Bad Faith and Antiblack Racism*" (forthcoming).

6. See Gordon, *Bad Faith*, chaps. 13–14; Lewis R. Gordon, "'Critical' Mixed-Race?" *Social Identities* 1, no. 2 (1995), pp. 381–395; and Tommy Lott, "Du Bois on the Invention of Race," *Philosophical Forum* XXIV, nos. 1–3 (Fall–Spring 1992–93), pp. 166–187.

7. The most well-known proponents of this basis for rejecting the concept of race are Anthony Appiah, *In My Father's House: Africa and Philosophy of Culture* (New York: Oxford University Press, 1992), and Naomi Zack, *Race and Mixed Race* (Philadelphia: Temple University Press, 1993). My criticisms of this position can be found in Gordon, *Bad Faith*, Part II, and Lewis R. Gordon, *Her Majesty's Other Children: Philosophical Sketches from a Neocolonial Age* (forthcoming), Part I. Zack's position also has an existential dimension. See Naomi Zack, "Race, Life, Death, Identity, Tragedy," in Gordon, ed., *Existence in Black*.

8. See Edmund Husserl, "Philosophie als strenge Wissenschaft," *Logos*, 1 (1910–11), pp. 289–341. This essay is also found in Edmund Husserl, *Phenomenology and the Crisis of Philosophy*, trans. and ed. by Quentin Lauer (New York: Harper & Row, 1965).

9. See Alain Locke's essays "Values and Imperatives" and "Value," in Leonard Harris, ed., *The Philosophy of Alain Locke: Harlem Renaissance and Beyond* (Philadelphia: Temple University Press, 1989), chaps. 1 and 7.

10. Maurice Merleau-Ponty, *Phénoménologie de la Perception* (Paris: Gallimard, 1945), *passim*; English translation by Colin Smith, *Phenomenology of Perception* (New York and London: Routledge/Humanities Press, 1962).

11. See Lewis R. Gordon, *Fanon and the Crisis of European Man: An Essay on Philosophy and the Human Sciences* (New York and London: Routledge, 1995), chap. 3.

12. Although I discuss this conclusion in my *Bad Faith and Antiblack Racism*, Patricia Huntington develops its implications for a critique of poststructural psychoanalyses of gender; again, see her essay, "White Gods, Raw Desire, Misogyny."

131

13. For discussion of Fanon's conception of phobogenesis, see my essays, "The Black and the Body Politic: Fanon's Existential Phenomenological Critique of Psychoanalysis," in Lewis R. Gordon, T. Denean Sharpley-Whiting, and Renée T. White, eds., *Fanon: A Critical Reader* (Oxford: Blackwell Publishers, 1996), and "Existential Dynamics of Black Invisibility," in Gordon, ed., *Existence in Black*.

14. See Gordon, *Bad Faith*, chap. 6, for a discussion of the spirit of seriousness, and Part III for a discussion of that attitude in an antiblack world; as well as Linda A. Bell, *Rethinking Ethics in the Midst of Violence: A Feminist Approach to Freedom*, foreword by Claudia Card (Lanham, Maryland: Rowman and Littlefield, 1993), *passim*. For the classic statement on the subject in philosophy of existence, see Jean-Paul Sartre, *L'être et le néant: essai d'ontologie phénoménologique* (Paris: Gallimard, 1943), conclusion; English translation by Hazel Barnes, *Being and Nothingness: A Phenomenological Essay on Ontology*, with intro. by Hazel Barnes (New York: Philosophical Library and Washington Square Press, 1956).

15. Think, for example, of black women who have been imprisoned for resisting white men's sexual advances and assaults. For discussions of the sexual exploitation of black women by the U.S. criminal justice system, see Calvin Hernton, *Sex and Race in America* (New York: Grove Press, 1965); Herbert G. Gutman, *The Black Family in Slavery and Freedom, 1750_1925* (New York: Vintage, 1976); and Gerald Horne, "On the Criminalization of a Race," *Political Affairs* 73, no. 2 (February 1994), p. 26–30. For a discussion of the supposed unrapability of black women, as it manifests itself in popular culture, see Joy Ann James and T. Denean Sharpley-Whiting, *High Tech Lynching and Low-Profile Rapes: Black Women and Sexual Violence in the U.S.* (forthcoming).

RACE, SEX, AND MATRICES OF DESIRE IN AN ANTIBLACK WORLD

16. Cf. Fanon, *Peau noire*, p. 9/*Black Skin*, p. 12.

17. See Gordon, *Fanon and the Crisis of European Man*, chap. 3, for discussion of typification. See also Maurice Natanson, *Anonymity: A Study in the Philosophy of Alfred Schutz* (Bloomington: Indiana University Press, 1986).

18. See Gordon, *Bad Faith*, Part IV.

19. See Merleau-Ponty's discussion in the preface to *Phénoménologie*, p. vi/*Phenomenology*, p. xii.

20. Fanon, *Peau noire, masques blancs*, Gordon, *Bad Faith and Antiblack Racism*, and Gordon, ed., *Existence in Black* address this dimension of theorizing about living in an antiblack/misogynous world. See also Bell, *Rethinking Ethics in the Midst of Violence*, and Cynthia Willett, *Maternal Ethics and Other Slave Moralities* (New York and London: Routledge, 1995).

132

GORDON

BODY BADGES:

Race and Sex

Kevin Thomas Miles

We are a sign that is not read....
　　　—Hölderlin, Mnemosyne

They've hung a black man...
For the world to see
　　　　　—Langston Hughes

IN THE wake of the narrative written by biological science it has become evident that feminism and emancipatory racial theory share a common interest in liberating the body from the oppressive limitations of metaphysical discourse. Both of these projects engage the body, as that phenomenon that can never be comprehensively addressed as a concept. The story biological science has been telling us about the body is written in the language in which science has long been fluent, the language organized by categorical opposition that makes classification possible in the first place, namely, the language of metaphysics. According to the rules of this language the body not only operates according to a logic (so that *bios* is read as the subject of *logos as science*), but it can also be understood as if it were logically fixed, that is, categorically determined as just another concept.

Biologizing the body in scientific terms is nothing less than the metaphysical enterprise of predetermining the universal category in which the original difficulty of *bios* (life) is summarily redacted by *logos* as logic. As such, biological science is more than an altruistic interest in knowledge that engages living organisms simply in the sense of "discovering" them; its metaphysical constitution inevitably promotes the domination of *bios* in order to ensure the continued rule of *logos* as that which has the singular authority to master-name whatever it finds in the world.

Feminist discourses have made the important observation that "the body has thus far remained colonized through the discursive practices of the natural sciences, particularly the discourses of biology and medicine.... Bodies are not inert; they function interactively and productively. They act and react. They generate what is new, surprising, unpredictable."[1] This kind of thinking has not, however, played as prominent a role in emancipatory racial theory as it should. The liberation of racialized bodies is still too often a project performed within the restricted limits of discursive science. Racialized bodies are not generally understood as being subject to the fluidity and ambiguity characterizing the bodies being discussed by feminists. Irigaray, Butler, and Grosz engage in discussions of sexuality while acknowledging its resistance to being "booked." No one following the path of what is at issue here makes the claim, because sexuality resists being comprehensively conscripted into the service of the biological sciences, that there is no such thing as sexuality. By contrast, in the interest of abolishing racial injustice, and because of the inability of the biological sciences to categorically identify "race," Appiah has made the claim that "the truth is that there are no races: there is nothing in the world that can do all we ask race to do for us."[2]

Appiah performs an important chore by demonstrating how the conception of race constructed according to the terms of the biological sciences is devoid of any epistemological value. The failure of biological science should not, however, be decisive in determining the status of the body for emancipatory racial theory. Perhaps Henry Louis Gates, Jr., offers a more tenable response to the relation this limited conception of biology has to race when he makes the qualified remark that "race, as a meaningful criterion within the biological sciences, has long been recognized to be a fiction. When we speak of the 'white race' or 'the black race,' 'the Jewish race' or 'the Aryan race,' we speak in biological misnomers and, more generally, in metaphors."[3]

Then, again, perhaps Gates does not go far enough. The metaphysically determined discourse biological science performs on the body is not alone in its use of metaphor because our narratives about sexual and racial bodies are themselves necessarily metaphorical. It is clear that Appiah's conclusion goes too far precisely because it depends upon the supposition that from the failure of biological science to locate the signature of race in the body, it follows that the body has no capacity for signifying race. The body undoubtedly discloses something of itself to biological science, but there is more to our biology than can be comprehended in any scientific discourse. Appiah's abandonment of the biological in favor of "culture" shows at least two things; that he has unnecessarily abandoned the body and that he has a limited understanding of the "biological" as that which comes under the dominion of a scientific logic. Under the aegis of this limited view he throws the body out with the biological and reveals the extent to which he is depending upon science. The *logos* of our *bios* does not readily conform to the framework of science. It involves, in the language of Merleau-Ponty, an "intertwining," a "chiasm" in which the body takes up and is taken over by *logoi* as histories or narratives that are written in our flesh as flesh. Even the ancient Greeks never understood *logos* univocally; it was a term that could simultaneously be understood as speech, narrative, account, reason, and rational faculty. We can, therefore, rightly understand the *bio-logical* as *bios-logos*, or as the narrative pertaining to a particular life. The life of our bodies cannot be master-named, "what we are calling flesh...has no name in any philosophy."[4]

There is no good reason why we cannot say of race what has been said of sexuality, specifically, that it "is incapable of ready containment: it refuses to stay within its predesigned regions, for it seeps across boundaries into areas that are apparently not its own."[5] In fact, it is this concern with the possibility of seepage, a psychotic fear of miscegenation, that betrays the degree to which racial injustice has always been preoccupied with our bodies. The ability the body has to "seep" across boundaries both sexual and racial is not simply scandalous on a social and political level, but more importantly, it is a scandal to reason itself. Bodies have a fluidity that is not contained by the logic of science, their movement and their being moved does not only and always behave according to the rules of a metaphysically determined *logos*. It is this thought, the thought of science's own limit, the thought of its own demise that seems to be the most disturbing thought it can think.

In her deliberations on the body Judith Butler refers to this movement in what seems to be a confession: "I could not fix bodies," she writes, "as simple objects of thought. Not only did bodies tend to indicate a world beyond themselves, but this movement beyond their own boundaries, a movement of boundary itself, appeared to be quite central to what bodies 'are.' I kept losing track of the subject.... Inevitably, I began to consider that perhaps this resistance to fixing the subject was essential to the matter at hand."[6]

It is equally as difficult to fix the subject racially as it is sexually. The racial body can be referenced in the same way Irigaray refers to the sexual body as that "real" which "may well include, and in large measure, *a physical reality* that continues to resist adequate symbolization and/or that signifies the powerlessness of logic to incorporate in its writing all the characteristic features of nature." The racialized body is certainly one of these features. As Irigaray goes on to point out, "it has often been found necessary to minimize certain of these features of nature, to envisage them, and it, only in light of an ideal status, so as to keep it/them from jamming the works of the theoretical machine."[7]

The theoretical machinery driving metaphysics has a long history of trying to avoid having its gears jammed. The history of metaphysics has been from the start a peculiar interest in preserving the notion of purity. As early as Hesiod's mythological description of human origins we can recognize the birthmark which still remains on the body of scientific discourse. The story Hesiod tells in *Works and Days* of the five ages of humanity is a story of gradual degeneration, a "fall," if you will, from the precious age of "pure" gold to the age of corruptible iron. Hesiod's paradigm, even if his "races" are "ages," bears an uncanny resemblance to some of modernity's racial theories in that his mineralogical categories are an attempt at creating discrete (read as "pure") identities for which one can express romantic longing.

The impurity of the human condition was a consistent theme in Greek mythology. Another tale of human origins involves Zeus' incestuous intercourse with his daughter Persephone, the mother of Dionysus. With the help of Zeus' jealous wife, Hera, the Titans attacked the infant Dionysus, cut his body in pieces and ate every part of his dismembered flesh with the exception of his heart which was carried off by Athena and returned to Zeus. In revenge Zeus blasted the Titans with lightning bolts that reduced them to ashes. From the remains of these ashes, the charred flesh of the Titans who had consumed the heavenly flesh of Dionysus, humanity is born as a mixture of the Titanic and the Olympian; good and evil; heaven and earth; corporeal and incorporeal; flesh and spirit; body and soul.

It should not be at all surprising that this mythological construction eventually makes its appearance as the philosophical distinction between the rational and the irrational, or the privilege given to reason over passion. Some of this concern is evident in the traditional readings of Plato's *Phaedo*. At that important moment before referencing the miscegenation of pleasure and pain, Socrates performs a hysterectomy on the setting in which the philosophical discourse on the soul is to be performed (60a–b) by having his wife, Xanthippe, hysterical with grief, removed so that the space is cleared for the *pharmacological charm* of reason to do its work undisturbed by the irrational.

Plato confirms the significance of "cutting off" (*koptomenān*, from the word *kopetos* translated as beating of the breast, a wailing, lamentation, can be translated as "cut off" because of its relation to *koptō*, to smite, cut, to cut off or down) the hysterical Xanthippe near the end of the dialogue. Just before Socrates dies from drinking the poison (*pharmakon*), one of his interlocutors described as the one who had never stopped crying, reduces the entire company to tears: "Apollodorus… now broke out in such a storm of passionate weeping that he made everyone in the room break down, except Socrates himself, who said, Really, my friends, what a way to behave! Why, that was my main reason for sending away the women, to prevent this sort of disturbance." (117d–e).

The Socrates Plato gives us in the *Republic* is also engaged in a discussion concerning the soul. Socrates tells the story of Leontius the son of Aglaion who, returning from the Piraeus, spotted dead bodies that had been publicly executed outside the city wall. Leontius simultaneously "felt a desire to see them and a repugnance and aversion, and for a time he resisted and veiled his head, but over-powered in despite of all his desire, with wide staring eyes he rushed up to the corpses and cried, There, you wretches, take your fill of the fine spectacle!" (439e).

Socrates concludes from this story that the human soul, like his notion of the *polis*, must be composed of three distinct parts so that one part separates the higher part of reason from the lower part of desire. Furthermore, this division suggests that the distinction between the rational and irrational parts of the soul is as profoundly fixed as the division between the worlds of being and becoming; they are worlds that do not "mix" even while standing in relation to each other as a relation.

Aristotle is also implicated in the purity project of preserving reason from the pollution of passion when he acknowledges in his *Politics* that females do indeed possess deliberative reason. He qualifies this possession by asserting that females have deliberative reason, but not as a controlling force: the deliberative element in the female "lacks authority" (1260a12). This is to say that it lacks the ability to dominate the other parts of the soul, namely, the passionate part that should be "cut off" from philosophical discourse. In our tradition this alleged lack of control is not simply a benign pollution, it is unreasonably feared as possessing not only the power to undermine the boundaries organizing society, but the structures of "pure" reason itself.

137

> In such a society, individuals who are regarded as especially lacking in control
> of their own boundaries, or as possessing special talents and opportunities for
> confounding the boundaries of others, evoke fear and controlling action from
> the rest of society. Women are so regarded by men in ancient Greek society,
> along with suppliants, strangers, guests, and other intruders.[8]

What Carson observes as the ancient Greek fear of a pollution disseminated by women, strangers, and intruders can still be observed in a modern fear of the black body. In the United States we have the events surrounding the crimes of Charles Stuart and Susan Smith to remind us that no image evokes more fear and the desire to control than the icon of a black man. Richard Lacayo sums up our cultural consciousness with disturbing brevity: "Susan Smith knew what a kidnapper should look like. He should be a remorseless stranger with a gun. But the essential part of the picture—the touch she must have counted on to arouse the primal sympathies of her neighbors and to cut short any doubts—was his race. The suspect had to be a black man.... Wasn't that everyone's most familiar image of the murderous criminal?"[9]

Projected images seem to be what it really comes down to in the end. It is not until the Hebraic influences of Christianity that the hearing ear receives a feature role in epistemological discourses. Aristotle has some things to say about hearing but for the Greeks it is the metaphor of sight that presides over what one knows: "see what I mean?" Images, like the play between light and shadow on the wall of Plato's Cave, can be projected, even on a body and then read as if they were proper to the body in the sense of being one of its "properties." As such the racialized body does not depend upon biological science for its identification because what is at work is not something wholly discursive. The image of the black body is signified, it is something *signed* and is, at least in this society, a sign of pollution evoking a response that is more visceral than rational.

This much is implied in Langston Hughes' poem, *Silhouette*, and is explicitly stated by Toni Morrison when she charges that "black people are rarely individualized.... Black people, as a group, are used to signify the polar opposites of love and repulsion. On the one hand, they signify benevolence, harmless and servile guardianship, and endless love. On the other hand, they have come to represent insanity, illicit sexuality, and chaos."[10] What Langston Hughes points to in the phenomenon of the lynched black man does nothing to contradict Morrison's observation, nor does it represent an exception. The lynching of an individual black man is exactly what Hughes says it is, something for the world to see; as such, it is a sign *of* black people.

This particular sign signifies something never fully comprehended by reason and thus, in a certain sense, is a sign that is never read. Why is this sign not read; is it illegible or unintelligible? No, this sign is not intended for reading, at least not in the sense in which what is read gives itself up discursively to the science of bio-*logic*. The registers for this sign are not at home with the reasons of science, but move about, if we must be compelled to name it, in that peculiar place to which Pascal alludes with his reflection that "the heart has reasons of which reason knows nothing." Lynching is paradoxically, and simultaneously, experienced as both sexual attraction and repulsion. It is experienced actually, factually, and as a particular memory in and of a body.

This is the disturbing reality behind the coincidence between race and sex; they are inextricably bound up in each other as signifiers that seep through the constraining boundaries of rationality by virtue of evoking responses that are more visceral than rational. This is not an extraordinary claim, Hughes and Morrison are only two of a number of people who have noted that lynching in particular and sex in general are profoundly implicated in the problems of racial injustice. In his autobiography published in 1933, James Weldon Johnson recalls having nearly been murdered when a woman with whom he was publicly keeping company was mistakenly believed to be white. The lesson Johnson says that he learned from this experience is that "in the core of the heart of the American race problem the sex factor is rooted, rooted so deeply that it is not always recognized when it shows at the surface. Other factors are obvious and are ones that we dare to deal with; but regardless of how we deal with these, the race situation will continue to be acute as long as the sex factor persists."[11]

Most assuredly Johnson was aware that had he been found socializing with a white woman he would have become what Hughes expresses poetically, "a sign for the world to see." But lynching is not simply a poetic devise, its signifying force is so monstrous, so violent, it transgresses the conventional force of law and order; "being a fact of both white history and black life, lynching is also the metaphor of itself."[12]

Frantz Fanon references the peculiar dialectic of this monstrous metaphor in *Black Skin, White Masks*:

> When a white man hates black men, is he not yielding to a feeling of impotence or sexual inferiority?...Is the lynching of the Negro not a sexual revenge? We know how much of sexuality there is in all cruelties, tortures, beatings. One has only to reread a few pages of the Marquis de Sade to be easily convinced of the fact.... If one wants to understand the racial situation psychoanalytically, not from a universal viewpoint but as it is experienced by individual consciousness, considerable importance must be given to sexual phenomena.[13]

James Baldwin also has some reflections on lynching and its association with castration. He recalls that his view from the plane, as he made his first trip to Georgia, provoked in him an image of a bloody heritage to which, as he believed, every black man in America felt himself a part:

> I was past thirty, and I had never seen this land before. I pressed my face against the window, watching the earth come closer; soon we were just above the tops of trees. I could not suppress the thought that this earth had acquired its color from the blood that had dripped down from these trees. My mind was filled with the image of a black man, younger than I, perhaps, or my own age, hanging from a tree, while white men watched him and cut his sex from him with a knife.[14]

In addition to this, Baldwin also claims that the issue of segregation in the schools "has actually nothing to do with education.... It has to do with political power and it has to do with sex. And this is a nation which, most unluckily, knows little about either."[15]

It would seem that almost every attempt at a serious consideration of what is at the bottom of racial injustice in America is necessarily compelled to take up the issue of how sexuality is implicated from the very start. Calvin C. Hernton claims that "there is a sexual involvement, at once real and vicarious, connecting white and black people in America...an involvement so immaculate and yet so perverse, so ethereal and yet so concrete, that all race relations tend to be, however subtle, sex relations."[16] Cornel West situates sexuality at the heart of the conflict in race relations as well: "black sexuality is a taboo subject in white and black America and…a candid dialogue about black sexuality between and within these communities is requisite for healthy race relations in America."[17] West also makes the observation that miscegenation is, as "social scientists have long acknowledged…the most *perceived* source of white fear of black people—just as the repeated castrations of lynched black men cries out for serious psychocultural explanation."[18]

There is no escaping the fact that a number of highly regarded thinkers have expressed no small concern about the way in which sex and race are involved with each other. This fact, however, is no guarantee that there will be a rush *en masse* to address this theme since it is, as West claims, "a taboo subject in America principally because it is a form of black power over which whites have little control—yet its visible manifestations evoke the most visceral of white responses, be it one of seductive obsession or downright disgust." It hardly seems incidental that West's "seductive obsession or downright disgust" echoes Morrison's "love and repulsion." This opposition is the site of the "chaos" of which black people are a sign, or, as West says, that "over which whites have little control."

The fact is that this preoccupation with a lack of control, as has already been suggested, implicates a good deal more than white people, it implicates every aspect of the metaphysical machinery driving the western tradition. The matter of how sexuality is signified in the issues of race is taboo not simply because it discloses a domain over which whites have little control, but rather because it signifies the *end* of reason in the double sense of its limit and purposivity. Reason discovers its "end" in this unsettling encounter with the body as that which can be taken up and over by a writing that is not discursively read by science.[19]

W.E.B. Du Bois may have been the first racial theorist to make an effort to understand the body in these terms. Forty-three years after the publication of "The Conservation of Races" Du Bois returns to the site of his failed attempt to reevaluate race with his essay "The Concept of Race." With Africa in mind he abandons his prior confidence in what science discloses:

> On this vast continent were born and lived a large portion of my direct ancestors going back a thousand years or more. The mark of their heritage is upon me in color and hair. These are obvious things, but of little meaning in themselves; only important as they stand for real and more subtle differences from other men. Whether they do or not, I do not know nor does science know today.[20]

Du Bois describes the bond connecting him to his African ancestry in terms of a narrative when he writes that "the physical bond is least and the badge of color

140

MILES

relatively unimportant save as a badge; the real essence of this kinship is its social heritage of slavery..." This is an affront to reason. In the terms of biological science a "real essence" is like real estate, its *solid*, you can buy it and build on it. But nothing seems to *stand* on the marks of heritage to which Du Bois refers, they *stand* for something, like signs on the body that confound the intentions of discursivity by not being read. This should remind us of what is quite likely Du Bois' most frequently cited assertion: "The problem of the twentieth-century is the problem of the color-line": because it too, as a line, is a sign drawn on the body that cannot be read by biological science.

Toni Morrison makes a point of noting the necessity for referencing the "bodies of black people" and their being subject to inscription in her analysis of the process in which Clarence Thomas was confirmed as a Supreme Court Justice. She candidly states that "a reference to a black person's body is de rigueur in white discourse."[21] She also contends that "as is almost always the case, the site of the exorcism of critical national issues [is] situated in the miasma of black life and inscribed on the bodies of black people."[22] A little later she reiterates and expands upon this claim concerning inscription in the context of "control":

> As in virtually all of this nation's great debates, nonwhites and women figure powerfully, although their presence may be disguised, denied, or obliterated. So it is perhaps predictable that this instance—where serious issues of male prerogative and sexual assault, the issues of racial justice and racial redress, the problematics of governing and controlling women's bodies, the alterations of work space into (sexually) domesticated space—be subsumed into the debate over the candidacy for the Supreme Court. That these issues be worked out, on, and inscribed upon the canvas/flesh of black people should come as no surprise to anyone.[23]

The body is, after all, the site of what concerns us most. Through our bodies we inherit the world and the problems with which we become concerned. This inheritance always involves mixture and impurity, it always involves intermediate lines that are both impossible and necessary to cross; lines from stories that have been written well in advance of appearing on any particular body. Our bodies take up and can be taken over by these lines in the same way that a badge or a scarlet letter is taken up as a sign signifying a message that need never be sent in order for it to signify something.

Most of our conversations about race are well past the point of believing in the idea of "race" as if "race means pure race."[24] The point at which we have not yet arrived, and the point at which we must arrive if we are going to engage in a serious discussion concerning racial injustice, is the juncture at which we become more critical about our love affair with the project of purity as a whole. We have been trying to dismantle the notion of purity insofar as race is concerned while staging attacks from the groundwork of pure reason. All sides of the debates have deployed methodologies and arguments executed as if reason itself could be something pure. We have been parading our reasons out onto the battlefields of discourse, as if they were Sir Lancelot of Arthurian lore, believing that the purest reason would always win the day. There can be no coming to terms with the myth of racial purity if we do not come to terms with the myth of pure reason and its magical power to destroy monstrous ideas.

Ours is an epoch that has been preoccupied by the mythology that reason is a pure, unstained *das Ding an sich* that works best when it keeps the body at bay. This kind of strategy should be recognized as psychotic since such a preoccupation signifies defective or lost contact with reality. If we can admit that our bodies matter even if they resist being booked as concepts, we should also be able to recognize that race matters as well, even if only provisionally, as a strategically deployed "construction" responding to the systemic injustice cultivated as a by-product of categorical thinking in search of purity. The attention feminism has given to the fluidity of our bodies is, in this regard, a clear indication that feminism and emancipatory racial theory share a common interest in liberating the body from the oppressive limitations of metaphysical discourse. It is also clearly indicated that the challenge confronting body politics in the twentieth century is the problem of addressing the "readings" of a sign that is not read.

NOTES

1. Elizabeth Grosz, *Volatile Bodies: Toward A Corporeal Feminism* (Bloomington: Indiana University Press, 1994), pp. x–xi.

2. Kwame Anthony Appiah, *In My Father's House: Africa in the Philosophy of Culture* (New York: Oxford University Press, 1992), p. 32.

3. Henry Louis Gates, Jr., "Writing 'Race' and the Difference It Makes," in *"Race," Writing, and Difference*, Henry Louis Gates, Jr., ed. (Chicago: University of Chicago Press, 1986), p. 4.

4. Maurice Merleau-Ponty, *The Visible and the Invisible*, tr. Alphonso Lingis (Evanston: Northwestern University Press, 1968), p. 147.

5. Grosz, *Volatile Bodies*, p. viii.

6. Judith Butler, *Bodies That Matter: On The Discursive Limits of "Sex"* (New York: Routledge, 1993), p. ix.

7. Luce Irigaray, *This Sex Which Is Not One*, tr. Catherine Porter (Ithaca: Cornell University Press, 1985), pp. 106–107.

8. Anne Carson, "Putting Her In Her Place: Woman, Dirt, and Desire," in *Before Sexuality: The Construction of the Erotic in the Ancient Greek World*, David M. Halperin, John J. Winkler, and Froma I. Zeitlin, eds. (Princeton: Princeton University Press, 1990), pp. 135–169.

9. Richard Lacayo, "Stranger in the Shadows," *Time* November 14, 1994, pp. 46–47.

10. Toni Morrison, "Introduction: Friday on the Potomac," in *Race-ing Justice, En-gendering Power: Essays on Anita Hill, Clarence Thomas, and the Construction of Social Reality*, Toni Morrison, ed. (New York: Pantheon Books, 1992), pp. xiv–xv.

11. James Weldon Johnson, *Along This Way: The Autobiography of James Weldon Johnson* (New York: Penguin Books, 1990), p. 170.

12. Morrison, p. xvi.

13. Franz Fanon, *Black Skin, White Masks* (New York: Grove Press, Inc., 1967), pp. 159–60.

14. James Baldwin, *Nobody Knows My Name: More Notes of a Native Son* (New York: Dell Publishing Co., Inc., 1970), pp. 86–89.

15. Ibid.

16. Calvin C. Hernton, *Sex and Racism in America* (New York: Anchor Books, 1988), p. 6.

17. Cornel West, *Race Matters* (New York: Vintage Books, 1993), p. 120.

18. Ibid., p. 125.

19. In his discussion of finitude in his *Science of Logic* Hegel writes of finite things that "the hour of their birth is the hour of their death." Later, under his discussion of 'Existence' he claims that "the essence of God...is the *abyss* [*Abgrund*] for finite reason." And then again, when discussing 'The Notion,' he writes: "The highest maturity, the highest stage, which anything can attain is that in which its downfall begins." (See G.W.F. Hegel, *Science of Logic*, tr. A.V. Miller (New York: Humanities Press, 1969), pp. 129, 483, and 611 respectively.) Kierkegaard's pseudonym, Johannes Climacus, follows these tracks where he notes that "the highest pitch of every passion is always to will its own downfall; and so it is also the supreme passion of the Reason to seek a collision, though this collision must in one way or another prove its undoing. The supreme paradox of all thought is the attempt to discover something that thought cannot think. This passion is at bottom present in all thinking."

20. W.E.B. Du Bois, *Dusk of Dawn: An Essay Toward an Autobiography of a Race Concept*, in *W.E.B. Du Bois: Writings* (New York: The Library of America, 1986), p. 639. Also see W.E.B. Du Bois, "The Land of the Burnt Faces," in *The World and Africa* (New York: International Publishers, 1965), p. 116: Du Bois puts even more distance between his thinking and science by conceding that one might provisionally say that there are "races" for the sake of certain discussions, "knowing well that no scientifically accurate definition of these races could be made which would not leave most of mankind outside the limits."

21. Morrison, "Introduction: Friday," p. xiv.

22. Ibid., p. x.

23. Ibid., pp. xix-xx.

24. Naomi Zack, "Life After Race," in *American Mixed Race: The Culture of Microdiversity*, Naomi Zack, ed. (Lanham, Maryland: Rowman and Littlefield Publishers, Inc., 1995), pp. 297–307.

THE AMERICAN SEXUALIZATION OF RACE[1]

Naomi Zack

Find out something that has the Use and Value of money amongst his Neighbours, and you shall see the same Man will begin presently to enlarge his Possessions.

—John Locke, *Two Treatises of Government*,II,v, Sec. 49.[2]

chapter 11

IT IS not immediately clear why Minerva should have an owl. Owls fly with heavy bodies, swooping down on ignominious prey in darkness. Minerva's bird should soar into the light with a flash of feathers like the flashing eyes of the goddess of wisdom, reason, and purity, and it should eat exalted things.[3] Hegel tells us, "The owl of Minerva spreads its wings only with the falling of the dusk."[4] One interpretation is that philosophers create knowledge only after the world has had its way with the subject matter—or that theory follows fact. This interpretation identifies theory as a product of the intellect; it also presupposes the empiricism of theory, as based on fact, while at the same time signalling that theory is always "after the fact." More generally, insofar as theory is about fact, a thinker could sort out an area of reality and construct an explanation of it. That explanation could be used as a basis for criticism, as well as for the control of fact in the future.

Thus, as philosophers, we ought to be able to construct theories about the cultural facts of race and use those theories to effect cultural change. One problem with this theoretical approach to race is that it sets up a metaphorical duality between the philosophical mind and the worldly body, which body is, in this case, races, racial identities, race relations, and so forth. Also, it is by no means accepted by all students of race that philosophers and other theorists are entitled to assume such high positions or even that their positions are high. In real life, truth is not exclusively given to the individual human mind through reason because the individual human body also receives and experiences truth through its physical modalities. The description of the world that corresponds to the body's truth can be at odds with the best description of the world we come up with using theory, or analytic reason, and information from the sciences. But even if truth always were what we had 'in mind' rather than 'in body,' it may not always be desirable or possible to substitute the truth of the mind for the "lies" of the body.

I want to suggest that while the empirical truth about the concept of race is a theoretical matter with immediate consequences for the philosophical world, it would be an error to assume that this truth could have an immediately positive effect in the lived world where the experiences of particular bodies, one's own and others', are so important. Indeed, much of the lived truth about race is an area of bodily truth that corresponds to social-psychological worldviews that are composed of illusions, gratuities, misrepresentations, and omissions. The intellect, and the will, insofar as it moves through practical syllogism constructed by the intellect, may have no immediate control over lived bodily experience. More perplexing, worldviews about race that directly influence lived bodily experience may not make sense to the intellect or to philosophical reason alone. Rather, the bodily experience of race in the United States may require wisdom in order to be understood.[5] Wisdom, unlike reason, often fails to rise above the most vulgar level of conventional opinion, and it is precisely for that reason that wisdom is necessary in order to live in the world. That is, Hegel was right to seize on the owl metaphor for knowledge, but it would be a mistake to imagine such a bird as a flashy courier of empirical truth born up in flights of pure reason. We have to fly down to the lowest level of the barnyard.

Race, as lived individual experience, is culturally constructed, but nonetheless physical. Americans experience race physically, in their own bodies and the bodies of others because the external social "soul" tells them that race is physical. If the individual soul were a system of beliefs and value judgements and the body so much insensitive stuff to be overcome by that soul, then Plato would have been right to say the "soul is…a helpless prisoner…in the body."[6] But the body is itself the location of immediate conscious experience and it is as much made up of sensation, perception, and motion as it contains internal vital processes or is moved by intentions based on conscious thought.

In lived experience, the body has sufficient sensitivity and accessibility as a processor of information to support Foucault's inversion of Plato to this effect: "the body becomes the prisoner of the soul."[7] I take Foucault to mean that our bodies move and produce sensations and perceptions as a result of the beliefs and value judgements that we hold "in" our souls. By "soul" I mean our consciously held beliefs and value judgments and their implications, including some beliefs and value judgments that others may ascribe to us which we might not recognize as belonging to us. In principle, every one of these beliefs and judgments and their implications could be described by sentences, so that the soul can be understood as a "text" instead of a kind of thing.

Sexuality is part of bodily experience, and in that dimension, as in all others, again, human bodies are not merely inertly material or instinctively biological, but receptive, responsive, and cognizant. I need to put a second, broader Foucauldian assumption to work here, namely that the forms, objects, and expressions of individual human sexual desire, are determined by, and in many senses appropriate to, specific cultural contexts.[8] From this second Foucauldian assumption, it can be concluded that the sexual desires, responses, and behaviors of individuals reflect not only the individual souls of the individuals whose bodies they are, but the broad social "soul" as well.

American racial experience is itself the result of beliefs that have been proved false according to our best reasoning and scientific information. The result of the historical intersection or connection between socially constructed sexuality and socially constructed race has been the sexualization of race in American lived experience. However, despite this doubling of social-construction, the phenomenological experience of sexualized race is no less natural and spontaneous than the phenomenological experience of any other bodily process. The sexualization of race means that the fictitious ideological machinery which posits and reproduces the existence of races, i.e., ontological racism, as well as the crimes and slights that whites have committed, and still do commit, against blacks in American culture, i.e., moral racism, are qualities and conditions of sexuality, for some individuals. The sexualization of race also means that the aesthetic standards and micro-judgments that in myriad ways express the devaluation of Americans designated as black, as well as reproducing that devaluation, are also part of individual sexual choices, judgments, reactions, and expressions.

The sexualization of race entails that sexual desire may have racial aspects. But, as socially constructed and determined by false belief as individual sexual desire may be, sexual desire cannot be changed at will in any immediate situation. The phenomenology of sexual desire requires that our specific desires be "given" to us as unpremeditated and not deliberately intended. This autonomous quality of desire is related not only to our inability to intend our sexual desires (in which case they wouldn't be desires), but to the real determination of our desires by factors over which we have no control and which, in the case of race, are based on beliefs or associations with which we would not necessarily agree, or might even strongly disavow, in our best rational moments. If we Americans choose to live physically as well as intellectually—that is, if we choose to *live*—then eventually we have to come to terms with the sexualization of race. It is not easy for thoughtful individuals to come to terms with such a bizarre cultural contingency. However, an historical understanding of how the contingency was originally construed (or cathected) may be the first step.

How did race come to be sexualized? At any given time in our culture there are myths about sex and race that float around in the popular soul (/"text"). These myths can be viewed as the flotsam of deeper historical connections between race and sex. Of course, 'history' in this context does not mean a chronology of public events, compilations of statistics, or even personal narratives from a 'primary record.' Here, 'history' means a reconstruction of motives in the past that can be used to explain present connections. Such a reconstruction is a genealogical account of current connections (or cathexions), and it can be assumed to be a (partial) analysis of racism, because it would be at best naïve to think that the American sexualization of race is racially egalitarian.

Toward that genealogical account, these are some commonly known facts about race and slavery: the modern concept of racial hierarchy with the white race on top and the black race on the bottom was invented by eighteenth- and nineteenth-century scientists on a flimsy empirical base;[9] since only "n"egroes could be enslaved, it was in the economic interest of white slave owners that all children of their black female slaves be racially classified as "n"egroes;[10] it was also in the economic interest of white slave owners to "breed" their female slaves as intensively as they could in order to increase their capital of human livestock; finally, there was considerable racial mixing between white slave owners and black female slaves, throughout the era of slavery, but especially after 1830 when it became illegal to import new slaves into the United States and the need for slave labor grew;[11] although white male–black female miscegenation was common and rarely condemned throughout the era of slavery, black male–white female miscegenation was always treated as a serious crime to be punished by torture, sexual mutilation, and death for black males.[12]

From the foregoing facts it is not difficult to construct a genealogical account of the sexualization of black race in the United States. First, it is important to emphasize that the American idea of racial hierarchy was a cultural invention that occurred during the era of slavery. Apart from a long European history of violence, including the rape of women from defeated populations, there seems to be no historical precedent for the sexualization of race in the United States, that is, no earlier cultural example of the assignment of a debased form of sexuality to an hereditary caste, over generations. At this point, I again acknowledge Foucault, for his claim, as quoted in the epigraph to this book, that sexuality is emergent. Applying that insight to the present discussion raises the consideration that the sexualization of American race was a new form of sexuality that emerged with the distinctive institution of slavery that was rationalized by new ideas of race. But, in addition to that broad insight, the foregoing historical facts permit a nuanced, causal, i.e., genealogical, account of exactly how sexuality, in the form of sexualized race, emerged during slavery.

The key to releasing the relevant nuances is *breeding*. Slaves were livestock to be bred as other livestock, for eventual monetary profit. Negro slaves were human beings and human beings are mammals. Mammals reproduce through heterosexual reproduction. Therefore, given the state of the art of bio-technology during the seventeenth, eighteenth, and nineteenth centuries, slaves were bred through heterosexual reproduction. So far, this stage of the model of the sexualization of race during slavery is no more than a literal biological model. The question is how race became sexualized, in degraded ways to be sure, but nonetheless in ways that resembled the sexuality that pre-existed (in the culture of white slave owners) before race was sexualized. A literal application of Foucault's emergent model of sexuality would be to speculate that the sexuality connected with race may not have significantly resembled the American white—or for that matter, black—sexuality that existed before slavery. But I don't think it is necessary to break off the historical analysis in that way. Rather, I would like to introduce into the genealogical account another commonly accepted fact about American history: An important dominant type of white American men is entrepreneurial. This type has a long tradition of "making money" that, in terms of its philosophical foundation, goes back at least as far as the seventeenth century, to ideas developed by John Locke in the Second Treatise of his *Two Treatises of Government*. According to Locke, individuals have a fundamental right to private ownership based on: the goodness of labor as decreed by God, the right of every man to own all of that with which he has mixed his labor, and the value of money as both a store of surplus goods and an incentive to labor.[13] White American men of the entrepreneurial type have traditionally regarded the making of money as an expression of moral virtue—which value they share with Protestant European and English forebears—and they have, and do, take a distinctive pleasure in making money. Successful American capitalism has always been great fun for successful American capitalists. This American pleasure in making money is not, strictly speaking, an erotic or sexual pleasure in the narrow sense, but it is a kind of infectious, self-justifying, self-celebrating gratification that is not altogether different from sexual pleasure, and, at the very least, is not incompatible with it. But even if the pleasure of making money had no resemblance to sexual pleasure, it is still possible that making money could result in specifically sexual desire in money-making situations, i.e., that making money could be what in nonscholarly usage is called a "turn-on."

This nuance of American capitalism suggests that the distinctively American sexualization of race might be understood through the American capitalization or monetarization of race. The monetarization of race required the mechanics of

149

mammalian heterosexual reproduction in order to be maintained and expanded in the way capitalistic enterprise requires. This is to say that black female slaves became objects of sexual desire to white slave owners because money could be made if they bred them, and more money could be made if they themselves bred them. For a white slave owner to breed his black female slaves himself, he would have had to have sex with them—ergo, the black female slaves were sexualized because they were literal objects of sexual desire, albeit primarily for monetary reasons—either "coldly" with deliberate monetary intent, or "warmly" in ways that resembled sexual desire in the absence of monetary motives. If it seems far-fetched that slave owners would have had sex with their female slaves for primarily monetary reasons, it should be remembered that the concept of self-validating and autonomous masculine sexual desire is an artifact of the later modern period, a final liberating pulse of romanticism. Before the eighteenth century, women were conceptualized as the sexual sex, and male sexuality was not construed as a prime moving force (persuasive though it may have been)[14] for getting into and maintaining male–female relationships. Until late in the seventeenth century, men married mainly for improvement in social status, economic gain, and reproduction if they were heirs who needed descendants to whom they could pass on legacies. Rarely did they marry primarily for love or the fulfillment of sexual desire.[15] While early modern masculine motives for marriage can hardly be posited as middle modern motives for sexual relations with female slaves, they offer a sketch of white male sexuality during the formative period of American chattel slavery which would be relevant to other relationships between men and women that were monetarily motivated. If sexual desire could be secondarily relevant to early modern marriage, then sexual desire could be secondarily relevant to middle modern breeding relationships with slaves, which, like early modern marriage, were undertaken in contexts set up for financial reasons—slave owning and breeding was primarily a form of American business.

If white slave owners can be plausibly viewed as having bred their black female slaves themselves for primarily monetary reasons, there are interesting implications about the motives behind the toleration of white male–black female miscegenation by the wives of slave owners. Miscegenated slaves were often more valuable commodities than presumptively "pure black" slaves, and for white wives who themselves may have married for economic reasons, the addition to household income that these miscegenated children represented may have sweetened the shame of the marital infidelity that they also represented.[16]

The foregoing account of the sexualization of black female race may seem too "cold," too quantitative, and altogether too *materialistic*. First, the account seems to exclude the possibility of white male sexual desire for black females that resembles what one would precritically recognize as genuine or sincere. However, as I noted at the outset, this account presupposes a racist social structure and the case of genuine white male–black female sexual desire would fall outside of that account. In more contextualized terms, it might be objected that for many ante-bellum white Americans, especially those "planters" who were a class of agricultural entrepreneurs, mammalian heterosexual reproduction was a powerful symbol of human sexuality in general. Since "n"egro slaves were bred on the mammalian model of reproduction, like other livestock, and black race itself was falsely construed to have an inheritable essence, it might follow that race itself became a symbol for mammalian heterosexual reproduction. Perhaps that association of symbols accounts for the American sexualization of race.

One problem with the association-of-symbols account is that whites as well as blacks are human beings who reproduce according to mammalian heterosexual mechanisms. Therefore, why wasn't whiteness as well as blackness sexualized in American history? One answer is that whiteness was sexualized but along more 'spiritual' or aesthetic or nonbodily dimensions, in accordance with its placement at the 'top' of a hierarchy of races. This superior placement, combined with reference to the white American tradition of physical self-denial generally and "puritanical" repressions of sexual attractiveness and desire, in particular, would imply that the sexualization of whiteness would be less physical and therefore less intense than the sexualization of blackness, especially for white women, who were assigned the gender virtue of being without sexual desire during at least part of the nineteenth century. The problem with this analysis is that it works too well as an account of differences in degrees of sexuality assigned by whites to blacks and whites, but it does not work well enough in explaining how reproduction has been sexualized for black women but not for white women.

The difference in the sexualization of black and white female reproduction persists to this day in common views of black and white maternity. White women with more than two or three children are viewed as nurturing, self-sacrificing, and perhaps asexual in motherly ways, as well as not very smart. But, holding social class constant, black women who have more than two or three children are popularly stereotyped as irresponsible, selfish, over-sexed, and scheming. Thus, for black women, but not for white women, maternity is read as proof of strong female sexuality. Motherhood is somehow able to spiritualize white women while at the same time it reveals what *whores* black women really are (as though prostitutes always took sexual pleasure in their work). Many contemporary social critics who want to deny public welfare payments to unwed pregnant black teenagers would do everything in their power to make sure that unwed white teenage mothers are informed about the "right to life" of their foetuses. This suggests that to this day, in the white cultural text, the offspring of black women are valued differently from those of white women. And this difference in value can be seen to have a monetary base. These days, what was once eagerly created, slave owner's capital, i.e., black progeny, has been reconceptualized (recathected) as the unearned plunder that black women, out of lust and greed, extract from an otherwise financially solvent system. But in either case, as the owned labor of slave owners or the begrudged

151

means of exploitation against capitalism, black children have been monetarized and their (presumably) black mothers thereby both monetarized and sexualized.[17]

The sexualization of black female maternity does not merely posit black women as sexual objects insofar as their reproduction of black children can be monetarized. In addition to their position as capital (or negative capital when their children are not wanted by white society), black women are imagined by white racists to experience sexual pleasure in the acts that result in the conception of black children. Why has their sexual pleasure been located just there? During the early modern period, it was commonly believed that a female orgasm was a necessary condition for heterosexual intercourse to result in pregnancy. It followed from this belief that pregnancy itself could count as evidence that women had not been raped in cases where charges of rape were under consideration.[18]

This early modern cultural link between female sexual pleasure (or, before the fact, female sexual desire) and pregnancy can be read as a reason for both an association of maternity with sexuality and the conceptual impossibility of classifying as rape some of the most brutal heterosexual assaults on the bodies of women. The link fits both the American sexualization of black maternity and the American tradition of failing to recognize, in law, and public and private morality, acts of rape which were committed against black women.

One might ask why the association of female sexual pleasure with conception was not discarded for black women when it was for white women in the later modern period. The answer lies somewhere in the general American tendency to assign separate and unequal resources to black people, on the grounds of race. Apparently, part of the cultural technique for constructing blacks as "primitive" has been to describe them in the terms of theories of human nature that, in comparison to the theories used to describe whites, are "primitive," or at least outmoded.

Thus far, I have considered the American sexualization of race in terms of black women only. What about the sexualization of black male race? Returning to slavery, one obvious nuance is the use of black males for breeding more slaves. But when whites themselves could and did perform this task, black male sexuality, on the monetarization of mammalian reproduction model, would have been rendered at best unnecessary and at worst a competitive threat to white men, insofar as their monetarization of black female reproduction resulted in white male sexual desire for black women. As literally *de trop*, black male sexuality would of course have seemed exaggerated from a white male perspective. As laborers, black males would be necessary enough, but insofar as their potential to produce more slaves was not literally necessary—because it could be fulfilled by white males—in times of surplus labor they would be more expendable than black female slaves (a situation perhaps echoed to this day in disproportionately high rates of unemployment for young black men). Furthermore, being deprived roles comparable to the most powerful economic, political, and social roles reserved for themselves by white men—in order to limit competition for the goods enabled by those roles—black

152

men have been deprived of some aspects of American masculine gender. This situation, together with perceptions of black male sexuality as exaggerated, because redundant, has occasioned precisely the kind of frustration for American black men that *everyone* expects to result in violence.

The white racist construction of black male sexuality can therefore be read as a direct result of the monetary sexualization of black female race by white slave owners. Within white racist constructions, black males have been insufficiently sexualized on the grounds of race because their sexuality has been viewed as though it ought to be dispensable given white prerogatives. There is also the question of how the denial of gender roles associated with power has effected black male sexuality. Overall, one would expect that the sexualization of race for American black men is in reality a combination of constructions originating within black culture and of fantasies and deprivations imposed by white culture. However, insofar as the sexualization of race is an artifact of American white racism, the sexualization of black male race is diminutive in comparison with the sexualization of black female race. Moreover, the white slave-owning intention to deny black males sexuality on the grounds of race can be read from white castration crimes against black males, as well as from hyperbolic fears about black male sexual desire for white females. Although, the sexual dimension of these fears should be viewed as derivative of economic and social domination, i.e., of the white-black power structure.

The preservation of a specifically white American male economic hegemony has always depended on the preservation of racial categories, especially that of a pure white race. The blackness of the black race has been compatible with white male–black female miscegenation, while the whiteness of the white race is incompatible with any kind of miscegenation. Therefore, it has been believed that the only way the whiteness of the white race can be preserved is to ensure that white females, who are the only females who can be the mothers of purely white children, have no way of breeding children who are not purely white. Of course, the preservation of whiteness has been differentially enforced according to social class and geographical area, and black-white interracial marriage has been legal throughout the United States since 1967, so that not all white women have been restricted to breeding purely white children. But when the restriction is applied, the sole necessary and sufficient condition for white mothers to have nonwhite offspring is for the fathers of their children to be nonwhite. On this model, sexuality is secondary to the exigencies of breeding, which is itself used to protect a socially constructed binary racial system that is the caste mechanism facilitating white-black power relations. In order for white males to exploit black males and black females on the automatic grounds of race, those grounds have had to be preserved by preserving the purity of the white racial category. Indeed, this purity—to be white one must not have *any* nonwhite forebears—is foundational for whiteness, and although it has been preserved by policing sexuality, sexuality is not its primary concern. Thus, in the preservation of whiteness, as well as the multiplication of blackness, sex is secondary to forms of power that are directly related to the advantage of American white men.[19]

The foregoing account of the American sexualization of race is limited by the heterosexual motif. I have said nothing about the sexualization of race in homosexual dimensions because the historical use of black females for breeding and the focus of white attention on that dimension of their gender automatically makes heterosexuality the subject. It is unclear how race could be homosexualized by white racism in a culture that is both homophobic and heterosexist with a strong tradition of monetarizing black children as either credits or debits to capital accounts.[20] But, of course, all of this raises the further question of the degree to which the sexuality of both white and black Americans has not been influenced by racism. A partial answer is that it would seem to be unlikely that black Americans, who unlike white Americans cannot neutralize or expunge race from their lived experience, can experience their sexuality as something completely free of racism. Going back to Minerva's owl, the relevant wisdom may include a sense that it is very difficult to understand what some areas of human experience would be like if conventional opinion had been different in the past.

Finally, the existence of personal genealogies of sexualized race should be noted. The texts of our individual bodies are formed not merely by the external culture but by the patterns of the sexual lives of our parents and grandparents. These forms of erotic life are socially reproduced in families from generation to generation, even though they may resist clear and direct reading by those who have learned how to reproduce them, and who know how to teach them to their children without knowing what they are doing. When we are able to read these forms clearly and directly, as they have molded us personally, it may be that the best thing we can possibly do is weep—because personal insights may not be sufficient to change private forms of behavior that are still shaped by public social conditions beyond individual influence.

NOTES

1. Some of my ideas for this paper were the result of a conversation with Lewis Gordon and Crispin Sartwell in New York, December 1995. I am grateful to John Pittman for discussion and comment on an earlier version of this paper, and to Linda Nicholson for clarifying editorial input on the penultimate draft.

2. John Locke, *Two Treatises of Government*, Peter Laslett, ed. (Cambridge: Cambridge University Press, 1991), p. 301.

3. For Minerva's attributes, see Edith Hamilton, *Mythology* (Boston: Mentor, 1940), pp. 29–30.

4. Georg Wilhelm Friedrich Hegel, *The Philosophy of Right*, T.M. Knox, ed. (Oxford: Oxford University Press, 1952), p. 13.

5. See John P. Pittman's discussion of the place of wisdom in contemporary philosophy, based on Cornel West's work on race, in Emmanuel Eze, ed., *Philosophy and the Postcolonial: African Philosophy in North America* (Blackwell, forthcoming).

6. Plato, *Phaedo*, in *Collected Dialogues*, Edith Hamilton and Huntington Cairns, eds. (New York: Pantheon), 82e, p. 66.

7. Michel Foucault, *Discipline and Punish* (New York: Pantheon, 1977), p. 30.

8. Michel Foucault, *The History of Sexuality*, Robert Hurley, trans. (New York: Vintage Books, 1980), Volume I: An Introduction.

9. For the flimsiness of the empirical base for race that in the nineteenth century included cultural traits, see Stephen Jay Gould, *The Mismeasure of Man* (New York: W.W. Norton, 1981). On the flimsiness of race as a biological concept, see my "Race and Philosophical Meaning," this volume.

10. Naomi Zack, "Mixed Black and White Race and Public Policy," *Hypatia* 10, no. 1 (Winter 1995), pp. 120–132, esp. pp. 123–4.

11. For a historical discussion of mixed race during slavery, see Joel Williamson, *New People* (New York: Free Press, 1980), pp. 8–10, 14–29.

12. See Gunnar Myrdal's often-quoted remarks on this in *An American Dilemma* (New York: Harper, 1944), p. 56.

13. John Locke, *Two Treatises*, II,v,Secs. 27–34 and 46–51, pp. 287–292 and pp. 299–302 in Laslett, ed. I discuss Locke's views on money more fully in *Bachelors of Science: Seventeenth Century Identity, Then and Now* (Philadelphia: Temple University Press, 1996), Chapter 14.

14. John Donne's often quoted "masculine persuasive force" was a reference to language:

> By our long sterving hopes, by that remorse
> Which my words masculine perswasive force
> Begot in thee,

(John Donne, "Elegie: On his Mistris," in Helen Gardner, ed., *The Metaphysical Poets* (Oxford: Oxford University Press, 1967), p. 20.)

15. Lawrence Stone, *The Family, Sex and Marriage in England 1500–1800* (New York: Harper and Row, 1979), pp. 37–81.

16. See W.E.B. Du Bois, ed., *Negro American Family* (New York: Negro University Press, 1969), p. 25.

17. As a test of the hypothesis that the American sexualization of race has been mediated through the eroticism of monetary profit, it could be predicted that in contexts where black people cannot be exploited or constructed as exploitative (in order to be thwarted), race will not be sexualized. Unfortunately, American life has not yielded many, if any, such contexts on which to perform the thought experiment.

18. See Merry Weisner, *Women and Gender in Early Modern Europe*, Cambridge: Cambridge University Press, 1993, pp. 46–47, 63–64.

19. On the "one drop rule" of racial inheritance, see Naomi Zack, *Race and Mixed Race* (Philadelphia: Temple University Press, 1993), chapters 2,3,8.

20. The problem with homosexuality in white capitalistic terms is that it cannot be monetarized or brought into racial grids of power through the mechanism of mammalian reproduction to which fantasies of racial inheritance have been attached. Thus, homosexuality may be reviled by "normal" Americans precisely because it is a crime against money, and only secondarily a crime against "nature." It needs to be more broadly recalled that mammalian reproduction has not been attached to ideas of race only, but that since World War II, it has been widely mobilized as the point of distribution for the products of the American consumer economy. When that primary blissed-out unit, which is styled by financial analysts as "Dick and Jane Six-Pack," makes its quarterly decisions about house, car, and big appliance purchases, not to mention Christmas shopping, corporate movers and shakers pay sober attention.

155

MIXED-RACE WOMEN

Maria P.P. Root

American Girl
No
I'm not feeling Asian today.
Or American.
And, no, I am not
Filipina Thai Samoan Hawaiian
Mexican Brasilian Burmese Siamese
Polynesian Tahitian Malaysian Moroccan
Egyptian Indo-Chinese Indonesian Micronesian
I have no race.
No country.
Only a soul composed of wars
mixed pride
and
agony.

—Velina Hasu Houston[1]

chapter 12

RACE AND gender co-construct each other in this country.[2] Nowhere is this more apparent than in the way a multiracial existence shapes the core of identity for the racially mixed woman.[3] In addition to being multiracial, the social value and pressure of physical appearance used to locate women in the social sphere adds a dimension to being multiracial that is not present to the same degree and meaning for most multiracial men. In this chapter the issues of uniqueness, acceptance and belonging, physical appearance, sexuality, self-esteem, and identity are discussed as they may surface during therapy with multiracial women. A case example is used to illustrate the subtle and not so subtle ways in which these issues surface and combine with one another.

Psychotherapy provides a context within which the confluence of social and political forces emerge. Therapy with multiracial people can prompt us as therapists to examine our assumptions about race and ethnicity and the degree to which we have internalized a pseudoscientific oppressive belief system. Therapy with multiracial women can prompt us as therapists to consider how perceptions and definitions of race and gender are intertwined.

The mixed-race woman seldom enters therapy overtly to resolve issues that have to do with her multiracial or multicultural heritage. However, the therapist's ability to understand the issues and themes related to this experience allows her or him to facilitate a relief of symptoms and/or strategize problem solving more quickly and in an appropriate context. A brief case summary is provided below as an example of how these issues and themes may be manifested in therapy. The ways in which the client benefits from therapy may inform and broaden the therapist's ideas and attitudes concerning race. (All identifying information has been changed; this case represents a composite of several clients.)

> Cherise was a twenty-eight-year-old, single, multiracial woman, the second of four children and second girl. Her mother was white and her father black. She reported their relationship to be positive, though there were tumultuous times during her adolescent years when her parents separated for 2 years. Her father had recently been diagnosed as terminally ill.
>
> She sought therapy to "sort out relationship issues." Cherise was in a four-year relationship with a man whom she met in college. This was her first sexually active relationship. She ended the relationship because she felt that something was missing: he didn't understand her perspective on life. Since graduating from college she had had several relationships. She had usually been the one to end the relationship for various reasons: the man put her on a pedestal; their backgrounds were too different; his family made judgments about her background; he didn't understand her; and so on. She wanted to have children and was worried that at the rate she was going she would never find a permanent partner. Her mother suggested that Cherise might be expecting too much from a partner; her friends suggested that Cherise just hadn't found her match, or alternatively, that she thought she was too good for the men she met. She was worried that there was something wrong with her ability to commit and relate in relationships.
>
> Meanwhile she reported withdrawing from social interactions, eating more, and avoiding the increased attention men appeared to be paying to her.

UNIQUENESS

Adolescence is marked by ambivalence about being different from one's peers. The adolescent laments on the one hand "being the only one who…," and on the other hand often makes stereotypical attempts to be unique. In some ways, the adolescent experience extends throughout the multiracial person's lifetime. The theme of uniqueness is a significant part of the multiracial person's experience; it interfaces with all the other themes to be discussed in this chapter. Whereas one might think that the multiracial person would derive a developmental benefit from her or his uniqueness, ironically it may pose an additional obstacle to establishing a positive self-esteem and identity. Additionally, many of the impersonal styles and defenses established to assert one's way of being and perceiving the world may be pathologized if misunderstood by the therapist.[4]

The multiracial woman may feel ambivalent about being special. Her uniqueness in the eyes of others is initially related to the ambiguity of her racial features, and subsequently, to her racially mixed heritage; she is often regarded as an object (e.g., exotic) or a curiosity (e.g., "I have never seen a bi-racial person up close"). This type of oppression perpetuates feeling "outside" of a group; she may feel hurt, angry, and/or incorporate this information into a negative sense of self-esteem (i.e., something is wrong with her). Conversely, many multiracials receive a great deal of attention and may feel deflated or less valued if something changes and their appearance or existence is no longer perceived as being so special. With either experience, a multiracial woman may feel alienated, anxious, depressed, and angry in response to events not apparently related to the personal problems she anticipates. Issues or feelings may appear more intense than the manifest issue warrants. A task in development is to understand if and how these feelings are related to the multiracial experience, how to interpret the feelings, and how to cope.

Women are particularly vulnerable to society's reactions to their ambiguous features. These reactions echo the overvaluations placed on women's physical appearance that play a critical role in the development of some unhealthy practices, such as eating disorders, cosmetic dieting, and some elective cosmetic surgeries. Furthermore, if a woman's uniqueness is seen as exotic, some women internalize this perception and will behave in ways to fulfill society's expectations of the exotic woman. As such, this experience interferes with self-discovery and the declaration of who one is apart from physical appearance.

In therapy, the experience of being the "only one" may manifest itself through the personalization of events and interactions that perpetuate feeling "different" or misperceived. The multiracial person may wonder "what if she had been monoracial?" How would the experiences of her life be different? And despite hypodescent rules, she will never know with certainty what life would be like without the questioning or accusing looks from other people. Such sensitivity may also originate in growing up in a family that was isolated by a community, isolated itself as a protective reaction against antimiscegenist responses, or was unable to provide proper socialization for coping with being multiracial. The repeated experience of being misunderstood may also contribute to the development of a style of communicating that attempts to provide a great deal of context in order to be better understood. However, this style can look compulsive and at times paranoid.

A lifetime of uniqueness may coincide with tremendous feelings of isolation and attendant depression and self-doubt. This observation is particularly relevant for women, who more than men derive validation from their shared experiences with significant people in their environment. Helping such a woman to connect her current feelings with her experiences of being multiracial can be particularly enlightening. Much benefit can be derived from a multiracial support group.

In contrast, the unique vantage point of some multiracial people has led to much questioning on their part of how the world works and given them more trust in their own perceptions than in those of others; this outlook does not necessarily result from a dysfunctional family, but from a dysfunctional society. This position at times may look as though the multiracial woman thinks that she is better than others or "entitled" in a way that appears narcissistic. It is important to consider that many multiracial women have grown up in communities and during a time in which the subtle governing rules of the social order are often illogical; many of them have also felt it necessary to be the representative or protector of their family and their parents, partly as a defense mechanism for their own insecurity. The style that emerges is "normative" for many multiracial persons.[5] Exploration of their emotional pain (hurt, anger, depression) needs to be conducted in a larger social context. The therapist can play a significant role in listening to the individual's reality and helping the woman to determine how she wishes to feel or act differently. Some individuals may wish to decrease their sense of self-consciousness and responsibility to others.

In the case of Cherise, there are at least two clues that suggest that the theme of uniqueness was contributing to her depression, anxiety, and feelings of isolation: (1) more than one partner had not understood her world perspective; and (2) her friends observed that she hadn't met her match or that she thought she was better than the men she dated. This latter point illustrates how "specialness" may convey expectations. Cherise was particularly distressed because although her perspective tended to be different from that of other people around her, it did work for her. But she was not so sure that she trusted her perceptions of herself. Increasing self-doubt and depression indicated that she was feeling misperceived and isolated in her experiences.

ACCEPTANCE AND BELONGING

At the core of the need to belong and to be accepted is that of connection, how one interpersonally experiences and is experienced in the world. This connection or grounding in one's social environment provides a foundation for positive self-esteem and identity. Many mixed-race people grow up with countless experiences that illogically and unnecessarily set them apart from others. For example, most multiracials have experienced being stared at and asked insensitive questions about their physical appearance (e.g., "What are you?"[6]), family experience, and cultural differences (e.g., "Where are you from?"). Connection is difficult when one is the object of curiosity, pity, or fear.[7]

There are rules about belonging to any group. Some of them become painfully apparent when dating starts, which for the biracial woman is potentially all interracial. For example, one light-skinned Eurasian woman described her high school dating experience as being "liked by everyone and dated by no one." She attributed her situation to being perceived as a person of color by whites, not really Japanese enough by the parents of her Japanese classmates, and not a person of color by her African-American friends. The multiracial woman needs strategies for coping with these situations.

Belonging can also be a broader experience than many monoracial women's experiences. Many respondents in Hall's[8] dissertation suggested that whereas their biracial identity resulted in their not fitting in perfectly to any situation, except perhaps with other mixed-race persons,[9] they had membership in multiple groups; sometimes the multiracial person will focus on the fact of not fitting in and feel isolated and alienated. A therapist can be particularly helpful to the multiracial person by validating these feelings and experiences and exploring how "the cup is half full" rather than always "half empty" (i.e., the advantages and comfort they have in initially being part of different groups).

The history of race relations in the United States contributes to the concern and even preoccupation with "acceptance" that some multiracial people experience; society's efforts to preserve color lines put the multiracial woman in a peripheral position.[10] Many communities of color have narrow criteria for group membership; sometimes the criteria have sociopolitical significance (e.g., is this person visibly a minority person?); sometimes the criteria are very inclusive for political reasons (e.g., when number counts; sometimes the criteria repeat the elitist, senseless process of treating race as a scientific concept and confusing it with ethnicity (e.g., "full-blood" individuals being more valued than those with mixed blood). The criteria become painful, however, when differences are emphasized and similarities are dismissed, the former resulting in exclusion of the multiracial person. Subsequently, many mixed-race persons suffer in the communities to which they are socially assigned because they do not "look right," "think right," or "act right." Consequently, some multiracial people try extra hard to prove that they are African American, Native American, Asian American, or Latino because belonging and acceptance are so important. And because some multiracial people do not stereotypically look like people of color, they may attempt to prove ethnic group membership to the extent of engaging in negative, stereotypic behavior[11] or emphasizing identification with the cultural practices of only one part of their ethnic heritage.

The implications for therapy are significant. The multiracial woman may manifest social anxiety, general anxiety, detachment, or depression when she does not feel connected. These are reactions of powerlessness and alienation that may be based in a reality that at times is very subtle. Feelings of being an "imposter" might arise as a signal that she feels pseudo- or conditional acceptance within a group. The experiences that give rise to this feeling may also give rise to a lack of confidence in herself or lack of trust in how she perceives her environment. The ther-

161

ROOT

apist can provide a sociopolitical perspective to both explore this experience and increase the client's self-confidence, and also affirm that being different is not bad or inferior. It is helpful for the therapist to acknowledge that there are very real barriers in the social environment for mixed-race people that may heighten feelings of alienation and isolation, increasing vulnerability to depression and anxiety. The strategies one employs to fit in might also make one too dependent on validation from outside of oneself. Lastly, the therapist might explore whether the multiracial woman is denouncing parts of her heritage in order to belong. The therapist must be aware of the difference between ethnicity and race and the limitations of both of these concepts.

To return to our case study, Cherise's anxiety over her relationships opened the door to her talking about how she often feels "alone in a crowd." This experience was related to the themes of both uniqueness and belonging. She often felt she didn't quite fit. These feelings were subsequently linked to her experience of truly having a different perspective that was probably related to her multiracial background. She described an experience in junior high that conveyed the rules of belonging. Cherise, like other girls, was experimenting with her hair, clothes, and makeup. On several occasions she had been confronted with, "What are you? Black or what?" A popular girl told her that she had to "make up her mind and stick to it" or else people wouldn't trust her. Thus, in a matter of seconds, she was handed the illogical belief system about race. It is supposed to be a constant identity and status. Since then she has "acted" black, but worries about acceptance by the black community because she might not be "legitimately" black enough. The therapist started to support her identification as multiracial and multicultural—and encouraged the notion that she could even feel differently on different days.

PHYSICAL APPEARANCE

Perhaps the existence of the multiracial woman has been minimized because to acknowledge her existence is to confront a social order based on colorism, racism, and sexism within and between groups. The spectrum of appearance when races are mixed blurs the lines that are asserted because even the same combination yields a continuum of color and other racial features.[12] For example, Black Japanese can look stereotypically black, Japanese, Filipino, Hawaiian, Polynesian, or Eurasian. Black Native-American people can look black, Indian, Polynesian, and so on. Furthermore, although physical appearance plays an important role in ethnic identification,[13] Hall[14] found that it did not predict identity choices of individuals in her study of Black Japanese.

There are several unique experiences related to physical appearance that interact with other issues for many multiracial women. Three are discussed here. Sometimes a name does not match what people expect to see. For example, a young woman with a German surname looks very Asian. People ask her if this is a married name, adopted name, and so on. A second unique experience is that of being stared at countless numbers of times. This experience fosters a self-consciousness that can exceed the adolescent years and is more intense and often more self-critical than the average self-consciousness of teenagers and young adults. It can be translated into feeling that one is being judged and evaluated, which may have a basis in fact. With the popularity of cognitive therapy, the therapist is advised to apply cautiously techniques that challenge irrational self-statements. The therapist should seriously consider the possibility that the multiracial person's experience is very different and the person may have a reality base for feeling "constantly judged and evaluated."

The third experience, a "flexible look" that changes with age, hairstyle, clothes, lighting, makeup, and who is looking, adds to the complexity of the multiracial woman's experience. First, because some multiracial women can voluntarily change how they are perceived racially, they can manipulate the types of subjective feedback and experiences to which they are exposed.[15] (Consequently, they have unique access to first-hand experience of more than one group of people.) However, the flexibility of this look is sometimes in the eyes of the beholder: any one person may "see" her in a way that does not correspond with how she sees herself, or to how most others see her. The result is that *the multiracial woman (or man) has to learn to establish a consistent, internal identity that resides within her and is not necessarily reflected back in the environment.* The flexible look and attendant social reactions also contribute to the self-consciousness that has been discussed and also specific self-criticism of various parts of the body related to racial features: eyes, nose, mouth, hair, and so on. A particularly difficult issue may have to do with hair, particularly for persons who are of African-American or Asian-American heritage. Hair can determine physical identification by others with a specific ethnic and racial group, and thus becomes a vehicle through which symbolic integration of a multiracial identity occurs. Asian people with lighter hair may wish for darker hair. Conversely, darker-haired Asian people may wish for lighter hair. The African-American biracial person may feel tormented by hair that isn't kinky enough. Conversely, she may be forced to grapple with issues of loyalty and authenticity if she straightens or relaxes her kinky hair. Lastly, individuals may "play" with their flexible looks beyond the adolescent years, when experimentation is considered normal. Some days they may strive to look "black," some days "white," other days mixed, and other days they may strive for an ethnic look that is not part of their heritage. Much as one may choose different color or style of clothing to suit one's mood, such behavior does not necessarily indicate pathology or lack of a stable identity or even a conscious or unconscious challenge to society's social order. In my clinical experience I find that women and teenage girls engage in this behavior more often than boys and men, since physical appearance and fashion have been made more of an issue for them than for men.

Successfully and sensitively working with a multiracial client requires that the therapist has explored and continues to explore how she or he has internalized

163

rules of racial categorization and accompanying ethnic stereotypes. For example, if a white-black woman looks as if she is trying to "pass for white" could it also be that at times she is trying to "pass for black"? And might it be that she is not trying to "pass," but that perceptions of passing reflect the therapist's implicit rules for racial boundaries? The therapist's clarity and flexibility and personal work to avoid prejudicial tendencies will provide her or him with an opportunity to distinguish dysfunctional from normative behavior and to help empower the client. The therapist can convey openness by asking the client to interpret her behavior and to provide explanations of her intent in different situations.

Although the issue of physical appearance is prominent for both multiracial women and men, it is embedded in a social context that classifies physical appearance as the most significant asset a women possesses. Together with striving for acceptance, struggling with identity, developing self-worth, and placing an external emphasis on physical appearance, some mixed-race women may be particularly vulnerable to developing eating disorders.[16] The multiracial woman is in a particularly odd position, as physical appearance may be a double-edged sword, a phenomenological juxtaposition of the beauty and the beast.[17] The unique integration of racial features may be quite aesthetically pleasing (the international modeling industry is increasingly capitalizing on "cosmopolitan" or "exotic" looking models who are of racially mixed heritage). However, stares and questions in everyday life can transform this same physical attractiveness into a burden.

Themes having to do with physical appearance were prominent in Cherise's life and subtly related to her experiences and choices of relationships. The confrontation she had with the girl in junior high school, mentioned earlier, had a profound effect on her. She learned that she was an "oddity" because of the flexibility of her racial appearance. Furthermore, she also felt anxious and powerless about trying to control the way people categorized her racially. Self-conscious about her appearance, she described her experience "as though people see in me what is most different from them." Accused of trying to pass for white she laughed, asking, "When have you seen a coffee-colored white?" And she said, "What is the problem if I look kind of white? That is part of me, too, but somehow I can only be one thing." The therapist supported a discussion of how situational context very much "colors" what a person sees in another person or themselves, and encouraged her to play with her racial and ethnic appearance to suit her mood, much like she had in junior high. Her personal belief system about racial classification and the meaning of these categories was explored. Cherise started to talk about how conscious she was of the color of the men she dated because she felt judged according to whom she chose to date.

SEXUALITY

The discrimination against multiracial women, compared to that of multiracial men, is especially great in the area of sexuality. The "exoticness" attributed to a multiracial woman is usually part of a male fantasy in which he seeks possession and dominance over the sexuality and sexual behavior of a type of woman about whom he has fantasized or is unfamiliar. Nakashima suggests that the attractiveness of the multiracial woman is partially linked to the stereotype of her being an unusually sexual being. She observes that

> the most constant off-shoot of this biological-psychological profile of people of mixed race is the stereotype that they are sexually immoral and out of control. This is especially true of multiracial women, whether they be "half-breed" Indian, Mexican "mestiza," "mulatta," or "Eurasian":... They are consistently imaged as extremely and sexually promiscuous.[18]

This fiction is portrayed in the pornography industry's stereotype of multiracial women. Nakashima further suggests that the mythology about the multiracial person's sexuality is perpetuated by oppressive stereotypes of American racial minorities as immoral, degenerate, and uncontrollable, particularly in their sexual impulses.

Multiracial women are especially vulnerable to internalizing the oppressive expectations of the exotic woman because of society's socialization of the importance of physical appearance, mixed messages about women's sexuality, and the oppressive beliefs about the sexuality of multiracial women. Accepting an "exotic" role may provide the permission to be sexual. Conversely, some mixed-race women may curtail the expression of their sexuality in order not to be stereotyped.

Lastly, the racially mixed woman may be more open to exploring sexual orientation. This openness often reflects the lifetime experience of flexibility in living aspects of racial identity[19] that may transfer over to viewing sexual orientation as flexible and sexual identity as mutable.

The racially mixed woman whose life experience has reduced her uniqueness solely to her appearance and discriminated against her because of her ambiguous racial social address may be starved for social acceptance. She may be more likely to accept partners who objectify her (as exotic) and seek to "possess" her; she may temporarily acquire a racial address when she is with a partner.[20] Such a relationship is likely to revolve around sexual relations that are fueled by fantasies loaded with racial and gender stereotypes. Ultimately, the racially mixed woman will feel emotionally unfulfilled. While there may be many paths of experience that lead to this type of relationship based on social attitudes toward mixed race, the therapist should also consider whether a history of sexual abuse, rape, or emotional abuse may account for her vulnerability to these relationships, as these experiences also objectify an individual and may result in the acceptance of unhealthy relationships for fear of being otherwise undesirable, unacceptable, or alone.

Cherise's sexuality was tied in with issues of self-esteem and physical appearance and had sometimes been a source of conflict on dates she had with men. She felt that she had dated several men who were attracted to her "exoticness," who sometimes thought she was of Polynesian background. She found that many of these men had fantasies that she would be "really different" sexually. In fact, Cherise described herself as often restraining or suppressing her sexual feelings for fear of contributing to these fantasies. Her recent avoidance of men was related to her feeling that she was tired of being treated like an object "to possess."

SELF-ESTEEM

Contemporary studies of nonclinical samples of mixed-race persons show successful adjustment and positive self-regard.[21] Nevertheless, some mixed-race people are in environments that make it difficult for them to feel good about themselves[22] because of negative messages and expectations regarding their multiracial heritage. Some multiracial people work very hard to excel at something to counter covert expectations that they are somehow inferior to monoracial persons. For example, one Latina black woman said it was essential for her to prove that she was better than most of her peers so that she would get respect for herself and her family. She equated excellence with acceptance and desirability; excellence resulted in her being sought out by different groups of people. She observed in retrospect that while she was aware at the time that she wanted respect, she only later related it to striving for acceptance and belonging, a theme in her life as a mixed-race person.

The mixed-race person may try extremely hard to "be good" or be an exemplary citizen in order to combat overt or covert negative evaluations of their parents' interracial union or their multiracial heritage. Some multiracial people counter negative expectations with a defense that magnifies Park's[23] suggestion that the multicultural person is the cosmopolitan of the world. This defense can appear narcissistic, since the individual believes that special things are expected of her or him. This foundation for self-esteem is fragile, and those who have it may feel devastated when they do not meet the expectations upon which they base their self-worth. For example, a twenty-three-year-old woman sought therapy for profound depression. She had been reluctant to seek help because she felt she should be able to overcome the depression herself. The onset of depression followed her failing the bar exam for her state, and since then she had been unable to seek work or study for the next exam. Although the therapist attempted to characterize her failure of the bar exam as normal (saying that a significant proportion of bright people fail it each time and that they should try to see whether test anxiety was a factor) the client could not think of herself as part of the norm. She was terribly afraid that her world would end if she failed a second time. In therapy it became apparent that her self-esteem had been predicated upon being perceived as exceptional, consistent with her destiny as a "special person," which was itself consistent with her completing law school at such a young age.

Much of a person's self-esteem comes from feeling special, valued, connected, and accepted. The mixed-race woman's evaluation of self may rest in how much she thinks others value her more than in how much she values herself. This mind-set is initially reflected by the family and later by the larger social environment. It is critical that parents understand their own racial beliefs, so that phenotypical differences are respected and do not have negative impact on a child's self-esteem and self-concept. Mothers particularly have carried on the responsibilities of the early socialization of their children. Parents need to provide primary interventions or inoculations against the dysfunctional attitudes of the social system toward women (i.e., historically women more often than men seem to base their self-esteem on whether or not they receive social approval). Parents should acknowledge the complex effects of physical appearance, provide direct education about the fantasies and stereotypes that people may have about multiracial people and interracial families, and teach a child psychological and verbal defenses that are empowering.

The majority of multiracial people I have worked with clinically, studied, or lived life with seem to be well-adjusted and feel good about themselves, despite some of the extra hardships of growing up. Cherise appeared to be no exception. A therapist with internalized oppressive beliefs about multiracial people might be ready to conclude that Cherise's difficulties in relationships come from low self-esteem. But that was not the case with this therapist, whose greatest concern was that Cherise's feelings of being misperceived, isolated, depressed, and anxious would start to change her image of herself in a negative direction of the stereotype of the tormented biracial woman.

IDENTITY

The sense of identity is a feeling of belonging. The theme of identity emerges, if not overtly through issues of belonging, then through feelings related to exclusion: isolation, depression, anxiety, and anger. The person who identifies herself or himself as multiracial possesses both multiracial and multicultural heritage and identity. For example, a major difference between African Americans and multiracially identified African Americans is not a fundamental difference in racial heritage but rather that the latter group identify themselves as multicultural, multiracial, feel a kinship with more than one group, or more comfortably move between racial groups on a social basis. Identity can be a political, social, cultural, and/or physical issue to resolve. And these aspects of identity are not necessarily congruent.

Socialization of a sense of ethnic identity is a unique feature of the lives of minority group members in American culture because this culture has made race such an issue. Miller and Miller observe the important role that parents of biracial children play. They reflect on the necessity to orient biracial children to a minority agenda or they will be "defenseless against a social reality."[24] Because little data exists, we do not know the extent of influence parents have on the ethnic identity choices of their children.[25] We know that parents play a role in other aspects of children's socialization including socialization to acquire psychological defenses to

live as people of color in this country.[26] Their attitudes and education of their children around the meaning of being biracial has impact.[27]

Wilson[28] observes that racial and ethnic identity for an individual may be different from one another and different also from phenotypic identity. Ultimately,
with people who do not know them, it is important that multiracial persons be
able to self-proclaim their identities. They may change them situationally because
their ethnic and cultural identities are not necessarily apparent to the observer,[29]
and without markers of racial address the individual may be excluded from the
very communities within which they were raised or identify if they move to a new
city. Given boundaries that are sometimes distinct between racial or ethnic groups,
and the authentic loyalties many biracial people have, the shifting of foreground
and background of identity may be required by the group which whom they interact. If race and its current codification, ethnicity, were not such important social
addresses in our society, these shifts might be less visible and less necessary.

Multiple identities do not pose an inherent problem for the individual, except
when a complex identity is viewed as abnormal by onlookers. Forbes reminds us
that we all have multiple identities, but that somehow we have assumed dichotomous and rigid approaches to race, often fusing it with ethnicity as though it were
a necessary and sufficient condition for "knowing a person." For example,

> some of the "cousins" will likely be in the "black" community, some are active
> "Indians," while still others may lead a dual life, sometimes being one thing,
> sometimes another. They may, for example, attend a "black" church where they
> do not publicly announce any Indian identity, and yet they may be Indian
> when visiting relatives or attending a pow-wow function.[30]

Duffy[31] concluded that such a duality may be viewed as a "simultaneously dynamic ethnic identity."

Ethnographic data on the choices multiracial women make in their partners is
sparse.[32] Society's dichotomies about race, a tendency to try to preserve color lines,
mistaken beliefs about miscegenation, and confusion of ethnicity with race would
suggest that the multiracial person's choice of partner has added complexity.
Beginning to date and make long-term commitments may expose the covert
racism of significant others and the larger social system. Virtually all dating or part-
nering may feel interracial or interethnic to the multiracial person. Sometimes
even dating another multiracial person may feel this way because of how the person locates herself or himself socially. Oftentimes, however, a shared experience of
life around the phenomenology of being mixed in society offers some implicit
understanding of life experiences around racial interactions.[33]

Many scholars in the area of multiracial identity[34] feel that left to her or his own
devices the multiracial individual would work out identity issues. However, social
forces complicate matters. For example, the U.S. Census Bureau, employers, health

insurance, and so on, expect racially mixed people to choose only one racial and ethnic identity. The dilemma for the multiracial person of Native-American, Filipino, and Scottish heritage might be to (1) remember what she or he checked the last time (and determine if the situation requires consistency); (2) consider the social, emotional, and historical implications of checking "other"; (3) consider the political and economic implications of checking "other" (would it deprive constituency, such as Native Americans, of the numbers needed for adequate representation?); (4) void the form by checking more than one identity; (5) write in an identity that will be ignored.

Some strategies used by multiracial people to reinforce and proclaim their identity may be misunderstood. Many of them center around names that are an important conveyor of ethnic identity and connections with their ancestors. Many mixed-race persons do not receive names that connote the multiple heritages. Therefore, they may change their names or add to their names, so as to strengthen an internal sense of belonging and/or identity with an important reference group and to provide historical continuity.[35] Others use middle names or reclaim formal names if their first names or nicknames obscure their ethnic heritage.

Sometimes people will fabricate ethnic identities that are more consistent with their appearance in order to avoid questions and negative reactions. For example, an adolescent black-white girl said she would tell people she was Egyptian because this made her more interesting and did not lead to intrusive questions about "whether or not her parents were married" or about her home life.

During the lifespan, there are experiences that sometimes facilitate clarification of identity (e.g., the birth of a child, the death of a parent, the choosing of a partner, the endings of relationships, or sociopolitical events). Sometimes the impact of these experiences results in a clarification of identity that appears to others to be a change in identity. Given society's belief that racial and ethnic identity are static, a change or clarification in racial or ethnic self-identification declared by a racially mixed person may be misinterpreted as pathological. The clarifications and changes observed in some multiracial persons might be akin to parents reevaluating a piece of their identity as children leave home, when they become grandparents, when their parents die, and so on.

SUMMARY

Therapy with multiracial people can prompt us as therapists to examine our assumptions about race and ethnicity and the degree to which we have internalized a pseudoscientific and oppressive belief system. In this chapter the unique pressures and experiences of multiracial women, and mixed-race people in general, have been highlighted. A concern at this time is the trend toward considering "exotic" looks intriguing, which may bring attention to multiracial people in this country, but also may continue the oppressive fantasies and the treatment of multiracial women as objects. Oppression insidiously affects mental health.

169

Despite oppressive mythology about miscegenation and the reality of multiracial people, mixed-race people tend to integrate their diverse experiences in a positive manner. Difficulties that arise from being multiracial are usually the results of an oppressive, dysfunctional environment that is perpetuated by ignorance and fear and falsely based notions of racial and cultural superiority. The distress that the multiracial women may exhibit can be congruent with symptoms observed in people growing up in dysfunctional homes. The therapist is advised to consider how the symptoms of growing up isolated from other multiracial individuals and families in a dysfunctional sociopolitical environment can mimic family dysfunction. Without this consideration the therapist may conceptualize distress in a way that invokes one of the nonrational hypotheses that have maintained the hostility toward miscegenation through several generations. Then, the individual's distress would be blamed on the family, ultimately the mother, and used to support illogical disparagement of interracial unions. In order to evaluate such biases, I have provided guidelines in this chapter to assess the validity and generalizability of a growing body of literature for professional and lay audiences. I have also drafted a Bill of Rights for Racially Mixed People that summarizes many of the issues discussed in this chapter.[36]

It is possible that the themes I have outlined in this chapter—uniqueness, belonging and acceptance, physical appearance, sexuality, self-esteem, and identity—will be less prominent issues in the lives of multiracial women in the future. Whereas the majority of multiracial people in this country at this time are biracial, the emerging generation will be multiracial. The next generation may benefit from biracial parents who can serve as role models and be empathetic to additional challenges of integrating a multicultural heritage, an experience largely absent for biracial people. Hopefully, as the number of multiracial people increases this will pose a concrete challenge to the racism that currently exists between and within groups. Consciousness is already starting to be raised in a way that is influencing theories and policies that affect our lives.[38]

NOTES

1. V.H. Houston, "American Girl," *Pacific Citizen* (December 1985).

2. H. Lerner, *The Creation of Patriarchy* (New York: Oxford University Press, 1986).

3. For racially mixed women both race and gender are secondary statuses. And within the construct of race in a monoracially constructed society, I infer that mixed race is a secondary status due to lack of official recognition by government bodies such as the U.S. Bureau of the Census that keep track of racial "counts." K. Allman, "(Un)Natural Boundaries: Mixed Race, Gender, and Sexuality," in M.P.P. Root, ed., *The Multiracial Experience: Racial Borders as the New Frontier* (Thousand Oaks, CA: Sage Publications, 1996), pp. 277–290. L. Jones, *Bulletproof Diva: Tales of Race, Sex, and Hair* (New York: Doubleday, 1994). G. Kich, "In the Margins of Sex and Race: Difference, Marginality, and Flexibility," in Root, ed., *Multiracial Experience*, pp. 263–276. C.A. Streeter, "Ambiguous Bodies: Locating Black/White Women in Cultural Representations," in Root, ed., *Multiracial Experience*, pp. 305–320. F.W. Twine, "Heterosexual Alliances: The Romantic Management of Racial Identity," in Root, ed., *Multiracial Experience*, pp. 291–304.

4. C.K. Bradshaw, "Beauty and the Beast: On Racial Ambiguity," in M.P.P. Root, ed., *Racially Mixed People in America* (Thousand Oaks, CA: Sage Publications, 1992), pp. 77–90.

5. Ibid.

6. The phenomenological experience of "What are you?" simultaneously infers lack of a "social address," creates a distance between the observer and the observed, and for the moment at least objectifies the individual. T.K. Williams, "Race as a Process: Reassessing the "What are You?" Encounters of Biracial Individuals," in Root, ed., *Multiracial Experience*, pp. 191–210.

7. M.P.P. Root, "A Bill of Rights for Racially Mixed People," in Root, ed., *Multiracial Experience*, pp. 3–14.

8. C.C.I. Hall, *The Ethnic Identity of Racially Mixed People: A Study of Black-Japanese* (unpublished doctoral dissertation, University of California, Los Angeles, CA, 1980). A condensed version of Hall's dissertation is found in C.C.I. Hall, "Please Choose One: Ethnic Identity Choices for Biracial Individuals," in Root, ed., *Racially Mixed People*, pp. 250–264.

9. T.K. Williams, "Prism Lives: Identity of Binational Amerasians," in Root, ed., *Racially Mixed People*, pp. 280–303.

10. Root, ed., *Multiracial Experience*.

11. T. Wilson, "Blood Quantum: Native American Mixed Bloods," in Root, ed., *Racially Mixed People*, pp. 108–125.

12. Hall, "Ethnic Identity." Hall, "Please Choose One." Williams, "Prism Lives."

13. A. Neal and M.L. Wilson, "The Role of Skin Color and Features in the Black Community: Implications for Black Women and Therapy," *Clinical Psychology Review* 9 (1989), pp. 323–334.

14. Hall, "Ethnic Identity." Another generation has matured since this study and the politics of race and mixed race have been attended to in a way that this study should not be considered definitive on this issue.

15. Allman, "(Un)Natural Boundaries."

16. M.P.P. Root, "Disordered Eating in Women of Color," *Sex Roles*, 22 (1990), pp. 525–536.

17. Bradshaw, "Beauty."

18. C. Nakashima, "An Invisible Monster: The Creation and Denial of Mixed-Race People in America," in Root, ed., *Racially Mixed People*, pp. 162–178; p. 168.

19. Allman, "(Un)Natural Boundaries." Kich, "In the Margins."

20. Twine, "Heterosexual Alliances." This acquisition of a social address through a partner is not limited through race, but recapitulates the ways in which women's social status and class belonging have been historically defined by the men they date and marry.

21. Hall, "Ethnic Identity." R.C. Johnson and C. Nagoshi, "The Adjustment of Offspring of Within-group and Interracial/Intercultural Marriages: A Comparison of Personality Factor Scores," *Journal of Marriage and the Family* 48 (1986), pp. 279–284.

22. J.T. Gibbs, "Biracial Adolescents," in J.T. Gibbs and L.N. Huang, eds., *Children of Color: Psychological Interventions with Minority Youth* (San Francisco: Jossey-Bass, 1989). J.T. Gibbs, "Identity and Marginality: Issues in the Treatment of Biracial Adolescents," *American Journal of Orthopsychiatry* 57 (1987), pp. 265–278.

23. R.E. Park, "Human Migration and the Marginal Man," *American Journal of Sociology* 33 (1928), pp. 881–893.

24. R. Miller and B. Miller, "Mothering the Biracial Child: Bridging the Gaps Between African-American and White Parenting Styles," *Women and Therapy* 10 (1990), pp. 169–180.

25. D. Johnson, "Racial Preference and Biculturality in Biracial Preschoolers," (unpublished manuscript, 1990).

26. B.A. Greene, "What Has Gone Before: The Legacy of Racism and Sexism in the Lives of Black Mothers and Daughters," in L.S. Brown and M.P.P. Root, eds., *Diversity and Complexity in Feminist Therapy* (New York: Haworth Press, 1990).

27. L. Funderburg, *Black, White, Other: Biracial Americans Talk About Race and Identity* (New York: William Morrow and Company, Inc., 1994).

28. R. Wilson, "People of Mixed Race Descent," in Y.I. Song and E.C. Kim, eds., *American Mosaic: Selected Readings on America's Multicultural Heritage* (Sacramento, CA: Ethnicus-Center for Multicultural Studies, 1991).

29. M.P.P. Root, "Resolving 'Other' Status: Identity Development of Biracial Individuals," in Brown and Root, eds., *Diversity and Complexity*. Omi and Winant also make this observation about the fundamental use of race as a location marker in society for individuals. M. Omi, and H. Winant, *Racial Formation in the United States: From the 1960s to the 1980s* (New York: Routledge & Kegan Paul, 1986).

30. J.D. Forbes, "The Manipulation of Race, Caste, and Identity: Classifying Afro-Americans, Native Americans and Red-black People," *Journal of Ethnic Studies* 17 (1989), pp. 1–51. Thornton also emphasizes this point recently. Stephan also researches and addresses the issue of situational identity in several publications. C.W. Stephan, "Ethnic Identity Among Mixed-heritage People in Hawaii," *Symbolic Interaction* 14 (1991), pp. 261–277. C.W. Stephan, "The Causes and Consequences of Ethnic Identity," in Root, ed., *Racially Mixed People*, pp. 50–63. C.W. Stephan, and W.G. Stephan, "After Intermarriage: Ethnic Identity Among Mixed-Heritage Japanese Americans and Hispanics," *Journal of Marriage and the Family* 51 (1989), pp. 507–519. In general, identity theories by race, gender, or sexual orientation often do not consider the multiple roles that inform our core identities. M.C. Thornton, "Hidden Agendas, Identity Theories, and Multiracial People," in Root, ed., *Multiracial Experience*, pp. 101–120.

31. L.K. Duffy, *The Interracial Individual: Self-concept, Parental Interaction, and Ethnic Identity* (unpublished master's thesis, University of Hawaii, Honolulu, 1978).

32. Twine, "Heterosexual Alliances." Williams, "Prism Lives."

33. Williams, "Prism Lives."

34. T. Wilson, "Blood Quantum." J.D. Forbes, *Black Africans and Native Americans* (Oxford: Basil Blackwell, 1988).

35. S. Murphy-Shigematsu, *The Voices of Amerasians: Ethnicity, Identity, and Empowerment in Interracial Japanese Americans* (unpublished doctoral dissertation, Harvard University, Cambridge, MA, 1987). This connection to one's lineage seems to have importance for many individuals' sense of belonging and well-being, particularly as our society becomes more anonymous and populated.

36. Root, "A Bill of Rights."

37. Root, "A Bill of Rights."; Naomi Zack, ed., *American Mixed Race: The Culture of Microdiversity* (Lanham, MD: Rowman & Littlefield, 1995).

PERFORMANCE

METHEXIS VS. MIMESIS:

Poetics of Feminist and Womanist Drama

Freda Scott Giles

FOR OVER two millennia Aristotle's *Poetics* has dominated Western dramatic critical theory, either as a guiding light for quantitative and qualitative analysis of a theatrical work or as a blinding beacon blotting out thoughtful contemplation of the conservative values Aristotle espoused—values which supported the Greek philosopher's ethos of religion, statecraft, class, and sex. When I was taught the *Poetics* as a theatre student, the ideas of the former tutor of Alexander the Great were presented to me as descriptive, rather than prescriptive, criticism; I was told that Aristotle was simply seeking to define and describe rather than pass value judgements, that the *Poetics* was the objective tool which molded Western dramatic theory.

When Europeans rediscovered Aristotle during their Renaissance, they formulated the Neoclassical Ideal, combining interpretations of Aristotle's ideas with those of the Roman critic Horace; a rigid formula for playwriting was one of the results. The Romantics (inspired by the resistance of Shakespeare and Lope de Vega) mounted a successful challenge to the restrictions imposed by this formula, but a number of its tenets, including the idea of universality, lingered on. The *Poetics* stood as a critical standard, and today it remains the basis for most popular contemporary theatre and film criticism. In the modern era, Brecht and Artaud led the charge against Aristotelian dramatic theory and criticism and its hegemony over dramatic structure. In the postmodern era, the constituencies Aristotle denigrated as unworthy subjects for drama or for tragic hero status are finally gaining a hearing, effectively responding to his proscription that "Even a woman may be good, and also a slave; though the woman may be said to be an inferior being, and the slave quite worthless…. There is a type of manly valor; but valor in a woman, or unscrupulous cleverness, is inappropriate."[1]

In order to explain the theory upon which feminist drama, a proactive implement in the feminist struggle, is based, Sue Ellen Case, Gayle Austin, Jill Dolan, and other feminist critics, have written extensively about the *Poetics* and the classical Greek theatre which predicated it.[2] The deconstruction and reinterpretation of the *Poetics* is a necessary step in re-educating students of Western theatre, and in the case of feminist theatre it is the first of a three-step process which Austin describes as:

1. Working with the canon: examining images of women;
2. Expanding the canon: focusing on women writers;
3. Exploding the canon: questioning underlying assumptions of an entire field of study, including canon formation.3

Austin's model serves any community omitted from or underrepresented in the canon of a culture in which it exists as a minority. The canon controls language, the primary descriptor of reality.

In his advice to the players, Shakespeare's Hamlet cautioned actors to "hold…a mirror up to nature." Aristotle described this mirror as mimesis, one of the creative building blocks of the dramatic impulse:

> …the instinct of imitation is implanted in man from childhood, one difference between him and the other animals being that he is the most imitative living creature, and through imitation learns his earliest lessons; and no less universal is the pleasure felt in things imitated.[4]

In her groundbreaking essay, "Classic Drag: the Greek Creation of Female Parts," Case explains that this mirror imitated a society which celebrated the suppression and disappearance of the female in public life, effectively excluding her from legal, economic, and cultural institutions. This disappearance is apparent in the reduction of the female element in the embodiment and worship of Dionysus, the god in whose name classical Greek drama became formalized in Athens, who had once been represented as male and female in perfect balance and whose chief adherents were his female acolytes, the maenads. In the theatre Dionysus' male mentors, the satyrs, took precedence. The dramatic and theatrical representation of women and ideas about women were totally within the province of men, and women became objects of conflict and opposition—the "other" which was better off suppressed. For a millenium, the female body itself would be represented by male actors and not seen in its own form except through the socially outcaste mimes.

Case points to *The Oresteia*, the tragic trilogy by Aeschylus, as a text central to the formalization of misogyny as a fundamental element in the tragedies and the state which those tragedies extolled. This trilogy, which commemorates the institution of the jury system in Athens, features, among a number of other anti-female elements, the rationale for the sole parental right of the father (the mother is ruled no more than an incubator); the stripping of power from the Furies (Eumenides), female deities; and the confirmation of Athena, for whom Athens was named, as a female in external representation only (not only had Athena no mother, having sprung full blown from the mind of Zeus, but she had forsworn her female sexuality).

The ideas of universality and of the tragic hero were effective instruments in molding the worldview of Athenian society into a cohesive unity which has persisted despite the efforts of resisting theorists to reveal this worldview's biases. Linda Kintz, author of *The Subject's Tragedy: Political Poetics, Feminist Theory, and Drama*, builds a complex argument against this worldview, which privileges the male, in her deconstruction of Aristotle's favorite tragedy, Sophocles' *Oedipus the King*. Kintz asserts that Freud's adaptation of the Oedipus myth to modern society serves much the same function that the original did—the story of Oedipus, who killed his father, married his mother, and fathered his brothers and sisters, was designed to "reinforce social organization":

> ...a mythological pantheon that retained traces of matriliny was being replaced
> by a patriarchal system of gods. Central to all these shifts was the inscription
> and ordering of sexual difference...one of the most important sites of orga-
> nizing the cultural representations of marriage and gender was tragedy.[5]

Thus, continues Kintz, "If Aristotle finds the story of Oedipus to be the most nearly perfect aesthetic production and if Western culture finds that the fate of Oedipus is the fate of every subject, a universal experience, then...Is every theory of the subject masculine?"[6]

Pro-feminist drama could be written within the confines of Eurocentric dramatic structure (well-made play, melodrama, etc.), but in order to shatter the false perspective of "objectivity" and "universality," feminist drama as a genre would undergo a reconstruction in form which would match content, reflecting profound differences in world view and the meaning of universality. One feminist theorist, Janet Brown, suggests that feminist drama represents woman's struggle for autonomy against the oppressive, sexist society: "When woman's struggle for autonomy is a play's central rhetorical motive, that play can be considered a feminist drama."[7]

Feminist drama is overtly political; its universality lies within the idea of equality and justice for all people. Since the Western idea of universality usually means "applicable to privileged white males," the whole claim that there can be nonpolitical "art for arts sake" is questionable. There are a number of meeting places in the human experience, but the interpretation of these "meeting place" events is as rich and varied as the human experience itself; common interpretation is virtually impossible, though the sharing of common cultural experiences and learning about the cultural experiences of others makes the understanding of a wide variety of these interpretations possible.

Brown has built her theory partially on a foundation provided by the rhetorical theory of Kenneth Burke, which rejects the separation of art from life, literature, or politics. According to Brown, authorship of feminist drama is not necessarily confined to the female author. In her critical analysis, David Rabe's *In the Boom Boom Room* is feminist, while Tina Howe's *Birth and Afterbirth* is not. In her book, *Feminist Drama: Definition and Critical Analysis*, Brown uses the plays *The Bed Was Full*, a nonrealistic farce by Rosalyn Drexler, and *Wine in the Wilderness*, a realistically constructed drama/comedy by African-American playwright Alice Childress, to illustrate issues and techniques in feminist drama. Brown extensively discusses *For Colored Girls Who Have Considered Suicide When the Rainbow is Enuff* by African-American poet/playwright Ntozake Shange as a feminist work. Brown closes with a chapter on the rhetorical strategies common to the works of feminist theatre groups, such as the short-lived but significant It's All Right to Be a Woman Theatre, which often compose theatre works collaboratively, reject the rugged individualism of the traditionally conceptualized hero in favor of a collective protagonist, and eschew "realism" and its concomitant linearism in dramatic structure. Brown does not discuss feminist performance artists who often add to these techniques the texturing of narrative through revision of the semiotic reading of their bodies, artists such as Holly Hughes, Karen Finley, and Rachel Rosenthal.

Generally speaking, Alice Childress, Ntozake Shange, and Adrienne Kennedy are the African-American playwrights most frequently cited by feminist theorists and critics as exemplars of feminist drama. Childress' plays are composed according to the linear plotting of the well-made play, but invariably feature strong, self-determined female figures who overcome attempts by others to constrict them on racist or sexist grounds. Shange, particularly in *For Colored Girls*, combines poetry, storytelling, music and dance, and a communal protagonist (a form which she has dubbed as the choreopoem) into what becomes a healing ceremony to offset the devastating damage the combination of patriarchal sexism and racism have

178

wrought on the African-American community. Adrienne Kennedy adapts Eurocentric avant-garde theatre techniques, combining symbolism, surrealism, and the fragmented semiotic landscape of Western culture, to reveal a psychological, interior portrait of the effects of racism and misogyny. A number of her plays, such as *Funnyhouse of a Negro* and *The Owl Answers*, are built around a central female character whose psyche has been shattered by internal conflicts over her racial and sexual identity.

Most feminist critics recognize a dichotomy between feminist and Afrocentric/womanist theatre theory, primarily by noting that the feminist experience in the United States frequently reflects the experience of the white middle-class woman: "The woman of color bears the triple burden of gender, racial and class oppression, while the white woman benefits from her class privilege of color."[8] Womanist theatre tends to foreground the impact of racism on the African-American woman and to frame the narrative of her experience according to Afrocentric dramatic and rhetorical precepts. Like feminist drama and Afrocentric drama, Womanist drama rejects much of the Western dramatic tradition.

Classic Drag for the African-American was the minstrel show. This form, in which troupes of white men swarthed in burnt cork impersonated their images of African-American men and women, molded the cultural consciousness of the United States from the mid-nineteenth century forward. The stereotypes of the mammy, the jezebel, and the tragic mulatto became the descriptors of the African-American woman; the residue of these images persists. When Alice Walker coined the term "Womanist,"[9] she codified the black feminist reclamation of identity definition and the self-empowerment of African-American women within the context of a unique history combined with an Afrocentric world view and culture.

In *Black Theatre: Premise and Presentation*, Carlton and Barbara Molette use Aristotle's *Poetics* as a point of departure in defining the elements of Afrocentric drama. Aristotle divided a play into six qualitative parts, valued in descending order: plot, character, thought, language, spectacle, and music. The Afrocentric tradition places primary value on the aural, visual, and rhythmic—language, spectacle, and music; the texture of the performance is as much or more a part of its meaning than whatever script there might be. The Afrocentric theatre event is tied to the African concept of time and space—the story is not necessarily told in a linear fashion, as time is not linear, but is more a circle or spiral where the past and present exist together. This theatre experience is holistic; there is no division of the intellect from the emotions—as much can be ascertained or learned through one source as the other. Nietzsche's idea of tragedy as the conflict between the Apollonian (intellect, after the god Apollo) and Dionysian (emotion, after the god Dionysus) would not apply: The Black theatre aesthetic grows out of an oral tradition that regards rhythm as the central factor in presentation. Improvisation plays a major role, and performer and audience may interact, or even trade places at any time. The event is communal and the manner of performance more presentation-

179

al than representational—that is, there is usually little or no "fourth wall" between performer and audience. Afrocentric drama serves functional purposes. It brings together a group of people in a communal celebratory act, creates spiritual involvement, and may effect some specific useful purpose.

The essence of African-American ritual-based theatre can be found in the traditional African-American church.[10] This communal theatre experience is described by the term *methexis*, a conceptualization of theatre oppositional to that of *mimesis*. Mimesis connotes emphasis on the solo performer (the hero) separate from the audience, who works from a predetermined, linear text, which Aristotle described as "complete."[11]

At a time when the African origins of much of ancient Greek culture, including the drama, are being more widely acknowledged by some scholars,[12] it seems only fitting that Afrocentric drama revive many of the ritual elements which informed the creation of classical Greek drama, including the idea of catharsis, cleansing through emotional release, which Aristotle defined as drama's sought-after endproduct. Contemporary African-American playwrights such as August Wilson ostensibly write in the Eurocentric well-made form, but they infuse so much Afrocentric myth and culture that their dramas take on a transcendent stylistic quality.

The Womanist dramatist mines the experiences of her foremothers, and her own experiences, passed through history, myth, culture, symbols, dreams, and inspiration, for the creation of the dramatic event. Glenda Dickerson, in her essay, "The Cult of True Womanhood: Toward a Womanist Attitude in African-American Theatre," describes this process as the act of a PraiseSinger: "A true PraiseSinger is a guardian of the archetypes of her culture's collective unconscious. Her function is not to invent but to rediscover and animate."[13]

A methexic Womanist theatre piece co-authored by Dickerson and Breena Clarke, *RE/MEMBERING AUNT JEMIMA: A Menstrual Show,* inverts and deconstructs the myth of the preeminent mammy figure, Aunt Jemima, to reveal her as an archetypal hero who perseveres from slavery days through the present. In the course of her satirical, often humorous, and sometimes tragic traversal of American history, presented in minstrel show format, Aunt Jemima, sexually abused concubine of a slave master, consort to Uncle Ben, lover to Two Ton (John Henry), indentured servant to the Quaker Oats Man, and immaculate conceptor, gives birth to thirteen daughters who march through time toward self-definition. Their adventures and misadventures are the stuff the African-American woman is made of. The experience of the African-American woman is reclaimed, revalued; the image dismembered by racism and sexism is re-membered:

> The painful, patient, and silent toil of mothers to gain a free, simple title to the
> bodies of their daughters, the despairing fight, as of an entrapped tigress, to
> keep hallowed their own persons, would furnish material for epics.[14]

Another strong example of methexic Womanist drama is *Praise House* by the collective, Urban Bush Women. *Praise House* invokes African-American religious imagery and ritual, dance, music, and folk narrative in celebration of the pain and passion which stimulate the creativity of the African-American woman. When the show tours, it often incorporates a local gospel chorus into its production. Performance artist Laurie Carlos, one of a powerful cadre of Womanist performers who are changing ideas about words and images in relation to the Black woman, often appears with the company. Such works "...reveal the complex interior landscape of black women's lives while at the same time looking outward and commenting on the world which impinges on their existence."[15]

Feminist and Womanist dramatic theories both recognize the need for reclaiming and revaluing the female experience, and that the process of doing so in the theatre involves the restructuring and reordering of both the language used in the drama (script, text, words) and the language of the theatre itself (the visual, aural, and internal language of performer, space, and audience). Womanist dramatic theory incorporates Afrocentricity into its perspective on the Black woman's historical, cultural, spiritual, and linguistic experience, and this has a particular influence on form and content: "Just as language cannot be separated from the community, form is integrally connected to content."[16]

Work with the canon, and with the magic power of the language, of which the word is only a part, continues. It has been slowly pressured into steps toward expansion, but has yet to explode, though a bulge appears here and there from time to time. The foundation for re-ordering is being laid, and the result will be the "transcendence of...gender-bent and race-rung perspectives"[17] which have inhibited Western drama's projections of universality:

> Regardless of the placement of the political narrative, there is an implicit sub-textual awareness of a larger communal context that is directly affected by even the most idiosyncratic protagonist's intimate search for meaning. Personal politics diversify the discourse and add new perspective to the global preoccupation with identity and survival of the species.[18]

When the concept of universality truly embraces representation of the totality of the human experience, when the action truly suits the word and the word the action, there will be no further need for new poetics:

> Women's writing. Men's writing. Gay and lesbian writing. Black writing. Such categories are only literary apartheid that marginalizes specific groups of writers. They are false commercial distinctions that have nothing to do with the quality of writing. There are only two kinds of writing. Good and bad.[19]

NOTES

1. S.H. Butcher, trans. *Aristotle's Poetics* (New York: Hill and Wang, 1961), p. 81.

2. The terms feminist, Black feminist, and Womanist are subject to a number of ideological, political, and philosophical definitions and interpretations; in this paper these terms are used loosely to describe the foregrounding, empowerment, and reclamation of women's experiences.

3. Gayle Austin, *Feminist Theories for Dramatic Criticism* (Ann Arbor: University of Michigan Press, 1990), pp. 16–17.

4. Butcher, p. 55.

5. Linda Kintz, *The Subject's Tragedy: Political Poetics, Feminist Theory, and Drama* (Ann Arbor: University of Michigan Press, 1992), p. 29.

6. Ibid., p. 14.

7. Janet Brown, *Feminist Drama: Definition and Critical Analysis* (Metuchen, New Jersey: Scarecrow Press, 1979), p. 1.

8. Sue Ellen Case, *Feminism and Theatre* (New York: Routledge, 1988), p. 97.

9. Alice Walker, *In Search of Our Mothers' Gardens* (San Diego: Harcourt Brace Jovanovich, 1967), pp. xi–xii.

10. Carlton Molette and Barbara Molette, *Black Theatre, Premise and Presentation* (Bristol, Indiana: Wyndham Hall Press, 1986), pp. 82–86.

11. Aristotle defined tragedy as "…An imitation of an action which is serious, complete, and of a certain magnitude; in language embellished with each kind of artistic ornament…; through pity and fear effecting the proper purgation of these emotions." (Butcher, *Aristotle's Poetics*, p. 61) Aristotle did make some comments on comedy, as an extension of fertility rites and dances, but his remarks on this genre are thought to be incomplete. (See Butcher, p. 2)

12. See Martin Bernal, *Black Athena: The Afroasiatic Roots of Classical Civilization* 1 (New Brunswick, New Jersey: Rutgers University Press, 1987). Bernal traces the myth of Dionysus to that of the Egyptian god Osiris; he also cites the plays of Aeschylus and Euripides as providing historical and mythic links between ancient Greece and more ancient Egypt.

13. Glenda Dickerson, "The Cult of True Womanhood: Toward a Womanist Attitude in African-American Theatre," *Theatre Journal* 40, no. 2, p. 187.

14. Breena Clarke and Glenda Dickerson, *RE/MEMBERING AUNT JEMIMA: A Menstrual Show* (unpublished manuscript, 1991), p. 22.

15. Margaret B. Wilkerson, *Nine Plays by Black Women* (New York: New American Library, 1986).

16. Joyce Ann Joyce, Warriors, Conjurers, and Priests: Defining African-centered Literary Criticism (Chicago: Third World Press, 1994), p. 33.

17. Sydne Mahone, Introduction, *Moon Marked and Touched by Sun: Plays by African-American Women* (New York: Theatre Communications Group, 1994), p. xiv.

18 Mahone, p. xxxii.

19. Aisha Rahman, introduction to *The Mojo and the Sayso* in *Moon Marked and Touched by Sun: Plays by African-American Women*, edited by Sydne Mahone (New York: Theatre Communications Group, 1994), p. 284.

PASSING BEYOND THE OTHER RACE OR SEX

Laurie Shrage

A WOMAN I know, whom I will refer to as "Mrs. C.," is raising two African-American daughters.[1] Mrs. C. is their biological mother and she is white. Their biological father is a man from Kenya, from whom Mrs. C separated when the children were young. Recently Mrs. C. told me that her daughters, now both in college, have become somewhat critical of her for not providing them with a stronger sense of their identity as African Americans. She had always identified her children as part Kenyan and part American, and she has attempted to raise them as she would have raised children of any skin pigment. That is, Mrs. C. seems to have chosen to be color-blind in matters pertaining to her daughters as a way of resisting a society that is not. Yet, this maternal strategy of blindness to "race" and "color"—a strategy that may have even seemed morally necessary to Mrs. C.—has not, from her children's perspectives, enabled them to negotiate successfully the racial system in the U.S.

and resist its oppressive dimensions. For notwithstanding Mrs. C.'s color blindness in regard to her daughters, these children will be racially classified in our society: most likely as black or African American.

It has become somewhat the common wisdom among progressives to see Mrs. C.'s decision to ignore race as a factor in raising her children as problematic—if not outright flawed. Instead we are likely to sympathize with her daughters' need for a racial identity and, in particular, their need to feel comfortable with, and even proud of, the one socially assigned to them. One of the most valuable aspects of recent work on race, gender, and sexual identity is that it forces us to reassess this common wisdom. While we can be sensitive to these children's problems in negotiating the American racial system, we might want to question their strategies of resistance to this oppressive system. For example, do the daughters' strategies, as young adults, of asserting African-American identities implicitly accept our society's arbitrary, asymmetrical, and pernicious culturally formed system of racial identification? If they do, then much like the mother's strategy of color-blindness, their strategies may fail to significantly challenge some fundamental elements of the racial status quo.

In thinking about the situation of families like Mrs. C. and her daughters, I find it odd that white women in our society can have children that are classified as racially different from themselves, but that it is often impossible for their children to be in the same situation vis-à-vis their own offspring. For example, should the daughters of Mrs. C. have children with men racially different than themselves, like their mother, their offspring would nevertheless, in almost all imaginable cases, be classified as belonging to the same race as themselves—i.e., black. Such a system of racial classification implies that the daughters are racially, and perhaps even culturally, closer to any of their future offspring than their mother is to them, which from the vantage of other classificatory systems seems absurd.[2]

Although Americans recognize, to a limited extent, the existence of persons who are racially or ethnically mixed, such persons exist, as many writers have shown, in the dominant social group's mythologies as tragic figures, incapable of integration into their own society. From the perspectives of those racially oppressed, "mulattos" or "coloreds" (in contrast to "Negroes" or "blacks") often represent a separatist and traitorous cultural elite that attempts to ascend existing social hierarchies by de-emphasizing its intimacy with black society and appropriating those things regarded as culturally "white." Therefore, to deploy racially or ethnically heterogeneous or ambiguous identities in a politically liberatory way requires some attempt to reinvent the category of the racially mixed so as to resist the "tragic mulatto" or "separatist elite" stigmas. If freed from these stigmas, the visibility of mixed-race, or multiply or ambiguously raced, persons might challenge a racial system that otherwise maintains the fictions of racial and ethnic purity and distinctness—fictions that are ever powerful despite the fact that the biological accounts supporting these distinctions have been overwhelmingly discredited.

Could the category "mulatto" or "mulatta" be reclaimed for the purpose of signifying multiracial identities, much as the term "queer" has been claimed by those in the gay, lesbian, bisexual, and transgendered movement, to resist the stereotyping and policing of human kinds that results from the use of identity categories? "Queer," in a sense, is an anti-identity identity, to be claimed by those who celebrate human diversity, and who want to resist the crude, essentializing ways we mark diverse sexual identities. Rather than sort out the real lesbians from the apparent ones, the real homosexuals from those who do not really qualify, queer is a status that is difficult to challenge. By claiming it one renders oneself queer and casts part of one's fate with other sexual dissidents and revolutionaries. Could the term "mulatta" serve a similar purpose in regard to racial identities? Many often claim that racial purity is an illusion; more of us are mixed than we acknowledge. Should those of us who want to emphasize our heterogeneous origins or contest the policing of racial borders describe ourselves as "mulatta"? Does the social act of claiming this status automatically put one in the category claimed so that the status cannot be challenged? Below I will take up some of these questions.

Recently, some scholars in feminist theory and gay and lesbian studies have attempted to articulate the relation of existing gender, sex, and sexuality categories to the perpetuation of sexism and heterosexism. For example, in her article "Interpreting Gender," Linda Nicholson encourages feminist theorists to be critical not only of biological determinism with respect to gender, but also what she calls "biological foundationalism."[3] In rejecting biological foundationalism, Nicholson asserts that not only is there no secure biological basis for existing gender norms, but there is no secure biological basis for the distinctions we make regarding sex and sexuality. Nicholson's work, like that of Judith Butler and others, examines the historical and cultural embeddedness of the categories of sex and thus calls into question the theoretical splicing of sex and gender. One's assigned sex does not necessarily determine the sex one lives, feels, or identifies with, much like one's assigned sex does not necessarily determine one's gender, understood in terms of the norms of femininity or masculinity. In some social contexts, for example, some "female-bodied" persons are not just masculine but male, and feminists homogenize human experience by treating all bodies with vaginas as female.

In a recent essay, Will Roscoe argues that understanding American Indian cultures and the traditional role of berdache persons requires that we recognize three or four gender categories that are embedded in belief systems "in which gender is not viewed as determined by anatomical sex or in which anatomical sex is believed to be unstable, fluid, and nondichotomous."[4] External genitals and biological reproductive capacity do not divide persons neatly into two sex/gender groups in these social formations. This example shows that, like gender and race, sex is not a purely biological concept—it is a theoretical construct that defines roles and identities in complex systems of social and biological reproduction and production. Roscoe's work suggests that the criteria of berdache identity vary across American

Indian societies, but in some it is more a function of one's spiritual ancestry rather than biological inheritance, and in others it is more a function of the type of productive activities in which one excels. One important implication of this understanding of berdache identity is that we are less inclined to view berdache persons as sexual hybrids made up of male and female traits and more inclined to view them as representing alternative possibilities to maleness and femaleness. Thus rather than see berdache persons as sexual misfits, defectors, or accidents of nature (i.e., similar to the way many Americans conceive gays, lesbians, transvestites, intersexuals, and transsexuals), Roscoe encourages us to interpret the Native-American berdache categories in terms of alternative, but legitimate and acceptable, social possibilities.

If the Berdache represent a third or fourth sex/gender category, then we can no longer conceptualize such folks as "passing": as women who are not really women, or men who are not really men. Indeed the common notion of "passing" seems to presuppose that there are stable, authentic sex or race identifications or designations that some individuals choose to conceal. If the daughters of Mrs. C., in my earlier anecdote, choose to assert identities as both white and black, either simultaneously or in different contexts, some would see them as inauthentic or as passing. Yet, it is unclear, to me anyway, what is socially or biologically most authentic for children with these family and personal histories. Our current system of racial identification assigns people to categories on the basis of visible pigment and known "facts" about a person's biological progenitors. Yet one's quantity of skin pigment or biological ancestry does not necessarily determine the race one lives, feels, or identifies with. By policing the categories of racial identity so that pigmented people must identify one way, and non-pigmented people another, we do little to challenge racialist notions about racial purity and distinctness.

Perhaps, when persons decide to confuse the apparent facts of racial inheritance or sex determination in their self-presentations, we should question the discomfort of those who see such individuals as alternately passing and being authentic, or who see these individuals as psychologically confused. In the realm of gender drag, there really is something quite powerful when so called "female impersonators" fulfill and exemplify the ideals of femininity better than many "female-bodied" persons do.[5] Such transgendered and cross-gendered performances indicate the potential that racial and ethnic cross-identifying has for rendering visible the socially constructed nature of our associations between body type or family ancestry, on the one hand, and social identities or cultural traits, on the other. I hope we can begin to consider strategies of resistance such as these without feeling vulnerable to charges of false consciousness, internalized racism, or homophobia.[6] Persons with mixed backgrounds or gender identifications are often socially cast into race/ethnic and sex/gender roles that are alien to them, and such strategies offer some means to resist the significant social pressure to know better their genuine roles and proper places.

186

In *Stone Butch Blues*, Leslie Feinberg describes the struggles of a young butch lesbian to live as a woman and then subsequently as a man in our society.[7] The book is extremely valuable for revealing the way sex identities are literally policed in our society. Feinberg describes the way persons who do not dress and act in accordance with their assigned sex are brutally harassed, assaulted, and mistreated by law enforcement officials, landlords, employers, family members and friends, and strangers. Persons who cross-identify in terms of our binary sex categories are marginalized as freaks, and their horrendous mistreatment is thereby tolerated or overlooked.

There is some literature documenting the ways persons who are designated as black and who are perceived as "whitening" themselves are mistreated in our society. However, I do not know of any studies that deal with the general treatment of persons who are designated white but who are perceived as inauthentically assuming a black identity. On a few occasions, I have seen young boys with blonde dreadlocks who have developed speech patterns associated with African Americans. I've often assumed (based on the pigment factor) that such boys are white (that is, have no ancestors that would qualify them in our culture for black identity). Though this assumption may be incorrect, it would be interesting to document the social experiences of these kids. Perhaps because the clothes, hairstyles, and speech mannerisms that mark racial identities are in some ways more subtle or complex than those that mark sex identities, the mistreatment of racial "cross-dressers" is somewhat different than that of sex "cross-dressers."

Many individuals who are contesting their assigned sex identities regard themselves as transgendered or transsexual. "Transgender," as a designation, is often contrasted with "transsexual." The latter is often understood to mean someone who is transitioning to the opposite sex and ultimately will seek bodily surgery to make one's chosen sex and body consistent with the body stereotype of that sex. A transgendered individual typically chooses to express one's sex identity in nonconventional ways and does not seek "corrective" surgery. Being transgendered or transsexual complicates one's assignment to other categories. For example, it is difficult to classify transgendered or transsexual individuals as gay, lesbian, bisexual, or heterosexual. If one is born with a vagina, lives as a man, but enjoys sexual intimacy with women, is one a lesbian? Is the partner of this person a lesbian too? Similarly, if one is born with a penis, lives as a woman, enjoys sexual intimacy with women, is one a lesbian?

Do people who live in multiracial families have obvious racial identities? Should the white parent of black children be designated "white"? Why are one's ancestors rather than one's descendants more relevant to establishing one's racial identity? If race is not biologically inherited (though bodily traits associated with particular racial groups are), why should biological ancestry be more important than existing social relationships? Perhaps the issue is not how, or only how, Mrs. C's daughters should identify—black or white—but how Mrs. C should identify. Would the designations "mulatta" or "transracial" help here, in the way the categories "transgender" and "queer" help to contest other pernicious systems of classification? Perhaps Mrs. C and her daughters could all be mulattas or transracial—identities that have the advantage of not distancing Mrs. C racially from her daughters.

In proposing such alternatives, I do not mean to subscribe to another version of the one-drop rule: those who socially mix with blacks are black or nonwhite. If Mrs. C were "officially" black with a husband and children who identified as white, then why should anyone deny Mrs. C a white identity if she should choose it? If racial classifications were made on the basis of social ties rather than blood ties, then race might come to be seen less as a biological or immutable characteristic.

Also, I do not mean to suggest that the only politically liberatory way to deal with conventional sex and racial classifications is to reject them. The strategy of affirming the stigmatized categories into which one is placed is also important. But this latter strategy has come to eclipse other possibilities for resistance. Moreover, these strategies need not be mutually exclusive. As a Jew who was not "raised Jewish" in some significant respects, I can both claim a Jewish identity but also know that at some level, when I compare my experiences with those of other Jews, I'm really faking it. For example, I remember when I was in high school in the late 60s and, in the wake of the student movement, it became useful in some contexts to have a non-Wasp identity. It was the first time in my life that the facts of my Jewish ancestry had some real social value for me. I remember consciously cultivating this identity for awhile—I started to wear a mezuzah necklace and to imitate what I thought was a New York accent. I managed to impress some of my more Waspy California friends and felt more valued socially for awhile. However, this affectation stopped when I went to college and met my Iranian Moslem boyfriend.

Not actively asserting my Jewish identity in the context of this relationship was also part of a struggle, though a different political struggle than fighting anti-Semitism. For my later behavior in college "passing" as a generic American occurred in a society in which Middle Easterners and Moslems are racially and ethnically stigmatized, especially by Jews and Christians. I realize that not all people have this kind of casual relationship to their inherited ethnicities. For some, these ethnic identities represent important community relationships and attachments. But there are others of us who feel that these identities can be worn on some occasions and discarded on others, and I do not feel this is wrong or an inferior way of appreciating one's own ethnicity and that of others. What this personal example is meant to suggest is that there is no single correct relationship to one's conventionally assigned ethnic, racial, or sex identity. There are contexts in which downplaying one's assigned racial or sex identity might be a good thing to do and contexts in which playing it up may be good. And there are contexts in which playing up a racial or sex identity one is conventionally excluded from may be good. There is at least no reason, other than a desire for conformity or tradition for their own sake, that we should be prudish about behaviors that "crossover" or "pass" into conventionally forbidden race or sex territories. I acknowledge that given existing body stereotypes, some people have more identificatory options than others. Yet because people who exercise their greater options often serve to denaturalize the categories of identity themselves, their nonconventional identificatory choices have the potential to open up liberatory possibilities for the rest of us.

Like Mrs. C's daughters, I have at times resented my parents for not providing me with greater exposure to "my" (in this case, Jewish) culture. Knowing more about a particular cultural group and one's own ancestors is generally a good thing. But I can also appreciate my parents' cosmopolitan values and their attempts to escape the social segregation that structured the lives of their parents. Participating in and even adopting the customs of social Others need not eventuate in self-annihilation. For just as Jewish and Gentile persons, or male and female or black and white persons, can persist side by side in a single community, Jewishness and Gentileness (maleness and femaleness or blackness and whiteness) can persist in a single individual. Taking parts of even dominant Others into ourselves need not obliterate subordinate identities, for we need to remember that these dominant cultures would not be what they are without the subordinate groups.[8] In a nonsegregated world, as individuals of different types live side by side, some of these individuals will create for themselves creolized personas that are as equally valuable as the presumably more "pure" ones.

We should perhaps vigorously resist the pressure to create more pure selves in terms of race, ethnicity, or biological sex, for this will surely lead us back to pernicious forms of social segregation. Certainly, one of the ways people have traditionally established their ethnic/racial/gender purity is to socialize more exclusively or share particular activities with only those like themselves. We are unfortunately too familiar with quests for self-purity that have generated fantasies of more racially and ethnically pure communities. Perhaps integration requires selves that are conceived less as biologically delivered pure types that persist over time and more as historical instantiators of valuable cultural options that persist over time. One's body type and personal history can constrain which cultural options one can instantiate, but the more integrated the society the less this will be so.

SHRAGE

NOTES

1. I am grateful to the Society for the Study of Africana Philosophy for providing me the opportunity to present some of the ideas and examples in this paper at their meeting in Boston, December 1994.

2. The U.S. historian Barbara Fields notes the absurdity of the "American racial convention that considers a white woman capable of giving birth to a black child but denies that a black woman can give birth to a white child." See her "Ideology and Race in American History," in J. Kousser and J. McPherson, eds., *Region, Race, and Reconstruction* (New York: Oxford University Press, 1982), p. 149. For other important studies on the social and historical contingency of racial classifications, see Virginia Dominguez, *White By Definition:*

Social Classification in Creole Louisiana (New Brunswick, NJ: Rutgers University Press, 1986); David Hollinger, "Postethnic America," *Contention* 2 (Fall 1992); Daniel Segal and Richard Handler, "U.S. Multiculturalism and the Concept of Culture," *Identities* 1 (1995).

3. *Signs* 20, no. 1 (Autumn 1994), pp. 79–105.

4. "How to Become a Berdache: Toward a Unified Analysis of Gender Diversity," in Gilbert Herdt, ed., *Third Sex, Third Gender* (New York: Zone Books, 1994), p. 371.

5. See Judith Butler, "Gender is Burning: Questions of Appropriation and Subversion," in *Bodies That Matter: On the Discursive Limits of Sex* (New York: Routledge, 1993). In the context of discussing the film *Paris Is Burning* (a film about drag balls in Harlem), Butler states "drag is subversive to the extent that it reflects on the imitative structure by which hegemonic gender is itself produced...." She also notes that "drag may well be used in the service of both the denaturalization and reidealization of hyperbolic heterosexual norms" (p. 125). See also Marjorie Garber's *Vested Interests: Cross-Dressing and Cultural Anxiety* (New York: Routledge, 1992). Garber considers the social meanings of double crossings: someone whose race and sex identities are blurred.

6. In "Ethnic Trangressions: Confessions of an Assimilated Jew," I argue that some instances of ethnic crossing may represent illegitimate cultural appropriation or the capitulation to hegemonic racist values, but that there are some crossings that challenge racist/racialist beliefs, and we should not treat all cases of ethnic crossing alike. This article is included in Naomi Zack's *American Mixed Race* (Lanham, MD: Rowman and Littlefield, 1995). See p. 294.

7. Leslie Feinberg, *Stone Butch Blues* (Ithaca, NY: Firebrand Books, 1993).

8. I am grateful to Daniel Segal for his insights on many of these ideas.

VOICED BODIES/EMBODIED VOICES

Judith Bradford and Crispin Sartwell

chapter 15

I.

THIS PAPER is about voices, bodies, social identities, and liberatory theory. In section one we discuss the specificities of our own voices, of how we speak and why we speak as we do and are heard in the ways we are heard. In section two we analyze the complex problems involved in "having a voice" or not having one. In the third part we go on to talk about the implications of this analysis of voice for social and political philosophy, especially in its liberatory versions. Unless otherwise indicated, the voice that speaks in this paper belongs to neither co-author: the text was worked out in close collaboration, and neither of us can tell which words are whose.

Race and gender cannot be compared because they are in fact inextricable; there are no unraced gendered persons, nor ungendered raced persons. Racing and gendering are social and political processes of consigning bodies to social categories and thus rendering them into political, economic, sexual, and residential positions. "Rendering" here means both "representing" and "boiling down"; the structures have the effect of radically simplifying identities, of making them comprehensible by selectively identifying certain physical or historical facts about those bodies and making them significant. The practices that race and gender bodies, however, do not remain merely external; they *use* bodies, flow through them, articulate forms of experience, modes of movement, and so forth. Thus, race and gender, though they originate in disciplines to which bodies are subjected, become relational in any given transaction; they are ways both of being a body and of interpreting persons. And since race and gender intersect in some way at every human body in and upon which they are rendered, they cannot be extricated from one another. The rendering of race and gender varies with context, and there may well be contexts in which they are absent, or in which they take up radically different forms. In the U.S., for example, there are white male bodies, but no bodies that are merely white. What we will discuss, however, is not primarily the raced and gendered renderings of bodies, but the intertwined emergence of raced and gendered voices. Of course, voices emerge precisely from bodies; it is bodies that speak or write. The categorization of the voices of bodies is a part of processes of consignment. This aspect of the rendering of bodies into social identities—the norms of voice—also acts at times to prevent expressions of resistance to the process of consignment; the voices of those who would protest their consignment to a social identity can be de-legitimated in advance by the expectation on the part of authoritative listeners that those voices do not count.[1]

We attach voices to bodies; we deploy expectations about the ways a female, dark-skinned body can speak or about the ways a male, light-skinned body can speak, for example. And that deployment conditions the way we can receive voices that proceed from those bodies. When a voice floats free of its body in certain respects, over the phone or on the radio, we imagine the body from which the voice emerges. When I read a text you have produced, I may search for signs of your embodiment and hence your social location in order to assess the authority of the voice to make the claims it is making. (Is the author's name the name of a woman? What kind of woman?) But voices disattach from bodies in another way; there are categories of appropriate voices that are heard as emerging from the bodies regimented by our systematics of body categorization. This normative attachment of certain voices to certain bodies can be used in many ways. It is a space in which one can try to erase one's embodiment, or to declare it, or to work against it and hence against the socially authorized taxonomies of bodies. One thing we hope to suggest is that the study of voicings shows very clearly how important it is that race and gender are interactive, and that it is a mistake to conceptualize them as separate variables that could possibly "add up" to a person's social identity.

CRISPIN SARTWELL:

I'm a white man, and I write, I think, in a particular "white male voice." I had to be trained in that voice. This is not to say that my writing is a kind of drag, a play with my own gender or race. Quite the reverse: the performance is not, for the most part, one that I take up consciously; it is perfectly ingrained. I learned it at my father's knee, as he argued me into submission and then presented me with a copy of *The Elements of Style*. I was taught how to write philosophy in measured, authoritative tones that sought to arrogate to myself certain forms of comprehension and, hence, of power. By an incredibly detailed process of placing marginal comments on my papers, and rewarding or penalizing me with grades and cash and letters of recommendation, I was initiated into a certain form of writing.

I have never doubted my right to argue with anyone about everything; I have never entered into a context in which I did not attribute to myself the right to speak. Now I have, of late, been trying to write against myself, to tear my own authority apart, and also to enter into contexts where I am anxious about my right to speak. That turns out to be much harder than I imagined. What voice I am able to produce is not determined solely by what I try to do with it, but also by what others are able to hear me saying. To change my voice effectively requires changing others' ears as well as my speech. No matter what I try to say, my voice gets heard through the norms that govern white male voices. The voice of the white male author, especially the white male academic author, speaks from on high, assumes that it ought to be heard, and is characterized by processes of abstraction and generalization associated with "reason." When I try to contravene the arrogance of the 'neutral' academic voice, and speak informally and personally, I am sometimes read as *more* arrogant than your typical white academic, as lacking the humility that the neutral voice is supposed to encode by erasing the flagrant signs of individuality.

The voice of the white male author is supposed to issue from no position. It is the one 'blank' in the race and gender taxonomy, the one location that takes itself to have no content, to speak for the neutrally human. That means, among other things, that it takes itself to be *voice* simpliciter; the white man takes himself to be that-which-speaks, that-which-writes, and we take others to be speakers and writers insofar as they speak or write like we do. We seek a certain form of erasure of our others from language. Thus, in an act of intense arrogance, we assign to ourselves the burden and the power and the right and the ability to speak *for everyone*. And we also assign to ourselves the task of *sorting* voices, of policing recognizability and comprehensibility. There are obvious political consequences: we white guys seek to control access to speaking positions, or to represent your experience in our voices, or to place your account of yourself into the record by our sufferance. That is, obviously, a position of power, and it also a position that erases its own location in power relations, that "naturalizes" that location.

193

SARTWELL

JUDITH BRADFORD:

Obviously, the 'blank' or 'neutral' academic voice does have content. Some of its contents are, in fact, listed above. It seems that the 'neutrality' of the white male speaking position has to do with what happens socially when white men speak it. The voice is presumed neutral when it issues from the appropriate body because its production from the appropriate body causes no remark; it is expected, and calls for no comment. Voices are shaped twice: once in the training of the body in the right kinds of production, and once (multiply) by the trainings of those who hear voices and respond to them.

When 'inappropriate' bodies learn to speak in this voice, the *unexpectedness* of it does bring comment. The 'neutral' voice can never operate in precisely the same ways for those whose bodies are not unremarkably attached to it. Such a voice is an achievement, or a sign of (sometimes admired, sometimes denigrated) irregularity. Persons whose bodies are not expected to produce such a voice sometimes achieve it only to find that overcoming the negative expectation does not place them in the neutral category but rather marks them out as irregular instances of their race or gender: tokens, exceptions, unusual cases.

As a "slip of a white girl," I've always wanted to speak words of power, in a voice that had authority, that compelled listening. This desire and its accompanying self-constructions are rooted firmly in my training as a *white* woman; my father wanted me to be a scientist, a thinker, with sexuality firmly sequestered in middle-class white femininity: all combed down and neat. As an undergraduate I was enraged by professors who assumed I could not reason, and brushed off my feminist claims with ostentatious yawns: This isn't *serious*; it's not really *philosophy*. So in graduate school I turned myself into an argumentative shark; I set out to speak in such a way that they would have to listen.

Of course, they never did, because the voice I trained myself to speak in graduate school was honed against different people, including fellow graduate students, who, I discovered to my chagrin, heard me as a destructively vicious arguer: someone who could, and would, destroy others. My 'philosophical voice' was heard differently than the philosophical voices of male graduate students. If I seek to represent my own experience in the philosophical field—and I do—then I must in some sense take on a white male voice, the voice recognizable as philosophical. There are limits, however, to the extent to which I can be heard as having such a voice; those limits are set by what the possible listeners and audiences of the philosophic field are able to hear. The possible listeners to my voice are not used to hearing such a voice issue from such a body, and do not hear my voice as I project it. But the difference between my voice and the voices of male students did not consist only in the gendered way I was interpreted by others in that particular instance; my voice *was* different, because I had something to prove that they didn't, and I was constantly conscious of that fact. Voices are relations of articulation and reception in social contexts; what will get understood is not up to me, or my listeners, but is made out of the interactions between them. The meanings of these interactions are set up by the intersections of my history and theirs, of the ways we have come to be out of our different experiences in certain contexts.

II.

Having a voice, then, is a relational characteristic: something that you have or don't have depending in part on the audience that your speech can, or can't, reach. Having a voice is not just a matter of speech proceeding from one's mouth. Almost all humans speak. But we don't all get listened to, and none of us can always get listened to in just the ways we want. Rather, the context of expectations in our culture, such as the expectations of what sort of voice is likely to emerge from what sort of body, conditions how we can get heard.

Having a voice in those different contexts depends on three things. First, can I actually *get* into some context—can I put myself into the physical position to speak to certain people? Second, once there, can I *speak*: can words proceed from my mouth, or typewriter? Third, if I can speak, can I get *heard*: will the people who physically read my text, or hear my voice with their ears, hear me in anything like the way I am trying to be heard? Or will the expectations of what people like me, with my race or gender, ought to say, or should be able to say, divert what I am trying to put across?

Ordinarily, when we use the term 'having a voice' we do not mean actually having a physical voice, being able to make linguistic noises, but rather having power to make one's voice heard. If someone 'does not have a voice' in some decision, for example, this doesn't mean that they can't say anything; it means that whatever they say will make no difference, will not be heeded, will have no power. I will have no voice in some decision if I do not know it is being made, or cannot get into a place where I could speak up. One way not to have a voice is not even to know *that* some ongoing decision-making process is affecting one in ways one might wish to address if one knew about it. For these cases, think about how little some people get to know about *where* and *by whom* certain decisions get made. Consider the economy, which is made up, among other things, of high level decision-making processes by powerful individuals. Most people who are affected by those decisions do not even know what they were, or how their lives are affected by them.

Even if we do manage to find out about such things, and figure out that some decision being made somewhere affects our lives, we frequently cannot get *in* to those spaces to say anything. And even if we do get in, do actually confront some persons who are making some decision, we may not speak a language recognizable to them, or their language of decision-making and deliberation may be a mystery to us. (Here is one place where the politics of theory making intrudes: what does it mean politically when one cannot understand the experts without having attended graduate school, and hence cannot enter an opinion that will be taken seriously?)

But the third kind of failure is the one that occurs when you speak in the right place but can't get heard. If the preceding two kinds of failure of communication are physical or linguistic, this failure is *epistemic*; you will not be taken to be able to know what you are talking about; or what you are expected to be able or likely to say limits what people are able to hear you saying. Such failures of reception take place very frequently along lines of race and gender expectations, and the history of discreditation of unauthorized voices is well documented.[2] This regimentation of voices through the expectations of effectively apportioned authority is under siege in the current American situation: one is no longer likely to hear, as one might have even fifty years ago, the exclamation "What would a woman know about politics?" or "What could a Negro know about culture?" Previously unaccredited voices are making significant inroads into the public spaces of debate, and the norms that kept them out of such positions are weakening.

We still have a long way to go in this regard. One version of this failure to hear people's voices is encoded in the liberatory theory of the last few decades: the move that disqualifies voices as representative of the experience of oppression *by the very fact of their speaking at all*. In contemporary social and political philosophy there are several views that hold that "the oppressed" cannot speak, or that they have no language, or that they speak only in self-betrayal, because the language they use is the language of their oppressors. We find it significant that such theories become prevalent just as the actual voices of previously discredited bodies have more power to enter claims and insist that they be considered.[3] We suggest that if voices are relational, rather than simply locatable in subjects, this sort of view is false and politically dangerous.

Of course, the claim that the oppressed cannot speak, or that Woman cannot speak, or women cannot speak, mean very different things in theories such as, for instance, Derrida's, or Luce Irigaray's, or Catharine MacKinnon's. The meanings of the claim depend on very different and quite complex views about speech, language, oppression, and gendering. Since there is no space to explain all these different meanings here, we will take, briefly, one version of them: Richard Rorty's in *Contingency, Irony, and Solidarity*. Consider the following passage, which follows a few pages after an approving mention of Elaine Scarry's *The Body In Pain*, which examines torture in relation to language:

> [P]ain is nonlinguistic: it is what human beings have that ties us to the non-language-using beasts. So victims of cruelty, people who are suffering, do not have much in the way of a language. That is why there is no such thing as the "voice of the oppressed" or the "language of the victims." The language they once spoke is not working anymore, and they are suffering too much to put new words together. So the job of putting their situation into language is going to have to be done for them by somebody else. The liberal novelist, poet, or journalist is good at that.[4] (Rorty p. 94)

The oppressed cannot speak, so we have to speak for them: on the face of it, that's a pretty bizarre claim, and it's worth trying to unpack what it could mean. Persons oppressed by race and gender and poverty speak all the time. At the very least, even if they can't speak to those who oppress them, they can often speak to each other. Oppression does not rip language away by its roots; oppression is not typically like torture, or, if it is, it is not constantly like torture. Even people who are in a great deal of pain often can point at what is paining them, can offer analyses of why they're being hurt and by whom. A lot of the time they talk about other things, too, besides what's hurting them and why. So "speak" can't mean quite what it normally does here. Rorty equates torture and oppression to make it seem that the "voicelessness" of the oppressed is like the breakdown of language Scarry examines in torture practices. But if this is a false equation, what work is it doing? What is elided in the collapse of oppression into torture?

If there is some reason the oppressed have no voice, it's not primarily a linguistic problem of the first sort we enumerated, nor, increasingly, the second. They make recognizable linguistic sounds, recognizable to each other at least, and increasingly are learning to speak the jargons and specialized languages of the sciences and humanities. Nor is the problem just one of access to speaking positions, although that is a big problem for very oppressed persons. If a liberal ironist wants to hear some oppressed voices, she could go listen to what some oppressed persons are saying, either in print or in person. So just what *does* the claim that the oppressed are voiceless mean?

Rorty has spent some time explaining how liberal ironic discourse runs the risk of being cruel by redescription, since everyone likes to be described using their own terms rather than another's. But why do we want to be described in our own terms? One obvious answer is that someone who is redescribed in terms other than her own feels or thinks that the redescription gets something wrong, or leaves something out, or distorts what the described person wants to say about herself. When you actually go and read what some sufferers of sexism and racism *say* about their own situations, they do not frequently claim that they have nothing to say, or that they have no language, or that they are suffering too much to put words together. Rather, the most common claim is that *you aren't listening.*[5] Rorty's redescription of the voicelessness of "the oppressed" makes that voicelessness a fact about *them* (that *their suffering* makes them incapable of speech) rather than something about the context in which they speak, or about whether anyone's listening, and, if so, who and how. Simultaneously, he relieves himself of the task of listening to those who are speaking. Is the problem that persons who suffer from racism or sexism cannot speak? Or is it that their conditions are such that it's dangerous to speak, so they try to keep their oppressors from hearing them? Or is it that no one who "counts" listens to them? Or is it that when the voices of oppressed persons do get on the radio or in the newspaper, they are not heard as they wish to be heard, or on their own terms, but rather heard through the powerful filters of raced and gendered expectations about authority, or through the constraints of someone else's theory about them?[6] Is the claim that those people can't speak performing the work of explaining why liberals don't have to listen to them, even while those same liberals claim to be trying to liberate them or avoid hurting them?

We agree with Rorty that there is no "voice of the oppressed" insofar as that means that there is no one voice of a unified category of social abjection. But the fact that there is no single "voice of the oppressed" does not mean that there are not plenty of persons who suffer from oppression who are capable, if allowed, to say what's on their minds. The category of "the oppressed" is taking the place of a complicated welter of different oppressed persons. The "voice of the oppressed" seems to hold the place of a stipulated silence out of which a theorist can speak "on behalf" of the oppressed; it explains a silencing, a failure to listen, by declaring that there was already a silence there.

Here is the crux of the last kind of failure to communicate that we set out to pinpoint in this section, the failure that occurs when the audience you are trying to speak to doesn't hear you as a possible representer of your experience of oppression *because* you're representing it, *because* you've managed to work your way into the physical and linguistic possibility of speaking, at long last, to those who need to know. It is a last-ditch protection against having to listen; if someone manages to overcome all the other difficulties involved in getting their speech heard—the physical and linguistic defenses of hegemonic authority—then whatever they say will not be heard, once they're there, just because they're there.[7]

198

III.

The blanket statement that the oppressed have no language strikes us as bizarre. The question has to be made specific, and it has to made much more specific than we will suggest below. White women speak. African Americans, both women and men, speak. And what each speaks is both conditioned by the modes of exclusion to which they are subjected and by the modes of nurturance that they have developed in resistance to that exclusion. On our view, gender and race are, equally, social constructions. They are, furthermore and obviously, interactive constructions; as applied to any particular body, they are inextricable from one another, as we argued at the outset. One might speak about the differing problematics of voice in the case of white women, in the case of African-American men, or in the case of African-American women in the contemporary American situation. In using those categories we do not want to suggest that these groupings are in any way natural, or that the groupings preexist the practices of dividing and consigning persons that we are describing.

All of those categories are constructed for white men by exclusions, isolations, excisions, silencings, segregations. But these take different forms in the different cases, forms that show the relations of bodies to particular distributions and configurations of power, and the relations of voices to differing relations and distributions of bodies. The taxonomy that consigns bodies to categories and attaches normed voices to the bodies so consigned does issue in the *specific* empowerment of voices. Not only is it not the case that the oppressed cannot speak, it is not the case that the voices they are expected and permitted to have are *simply* the "language of the oppressors." There exist specific white female voices, black male voices, black female voices, that are recognizable in our culture. These voices are taken to be authoritative about *specific* matters when they speak in specific ways; they are historical formations that result from the specific oppressions of persons and the way those persons have taken up their locations. These norms of voice are one facet of oppression, but also artifacts of complex struggles of oppressed persons with their specific problems of location, access, translation, and credibility.

Consider the voice of the white female moral spokeswoman: the abolitionist, the suffragette, the social purity reformer, the temperance unionist. This American white woman's voice is instantly recognizable and quite powerful; it stems in part from the separate-spheres doctrine of nineteenth- and early-twentieth-century Anglo gender arrangements, which assigned to white women the management of domestic life. From that social identity, white women were able to claim to speak for the proper morality of that sphere, and have spoken publicly, and recognizably, about it. White women have crusaded successfully for the defense of feminine virtue; this was one crucial rhetorical support of the abolitionist movement. (Judith Bradford has argued elsewhere that Catharine MacKinnon and other antipornography feminists speak in this voice and derive moral authority and recognizability from it.) The gendering of white women as normatively selfless both constrained and enabled the emergence of this voice; white women could not speak on their own behalf without being heard as selfish, but could speak powerfully (and often imperially) on behalf of others' suffering. This voice is one that has been taken, in some contexts, as 'women's' voice, but it is crucial to point out its normative whiteness; it is the voice in which white women have claimed, falsely, to represent black women.

A similarly recognizable voice is that of the African-American male preacher, who is authorized first within the black community, and subsequently, often, is authorized to speak on behalf of that community to the centers of power in white culture. The notion of voice here is quite literal: this figure speaks in specific cadences, patterns of repetition, and inflections. (These were set out systematically as early as the 1930s in a series of essays by Zora Neale Hurston.) Figures such as Jesse Jackson, Malcolm X, and Martin Luther King, Jr., have spoken this voice publicly whether they were actually preaching or not. The figure of the African-American preacher has been taken in certain spheres of white America to speak with great moral authority not only about the conditions of African Americans, but about the moral state of white America. This voice too has been shaped in a situation of oppressions; the centrality of the black church in the segregated community, the moral resources of the church traditions, the normative masculinity of

199

the voice that could speak. The meaning of its masculinity is filtered through race (white and black masculinity are different and related constructions); roughly, there are no black female preachers.

Black women such as Patricia Collins have written about the ambivalent situation of black women in the black church; they were its main supporters, but they were also unable to speak in certain ways in that context. But Collins identifies several recognizable voices of black women's resistance: the blues singer, for example, and the black mother who must simultaneously protect her children from racism and enable them to survive and resist it. Black women speak (or sing) recognizably, and in some contexts authoritatively, about passion and suffering, sex and motherhood. The voices of black female resistance that Collins describes are differentially audible and recognizable across political and social contexts and are also very much shaped by specific dangers, exclusions, and the forms of expression possible in those locations. Such voices are taken up into literary contexts such as the work of Toni Morrison: the black female literary figure is now, or is emerging as, a recognizable "norm" that both constrains and enables black women writers. The recognizability and authority of this emergent voice is being shaped right now by the labors of black women writers and the changing circumstances of their reception.

What this cursory tour of voices is meant to show is that the problem with such normed voices is not that they cannot speak, but that what they can be heard as speaking *about* is historically shaped in a way that makes it difficult for them to enter and sustain claims about anything else: even when they *do* talk about other things, some audiences (say, white literary critics) will still *interpret* them as talking about the things they are *supposed* to be concerned with. Zora Neale Hurston, for example, was a novelist, but she was also a folklorist, an anthropologist, an essayist, a theorist. But she is now firmly ensconced and authorized in an emerging canon of African-American women novelists, and her other works, if mentioned, are interpreted in that light. The norm of the black female voice as literary voice is a problem, for instance, for black female writers who wish to be heard as theorists rather than storytellers. It would be a serious mistake to claim that these voices were unproblematic, or that they are not shaped in oppressions of various specific sorts, or that they do not constrain the ways in which persons can be understood. But it is equally a mistake (and rather insulting) to think that speaking those voices must be a betrayal, or a dead end, or a mere reiteration of oppression. They are complex achievements, and important resources for public speech as well as for connecting oneself to traditions and histories.

Finally, there is also a *set* of recognizable voices that attach to the bodies of white men, that people expect to hear white men speaking. Academics, for example, speak the white male voice characterized by a passionlessness or detachment that is a foil for the other voices we have described. This voice takes itself to be authoritative roughly about everything, including the experiences of others: a pure describer, *just* a voice. This voice has a very different location in the power struc-

SARTWELL

ture than the other voices we have described: it is the voice that takes itself to be voice simpliciter, language simpliciter. But it is equally relational, equally an artifact of power relations, equally specific, equally a construction, equally gendered and raced. It is not 'voice' (if it were, white guys *would* have to speak for the oppressed), but *a* voice. And this voice not only provides white men with great privileges, it limits the ways they can be recognized as speakers.

All of these voices are problematic in certain respects; the recognizable voices of the oppressed *are* implicated in the power structures that they sometimes speak against, and can allow those voices to be more or less easily re-contained in the processes of authority distribution. Yet each of these voices is *in process*: emerging in different contexts, being turned to different political or social purposes, shifting its rhythms. Catherine MacKinnon is not Carrie Nation, even if the two can be connected in similar processes of authorization in some respects. Malcolm X and Martin Luther King, Jr., turned the voice of the black preacher to different purposes and aimed it at times at different audiences. The normative white male voice is undergoing flux due, in part, to the changing possibilities of bodies that can appropriate it. All of these voices are minted in relations of oppression (though not only *by* oppression; they have creative sources in the cultures from which they emerge) and carry various subversive capacities. Locating the 'neutral universal' voice as one voice among others would possibly destroy that voice as it is currently configured; but even it contains possibilities of subversion of the existing distributions of power, depending on who speaks it and to whom.

That these voices are 'in process' means that the modes of speech are constantly changing, and the expectations about who can speak in what ways are shifting. Also, however, it is important to remember that if voices are interactive events, voices are also in process as the *abilities of listening* of different audiences change. Whether a voice is recognizable and how it is recognizable depends on the way people hear and respond to it. How to speak is one problem; how to listen is another. What we find lacking in some versions of philosophical liberatory theory (although not all) is sufficient attention to the problem of *how to learn to hear* people's voices. If a theorist is hearing someone's voice *as* the "voice of the oppressed" or the "voice of Woman" or the "voice of black America" something has already, on our view, gone wrong. Just what has gone wrong may be a matter of considerable complexity. If there are no persons who are simply raced or gendered (that is, if everyone takes up positions along both racial and gendered lines) then there are no voices that can simply represent 'race' or 'gender.' (Often, in fact, such claims to represent some category of oppression are made by those who are relatively privileged along some other axis of social accreditation.) The categories of race and gender are abstracted from a very complicated welter of bodies, voices, and practices; it should not be surprising that the attempt to find a *person* who could speak 'for' such an abstraction would be fraught with pitfalls.

201

SARTWELL

Rather than focus on who can speak and how, we wish to shift some attention to the question of who can hear what is said and how they can hear it. The problem of the 'voicelessness' of the oppressed has led, on our view, to a mistake insofar as that voicelessness has been taken as a fact about oppressed people, rather than as an interactive fact that emerges between oppressed and oppressors. This mistake has led well-intentioned persons to search for the 'authentic voice' of an oppressed group, rather than look for what it is about the *oppressors* (where they are physically, how they are protected from having to hear others, how they are not trained in the right ways to understand others) that produces the situation called 'voicelessness.' Even more troubling is the way in which the discourses of the 'voice' of some oppressed group can serve to delegitimate members of that group as representative of what they are.

We want to suggest, finally, that the situation is messy, but that the immediate need is simply to recognize *everyone* as an authority of a certain sort about *their own* experience, to perform the fewest possible and the least pervasive possible undercuttings of persons' voices. Every recognizable voice is a construct of histories of constraint and empowerment, a dialectical formation; the point is not to find out *in advance* what kinds of voices are the right ones, but to listen very carefully to how people speak and what they are trying to do with their voices. Our goal is not to speak for the oppressed, but to allow more persons to speak authoritatively of their own sufferings and of their own pleasures. And thus the goal is a growing multiplicity of recognizable voices, and the skills to recognize them.

202

NOTES

1. See Walker, Margaret Urban, *Moral Understandings* (New York: Routledge, forthcoming 1996).

2. These kinds of qualification and disqualification regarding audience contexts have been written on extensively. Maria Lugones' article "World Travelling and Loving Perception" is a very fine analysis of the way voice varies with context shifting and power relations, and how one can be taken as representative of a "they" that one doesn't even agree *exists*. See Lugones in Deane Curtin and Lisa Heldke, eds., *Cooking, Eating, Thinking: Transformative Philosophies of Food* (Bloomington: Indiana University Press, 1992). Also, David Halperin's *Saint Foucault* is concerned with the problems of disqualification faced by persons with certain backgrounds. See Halperin, David, *Saint Foucault* (New York: Oxford University Press, 1995).

3. For an analysis of the politics of postmodernism relevant to this claim, see Rosi Braidotti, *Patterns of Dissonance* (New York: Routledge, 1991).

4. Richard Rorty, *Contingency, Irony, Solidarity* (New York: Cambridge University Press, 1989) p. 94.

5. Patricia Collins' account of the situation of black women and their speech says nothing about lacking language, but a lot about being ignored or misunderstood or threatened; black female resistance has been *spoken* mainly in the home where it's safe, or given expression in genres such as blues. See Patricia Hill Collins, *Black Feminist Thought* (New York: Routledge, 1990).

6. Take the case of MacKinnon's advocacy of former porn actress Linda Marchiano, who is seeking legal redress for having been, on her own account, forced to appear in the movie "Deep Throat." Introducing a speech by Marchiano, MacKinnon says that "it is a miracle that you have heard from her." But surely this miracle can be accounted for by less mysterious forms of explanation. Marchiano is being heard in the places she is, and heard as an authority of a certain kind, because Catharine MacKinnon was able to get her there and set up the possibility of her being heard *as* representative of the brutal subordination of women. But why Marchiano in particular, rather than Margo St. James, or Annie Sprinkle, or any other current or former sex worker? Because Marchiano's account of her harm matches perfectly MacKinnon's theory of gender oppression, while the analyses of other politicized sex workers do not. Carol Jacobsen writes, in "Fighting for Visibility" (*Social Text* #37), of having her exhibit at a Michigan conference about sex work and gender oppression actually *confiscated* because of pressure from MacKinnon and John Stoltenberg. MacKinnon deploys her considerable power and authority as a prominent law professor as though that power to silence or empower speech were actually morally supported by her self-claimed status as the representative of the powerless. Her claim that women cannot speak is thus a complicated trick, enabling her to hide her own power by claiming to represent an oppressed category that cannot speak, while in fact exercising power to determine who can and cannot get heard. On "the politics of theory" and the issue of accountability, see, for example, Maria Lugones and Elizabeth Spelman, "Have We Got a Theory For You! Feminist Theory, Cultural Imperialism, and the Demand For 'The Woman's Voice,'" in *Women's Studies International Forum*, no. 6 (1983), p. 573–81.

7. This is one version of what Margaret Walker has called the "epistemic firewall" that prevents entire groups of persons from having their complaints heard. See Margaret Urban Walker, *Moral Understandings* (New York: Routledge, forthcoming 1996).

MALCOLM X:

Masculinist Practice and Queer Theory

John P. Pittman

I WILL examine Malcolm's account, in *The Autobiography of Malcolm X*, of his public persona, and argue that this persona represents a particular style of enactment or performance of black male identity. This will be juxtaposed to a reading of Malcolm X's latent metaphysics as found in the *Autobiography*. These two facets of Malcolm's world will be examined with a view to discussing two questions. First, I want to examine whether—and if so in what sense—Malcolm's black male identity is subversive or transgressive. Second, I want to suggest the relevance of Judith Butler's performative account of gender identity for race and racial identity.[1]

Malcolm's *The Autobiography of Malcolm X*,[2] "as told to Alex Haley" during the period in which he broke with the Nation of Islam, was left unfinished by his assassination on February 21, 1965. The book recounts the fall and moral regeneration of Malcolm through conversion to the Nation of Islam.

When he began the project of composing it, Malcolm was a disciple of Elijah Muhammad and one of the most powerful ministers in the national organization. At the outset of its composition, Malcolm presented Haley with a dedication of the book to Elijah Muhammad: it was intended as a morality tale, showing "how Mr. Muhammad salvages black people."[3] After his break with the Nation of Islam, the character of the book changed (it's dedicated to his wife and kids). But clearly the conversion in prison is the central and redemptive episode of the narrative of his life.

There is, despite that, a continuity that seems significant to me. In the *Autobiography*, Malcolm is always keenly aware of how others take him, of how he is perceived. He is not only aware, but ceaselessly calculating how to use those perceptions to his advantage. The continuity I have in mind is that of the actor: Malcolm is always performing, acting out a role. This is borne out by the titles of many of the chapters, which identify roles he assumed at different stages of his life's career: "mascot," "homeboy," "hustler," "satan," "Minister Malcolm X." Many episodes of his life as hustler involve the uses of deception and role-playing to get what he wants: he evades the draft by acting crazy; instills fear in his criminal colleagues by acting fearlessly; caters to patrons as a dining-car waiter by a kind of dissimulating obeisance. In the period after his conversion Malcolm quickly became Minister Malcolm X, whose amazing personal attributes electrified a nation in and through the public persona of spokesman and disciple. Indeed, the very terms in which he describes the conversion suggest the sloughing off of a persona: he says that "my previous life's thinking pattern slipped away from me.... It is as though someone else I knew of had lived by hustling and crime. I would be startled to catch myself thinking in a remote way of my earlier self as another person."[4] Significantly, there followed another such conversion, in effect: a shaking off of the tutelage under which he worked for Elijah Muhammad.

The presence of violence, the incessant intimations of violence, the preparedness for it, also resonate backward and forward throughout the narrative of Malcolm's life. The first half of his life is engulfed in violence, beginning with the violent murder of his father; his growing "degradation" is marked by his becoming more and more violent himself; the book ends with his (correct) prediction that his life would be taken before the book was published. This sense of immanent and constitutive violence permeated his skin: remarking that he was the lightest of seven children, he adds that "I learned to hate every drop of that white rapist's blood that is in me."[5] This violence that is physically constitutive of Malcolm's bodily self is the condition of a rage which is his most basic orientation toward the social world, both before, and in another way, after his prison conversion.

Physically Malcolm was always big, and one consequence of this was his being frequently taken to be older than he actually was. This misperception he frequently used to his advantage, as he often remarks in the *Autobiography*; he successfully impersonated an older man, "passing" as older to get jobs and "get over" hustles in ways that would not have been possible had he looked his age. His size added to his striking appearance; it also seems to have figured in his physical courage. For despite being a failure in his juvenile attempts at boxing competitions, most of his hustling exploits—and others—demanded a considerable degree of nerve: the many stare-downs, confrontations, fights, and encounters with "the law," not to mention plain old crackers. Here is his account of one such encounter, which took place on the "Yankee Clipper":

> I was working down the aisle and a big, beefy, red-faced cracker soldier got up in front of me, so drunk that he was weaving, and announced loud enough that everybody in the car heard him, "I'm going to fight you, nigger." I remember the tension. I laughed and told him, "Sure, I'll fight, but you've got too many clothes on." He had on a big Army overcoat. He took that off, and I kept laughing and said he still had on too many. I was able to keep that crack-er stripping off clothes until he stood there drunk with nothing on from his pants up, and the whole car was laughing at him, and some other soldiers got him out of the way. I went on. I never would forget that—that I couldn't have whipped that white man as badly with a club as I had with my mind.[6]

The cracker had been whipped, outwitted by a younger, craftier, larger man.

Finally, Malcolm's directness and honesty were also significant features of his personification of black masculinity. Here was someone for whom there was no need to hide behind a mask, someone for whom the clearly perceived and direct-ly stated truth provided the antidote, the supreme weapon, against all hypocrisy, pretense, and deceit. Honesty may be a pose, a pretense all its own, but directness could not be so. It is rather a style of presentation, of attack; a way of life, but also a tactic or rhetorical strategy. It is a part of, and a mark of, Malcolm's strength—a strength which has burnt off the inessential and is simple and pure. This directness is both a deeply ingrained personal style—one that predates his conversion and nationalist awakening—and the trace of an open-eyed encounter with a world negotiated at the lowest levels. It bespeaks an urgency, a worldliness, and a project of unmasking—and self-revelation—that combines the authority of the raw wit-ness with the tenacity of the fighter accustomed to the trading of body blows.

I have suggested a number of elements of Malcolm's self-presentation as depict-ed in the *Autobiography*: a bodily self constituted by violence; an orientation toward the world framed by the consequent rage; a life career steeped in impersonation, role-playing, and a performative transposition of "identities"; a demeanor—and an experience and self-confidence—beyond his years; a fearless directness and com-bative determination. There are two questions about this enumeration that I can forestall only by noting them briefly here. First, these might be only figments of a self-(re)presentation untrue to the Malcolm others knew. I take it these represen-tations have been confirmed and constitute some core of (the myth of) Malcolm.

207

Second, the question may be posed: why *these* features as aspects of Malcolm's pre-sentation of black *masculinity*? Perhaps the best answer is this: these elements do not by themselves, taken singly or even in combination, signify masculinity. But they do so as organized through the two consecutive configurations of agency they make possible and through which they are mobilized: those of the "predatory" hus-tler and of the minister as messenger of the faith. These, each in their own way, are meta-enactments of distinctly American male characters, two instantiations of the bourgeois possessive individualist: the outlaw-gangster and the organization man. It is from these elements that sprang the myth of Malcolm, who is characterized in its most telling formulation successively as the "gallant young champion," "master," "bold young captain," "our living black manhood," and "our shining black Prince, who didn't hesitate to die, because he loved us so."[7]

I am not concerned to dispute the terms of this myth; instead, I propose to examine the gendered, racialized, and sexualized categories through which Malcolm thought and lived out this representation of masculinity. The narrative of the *Autobiography* is underpinned by three closely interconnected tropes of degra-dation and rebirth, by which the consecutive configurations of agency identified above are related to one another through the oppositions of "brainwashing" to enlightenment, self-delusion to self-understanding, slavery to freedom. These tropes are those of the "true," "natural" gender difference between "man" and "woman" and their degraded, overturned enactments; of the original state of racial purity and its degraded condition consequent to race mixing and miscegenation; and finally, subsuming the first two, the taboo lust of black men for white women, which is the ultimate source of weakness and corruption. These three are prefig-ured imperfectly in the account of the relation between Malcolm's parents, come to be fully realized in Malcolm's own degraded life as hustler, and are resolved and ideologically foregrounded as problematic expressions of racial oppression through Malcolm's reflective coming to self in—and beyond—the Nation of Islam. Here a brief and sketchy overview of these strategies of figuration must suffice.

Malcolm's "gender ideology," and his uncritical acceptance and perpetuation of a naturalist account of gender domination, has been noted and commented on by many writers.[8] Malcolm discusses gender roles and advances his views about the "natural" constitution of gender at various points in the *Autobiography*; Patricia Hill Collins takes stock of some examples, and goes on to argue that because Malcolm didn't see the parallels between gender and racial oppression, he didn't see that "the logic of his own arguments concerning racism" would show his own views about gender domination to be "unacceptable."[9] Collins discusses an episode in which Malcolm, while visiting his friend and partner in crime, Sammy, strikes Sammy's "newest woman," who is a "flashing eyed, hot-headed Spanish Negro woman." Sammy drew his gun, trying to kill Malcolm. Malcolm comments that Sammy's reaction "was the only weak spot I'd ever glimpsed" in Sammy. Collins notes that this incident shows Malcolm's "unquestioned acceptance of black male violence against black women."[10] Collins doesn't note that on a subsequent visit, Malcolm finds that:

> Sammy had gotten weak for that woman. He had never let any other of his women hang around so much; now she was even answering his doorbell. Sammy was by this time very badly addicted [to cocaine]. He seemed hardly to recognize me.[11]

That scene, the last time Malcolm saw Sammy, suggests the danger which serves to legitimate Malcolm's violence and the "ideology" of gender domination inscribed in the narrative of Malcolm's own degradation and redemption.

Of course the main figure for Malcolm's degradation used in the *Autobiography* is that of what might be called his "racial flight": his acceptance of the "brainwashing" ideology of black inferiority. Indeed he identifies his "first really big step toward self-degradation" as his first conk, which turned his kinky hair into "this thick, smooth sheen of shiny red hair—real red—as straight as any white man's."[12] Malcolm came to be known, for the duration of his hustling days, as "Red," because of both his conk and the "reddish-brown marriny color"[13] of his skin. Significantly, and characteristically, this "first really big step" occurred *after* he began habitually drinking, smoking, and gambling: clearly self-degradation is not for Malcolm a matter of small morals, but of a renunciation of identity conceived, here, in a racialized way. It's worth recalling Malcolm's comment about hating "every drop of that white rapist's blood that is in me."[14] Coming on the second page of the book, this suggests an effort to purge himself figuratively of his "white" "blood" in a reflexive reversal of the act of "literally burning my flesh to have it look like a white man's hair." Here it is more than an ideology that is at issue; the very "natural elements" of Malcolm's bodily being—blood, hair, skin—become sites of contestation in what becomes, in the fullest elaboration of his black nationalism, a Manichean struggle.

The overall outlines of the Nation of Islam line Malcolm came to preach are perhaps familiar. When Malcolm describes "the true knowledge" as he encountered it in prison, one of the first principles is that:

> [T]he black man in America was the earth's only race of people who had absolutely no knowledge of his own true identity. In one generation, the black slave women in America had been raped by the slavemaster white man until there had begun to emerge a homemade, handmade, brainwashed race that was no longer even of its true color....

"This rape-mixed race"[15] of American "Negroes," racially impure, suffers from the fate of Mr. Yacub's "bleached-out white race of people": "as they became lighter and weaker, [they became] progressively also more susceptible to wickedness and

209

evil."[16] Ultimately, they became "devils." The idea of a "homemade, handmade" race through forcible miscegenation clearly contrasts with the "Original Man" who was black; notice that the loss of true identity proceeds apace with the "bleaching" and loss of "true color." This "homemade" race is "brainwashed" in that "he" has no knowledge of his true identity.

In all of his discussions of the bleaching out of the black race and its subsequent weakness, immiseration, and degradation, there is absolutely no mention of white women bearing mixed-race offspring to black men. The mechanism of race mixing is always one of white on black rape, or of the scientific engineering of Mr. Yacub. This is particularly noteworthy because the theme of black men's lust for and pursuit of white women is a constant one throughout the *Autobiography*. It seems that here we see the effect of the standing gender subordination of women: in a masculinist world black men fathering mixed-race children with white women could not be a figure for the degradation *of black men*.

When Malcolm comes to describe his relationship with a white woman ("I'm going to call her Sophia"[17]), a relationship that lasted until prison and redemption, his first remark is that "to have a white woman who wasn't a known, common whore was—for the average black man, at least—a status symbol of the first order."[18] It is on that level, it seems, that Malcolm experienced and thought their relation at that time: "having her" gave him "some real status in black downtown Roxbury."[19] But the whole story of Malcolm's first encounter with Sophia is in a chapter titled "Laura," after the young black woman Malcolm dropped to pursue Sophia. Laura is described as a studious, ambitious, and talented middle-class girl. She gets involved with Malcolm, only to be dropped when he takes up with Sophia. Malcolm's abandonment of Laura for a white woman signifies both the first push initiating Laura's corruption as well as one further step in Malcolm's own downfall. In concluding his account of that episode, Malcolm writes of Laura:

> The next time I saw her, she was a wreck of a woman, notorious around black Roxbury, in and out of jail. She had finished high school, but by then she was already going the wrong way. Defying her grandmother, she had started going out late and drinking liquor. This led to dope, and that to selling herself to men. Learning to hate the men who bought her, she also became a Lesbian. One of the shames I have carried for years is that I blame myself for all of this. To have treated her as I did for a white woman made the blow doubly heavy. The only excuse I can offer is that like so many of my black brothers today, I was just deaf, dumb, and blind.[20]

Malcolm's pursuit of the white woman Sophia is a symbol of his degradation, of his being brainwashed. But notice that the evil caused by his act is depicted as causing a degradation and corruption in its turn, Laura's turn away from men and her becoming a lesbian.

To the three tropes of racial purity and degradation, gender domination and the degradation that comes of abandoning it, and the corruption that is symbolized by black male lust for white women, can now be added a fourth, "homosexual"—and specifically lesbian—danger to the naturally constituted order of race, gender, and sexuality. These tropes are interconnected and constitute often parallel or homologous naturalizations of oppositions of purity and danger. They are the constructs through which Malcolm thinks the style of masculinity that he personifies, but they come to be ultimately inconsistent with that enactment, and so, as I will argue later, he gives up the Nation of Islam Manicheanism. This combination of a set of metaphysical oppositions and a performance of gender that underlies them is in keeping with Judith Butler's "queer theory" of gender. I now turn to a brief account of that theory.

Judith Butler has developed an account of gender that is substantially at odds not only with conventional commonsense views of gender but also with established critical feminist takes on it. The account she provided in her first book on the subject, *Gender Trouble*, put her in the forefront of what has come to called "queer theory."[21] A further work, *Bodies that Matter*,[22] addresses some of the criticisms of *Gender Trouble* and attempts to develop her views more fully. I want to briefly sketch what I take to be the main lines of her argument in the first book, when necessary noting clarifications she has provided since.

Gender Trouble begins with two concerns of recent feminist writing: the attempt to identify a category or concept of *women* that is the subject of feminism, and the sex-gender distinction developed as a first theoretical attack against a male-centered and sexist essentialism which justified male superiority and 'patriarchy.' In a sense, these two concerns can be seen in De Beauvoir's claim, reiterated by Butler, that "one is not born a woman, but, rather, becomes one." This claim involves a rejection of the view that "biology is destiny," and so contains implicitly the distinction between sex, taken to be the biological category evident at birth and marked by distinct natural physical features, and gender, the socially and culturally mediated forms of expression through which distinctly sexed individuals live and express their sexuality as and through social relations. This distinction allows for the possibility of radically transformed gender roles freed from oppressive patriarchal power relations. But that depends on the agency or social subjectivity of women as transformative of their own self-definition and of social and cultural relations simultaneously.

Butler contests the traditional account for preserving the assumption that there are/should be two genders in a binary opposition that mimes the presumed givenness of the male/female biological categories. Further, the suggestion that "one becomes a woman" presupposes a "one" that preexists the becoming of the gendered self; this must be a genderless *ego* or subject that is then seen as choosing to become or coming-to-be gendered through a process that can only be a modification of a genderless being. This view seems to either undermine the escape from determinism or commit one to a voluntarism of gender as an inessential modification of self.

Butler argues that this traditional account displays the effects of what she calls "compulsory heterosexuality," in part by reproducing in gender binariness the presumed givenness of biological sex categories. Insofar as sex categories are taken as capturing "natural" and preexisting biological differences, and an unquestioned gender binarism is postulated as a cultural superaddition upon those binary sexual categories, sex becomes a "regulatory ideal" enforcing heterosexuality by making its other unthinkable, impossible, and invisible. The possibility of stable identity is constituted by discourses and regimes of power: the medicolegal discourse of biological sex, the psychoanalytic discourse of gendered identity, and the masculinist discourse of heterosexual desire converge to subject human bodies to an internal coherence of gender, sex, and desire. This coherence of identity is grounded in the "metaphysics of substance," the tendency in common (Butler would say "hegemonic") language to substantivize sex and gender as modes of *being* which thereby take on a reality—"presence"—as self-identical. This obscures not only the purely relational and hence dependent status of every identity-position with respect to its binary other but also the constructedness or arbitrariness of these oppositions. Butler further characterizes these constructions as performative in the sense that they are constituted through and as the effect of discourse. Gender, on her view, is a style of enactment of the bodily; she suggests that some enactments can be transgressive and disruptive of the entire system of biological sex, binary gender, and heterosexual sexuality insofar as they contribute to the deconstruction of gender and the problematizing of stable identity.

The order of naturalized racial, gender, and sexual distinctions and roles expressed latently in Malcolm's *Autobiography* forms a system of mutually interlocking and mutually reinforcing hierarchical relations. It should be noted, first of all, that Malcolm's parents' relations, as depicted in the *Autobiography*, exhibit this interconnection. Malcolm consistently refers to his father's blackness, his mother's lightness; he depicts his father as strong willed, courageous, and independent, while his mother ultimately falters, loses her way, becomes mentally "sick." His father is proud of his own blackness; his mother is ashamed of her light coloring. He describes frequent beatings his father inflicted upon his mother and justifies them, in effect, as a matter of his putting her in her place. His father is seen as a threat to the hostile surrounding world and dies violently because of it; his mother attempts to negotiate a life within that world, and is destroyed mentally as a result.[23]

The interconnection of these distinctions becomes more fully realized in Malcolm's account of his hustling life, and that interconnection is thought out by Malcolm subsequently in terms of the category of race. The racialized version of gender domination becomes splayed on the axes of white male—black female and black male–white female desire. Both of these possibilities signify the degradation of the black race on Malcolm's account. White male—black female desire is real-

ized most characteristically as rape, a violent form of physical domination as sexual expression. Black male–white female desire is ultimately a desire for whiteness:
"having" a white woman—notice the proprietary construction of the relation—
being a status symbol among black men. It is as though one has taken the place of
the white man by possessing "his woman." Malcolm depicts such desire as an obses-
sive preoccupation of (many) black men which stands as a deeper signifier of "racial
flight" than conking. Such racialized desire seems to be exclusively masculine
(Malcolm indicates bewilderment at Sophia's motivation for being with him). Such
desire is thus conditioned by and conditions gender domination, but its overall
meaning is a racialized one. He treats the cases asymmetrically: first, in that they are
both signifiers of black degradation, but not white; second, that degradation is conceived not merely in psychological, but also in biological-metaphysical terms. It is
the "Negro race" that is described as "handmade, homemade" and "bleached" of its
original and true identity by the acts of rape that bring it into being. But because
this account is formulated in biological-metaphysical terms, the same degraded status should characterize the children of black male–white female relations as well.
Yet Malcolm virtually never mentions such an issue. This suggests that the asymmetry is in some basic respect a class one because it bears the mark of two closely
connected phenomena that are not in themselves matters of gender: the ownership
of black *people*, and the one-drop rule.

If the black man's desire for the white woman is a symptom of racial flight, it
assumes the character of a self-frustrating and inherently unsatisfying project. By
contrast, the white man's rape of the black woman, an expression of racialized
physical gender domination, is an enactment and display of realized or achieved
power: it is self-affirmative and so a plenum of self-identical meaning. These psychologically conceived relations of domination are latent in Malcolm's narrative
but in an ahistorical form, which finds its correlate in the metaphysical biology of
race and race mixing Malcolm borrows from Elijah Muhammad. Yet the structural asymmetry mimics that of the property relations of slavery as enforced juridically by the one-drop rule. Race mixing, in either of its modes as the expression
of desire, contributes to the degradation of the black race: any mixed-race person
is juridically marked as "Negro" and so in principle, if not actually, chattel. In the
nationalist mythology Malcolm puts in the middle of his life story, race mixing
marks the fall of the black race because impurity is itself a weakness which finds
expression in the black man's obsession with white women. But the issue of the
successfully achieved project of that black male obsession is also, because mixed-
race, in principle chattel and so degraded. That is to say, given patriarchal gender
hierarchy and white supremacy, the black man's attempt to usurp the place and
property of the white man—the proprietary domination of the white woman—is
defeated by the white man's claim to proprietary domination of mixed-race progeny through the one-drop rule. Thus, desire across the boundary of race is inher-

213

ently degrading (in both an individual-psychological and a biological-racial-metaphysical sense), its issue governed as property by the one-drop rule.[24]

Malcolm—that is, Minister Malcolm X—counterposes to this transracial desire, resulting in pollution and degradation, the desire for "racial cleansing," for purification and the restoration of the black race to an (imagined) original state of strength and self-subsistent meaning. Because the condition of degradation is conceived both as an individual-psychological problem of disorientation and derangement—"brainwashing"—and a metaphysical-biological problem of race-weakness, the cure has the double aspect of what Cornel West has labelled "psychic conversion"[25] and race separation. Malcolm recounts in detail the conversion that began with his brother Reginald's telling him, "The white man is the devil." This makes sense to Malcolm, in part, it seems, as an account of his own degradation, or, as he puts it, his "guilt": "The very enormity of my previous life's guilt prepared me to accept the truth."[26] The "crime" for which he and his accomplice Shorty were jailed was not burglary but taking "the white man's women."[27] But what he was guilty of, in the black Muslim terms he came to accept, was both the racial flight of his conking, white-woman lusting days, *and the original sin signified by the rapist's blood flowing in his veins.* These represent the degraded enactment and the degraded outcome of transracial desire.

Salvation took the form of a *practice* of religious purification under the authorizing gaze of a divine messenger: this represented the recuperation of self through a performative identification with the role of the disciplined and self-disciplining, under the aspect of submission to an authority, as befitted the penitent sinner. And in very short order, Malcolm himself became a messenger, through the force of his personification of those traits of masculinity mentioned before: fearlessness, directness, sensitivity to how one is being perceived, physical impressiveness, and wits. But if Malcolm had to be "saved" by divine intervention from the self-destructiveness of his first enactment of black man as degraded fugitive from blackness, he outgrew his second enactment of black man as submissive messenger of racial purity and separation. Malcolm's enactment of black masculinity was increasingly organized through the performative utterance of accusation and affirmation. What Malcolm effects by deploying the black Muslim ideology in the way he does is a transvaluation of racialized values: blackness becomes an affirmation of the humanity of those called "Negroes" in a civilization organized by the "devil" white man. But he does this, carries it off, in the first place because of a style: the in-your-face streetness of the hustler proportioned to the eloquence of the self-taught intellectual, the honesty, the fearlessness, the violence of approach. It is because Malcolm *enacted* the pride, assurance, and canniness of the "black man" that he became such a wildly popular and effective voice of the Nation of Islam. Here West's notion of "psychic conversion" is importantly right—blackness is the key, the affirmation that is exchanged for the brainwashing of "the white man"—but it is an affirmation personified, enacted; an affirmation and an accusation: "the devil white man."

214

The force of these performatives, carried as a charge into the ranks of "the white man" by a style of oratory, was the condition of blackness' credibility.

But there is another aspect to the Malcolm who was soon to become the Minister: a sense of deep shame, of being (in) a "polluted" body, of being a "weak self." This sense came to be increasingly at odds with the power of the public persona which he lived, the force of the utterances, the effect they had on those who listened to him. His nationalist message was a style of black manhood, it came to be seen that way, it was taken to be so, he spoke and thought it in those terms. Within the Nation of Islam, Malcolm could not but sit on the accumulated debris of the inverted but still live and active binary hierarchical oppositions. He sat on them because they made sense of his own story up till that time, of how he had lived out his redness, his criminal manhood in the streets of Roxbury and Harlem. But he outgrew that system of oppositions, because his style and personification of pride and self-awareness could not be confined by the organization nor the ideology that put so much of its weight upon his voicing of it.

Malcolm's life can be understood in terms of queer theory, while also showing that theory to be limited in a couple of crucial ways.[28] Thus, while Malcolm's masculinist style was not transgressive but virtually conventional in its gendered self-identity, it was nonetheless a crucial condition for the sort of racial transgression, or transvaluation, that Malcolm worked to bring about. And one sign of this is the extent to which the myth of Malcolm has been framed in terms of his black masculinity, his personification of it in a way that is (racially) transgressive.

At the same time, Malcolm thought and spoke his own experience as a black man in terms of an implicit metaphysics of hierarchically opposed and naturalized racial, gendered, and sexual categories. Malcolm's thinking in these terms seems to support Judith Butler's view that gender binarism and the compulsory "heterosexual matrix" are closely connected elements of any articulation of a stable gender identity, given a context of the metaphysics of substance and of the social regulation of desire generally. In this light, what I have identified as Malcolm's preoccupation with transracial desire, particularly black male desire for white women, suggests a racialized binarism and its effect of enforcing a regulation of desire in accordance with the one drop rule. But this racialized binarism is not simply an "additional" polarity taking its place next to the others: the fear of transracial desire seems to assume a prominence indicative of a nexus of prohibitions and oppositions. Sexual hierarchies, racialized, are not just given another color: they are transmuted and supercharged.

And this suggests the need for rethinking queer theory, or at least Butler's version of it, in racialized form. The problem of identity-formation, which Butler attacks using the tools of a poststructured psychoanalytic model, is one close to the core of "race" as it is to "gender" and "sex." But these problems cannot be solved one at a time, seriatim—neither on a theoretical nor a practical level. The uneven development represented in Malcolm's performative transgression of American

215

racial codes by relying on patriarchal sexuality suggests, as a number of writers have pointed out, that emancipation from the hierarchized oppositions of modern society cannot be achieved piecemeal. A final lesson, which we can learn from a reading of Malcolm's life, is that, as another forerunner of queer theory put it, "the master's tools will never dismantle the master's house."[29]

NOTES

1. I want to thank Naomi Zack for helpful discussion of an earlier version of this paper.

2. Malcolm X (as told to Alex Haley), *The Autobiography of Malcolm X* (New York: Ballantine, 1973).

3. Ibid., p. 386.

4. Ibid., p. 170.

5. Ibid., p. 2.

6. Ibid., p. 77.

7. Ossie Davis, "Our Shining Black Prince," in John Hendrik Clarke, ed., *Malcolm X: The Man and His Times* (New York: Macmillan, 1969), pp. xi–xii.

8. See especially Angela Davis, "Meditations on the Legacy of Malcolm X," and Patricia Hill Collins, "Learning to Think for Ourselves: Malcolm X's Black Nationalism Reconsidered," as well as Marlon Riggs, "Sexuality, Television, and Death: A Black Gay Dialogue on Malcolm X," all in Joe Wood, ed., *Malcolm X: In Our Own Image* (New York: Doubleday, 1992).

9. Collins, op cit, p. 81.

10. Ibid., p. 80.

11. *Autobiography*, p. 131.

12. Ibid., p. 54.

13. Ibid., p. 2.

14. On the figuration of "blood" in racial ideology, see Naomi Zack, *Race and Mixed Race* (Philadelphia: Temple University Press, 1993), p. 14.

15. *Autobiography*, p. 162.

16. Ibid., p. 165.

17. Ibid. p. 67. This seems to be the only case in the book of Malcolm giving a fictive name to one of the characters.

18. Ibid., p. 67.

19. Ibid., p. 68.

20. Ibid.

21. Judith Butler, Gender Trouble: Feminism and the Subversion of Identity (London: Routledge, 1990).

22. Judith Butler, Bodies That Matter: On the Discursive Limits of "Sex" (London: Routledge, 1993).

23. See Collins, "Learning to Think for Ourselves," for an extensive treatment of these matters.

24. But see the substantially different treatment of these matters developed by bell hooks in *Ain't I A Woman: Black Women and Feminism* (Boston: South End Press, 1981), especially chapters 1 and 2.

25. Cornel West, "Malcolm X and Black Rage," in Cornel West, *Race Matters* (Boston: Beacon, 1993).

26. *Autobiography*, p. 163.

27. Ibid., p. 150.

28. Although I have taken Judith Butler's account of gender as an exemplar of "queer theory," I do not want to suggest that it is the only or the best such account, nor that it best fits with the "facts" of Malcolm's life. Indeed, I do not discuss Malcolm's life as such at all, but only that representation of it which has been most influential generally. I have tried to use Butler's writing to bring out two things: the inextricable connections between gendered and racialized hierarchies in the implicit metaphysics or ideology of the *Autobiography*, and the significance of Malcolm's enactment of a particular style of black masculinity as a condition of both his public persona as messenger of black nationalist ideology and his subsequent break with that role and that ideology. In thinking about these things I found Butler's work suggestive. There are nonetheless questions internal to Butler's writing that need answering, tensions that need attention (involving the notions of performance and "performativity") but cannot be addressed here. Finally, though my analysis focuses on the Malcolm presented in the *Autobiography*, and especially the first half of it, that is not because I want to downplay the importance of the breakthroughs Malcolm achieved late in his life (discussed by Angela Davis, Patricia Hill Collins, and bell hooks), which were significant though undeveloped and untheorized by him.

29. Audre Lorde, *Sister Outsider* (Trumansburg, NY: Crossing Press, 1984), p. 110.

217

SELECT BIBLIOGRAPHY

Allman, K.M. "(Un)Natural Boundaries: Mixed Race, Gender, and Sexuality." In Root, ed., *The Multiracial Experience*.

Althusser, Louis. *For Marx*. London: Pantheon,1969.

Appiah, Anthony. "Racisms." In *Anatomy of Racism*. Edited by David Theo Goldberg. Minneapolis: University of Minnesota Press, 1990.

Appiah, Anthony. *In My Father's House: Africa in the Philosophy of Culture*. New York: Oxford University Press, 1992.

Aristotle. Aristotle's De Partibus Animalium I and De Generatione Animalium I (with Passages from II. 1*f*3). Edited by D.M. Balme. Oxford: Clarendon, 1972.

Aristotle. *Aristotle's Poetics*. Translated by S.H. Butcher. New York: Hill and Wang, 1961.

Austin, Gayle. *Feminist Theories for Dramatic Criticism*. Ann Arbor: University of Michigan Press, 1990.

Ayer, A.J. *The Problem of Knowledge*. New York: Penguin, 1956.

Ayres, B. Drummond. "California Board Ends Preferences in College System." *New York Times*. July 21, 1995. Pp. A1, A14.

Baldwin, James. Nobody Knows My Name: More Notes of a Native Son. New York: Dell, 1970.

Barker, Martin. *The New Racism*. London: Junction Books, 1981.

Beauvoir, Simone de. *Le deuxième sexe*. Paris: Gallimard, 1949.

Bell, Linda A. *Rethinking Ethics in the Midst of Violence: A Feminist Approach to Freedom*. Foreword by Claudia Card. Lanham, MD: Rowman and Littlefield, 1993.

Bishop, Sharon & Marjorie Weinzweig, eds. *Philosophy & Women*. Belmont: Wadsworth, 1979.

Bleier, Ruth. *Science and Gender*. New York: Pergamon, 1984.

Blos, Peter. "The Second Individuation Process of Adolescence," *Psychoanalytic Study of the Child* 22 (1967): 162–186.

Bracken, Harry. "Essence, Accident and Race," *Hermathena* 116 (Winter 1973): 81–96.

Bracken, Harry. "Philosophy and Racism," *Philosophia* 8, no. 2 (November 1978): 241–260.

Bradshaw, C.K. (1992). "Beauty and the Beast: On Racial Ambiguity." In Root, ed., *Racially Mixed People*.

Braidotti, Rosi. *Patterns of Dissonance*. New York: Routledge, 1991.

Brennan, Teresa. *The Interpretation of the Flesh: Freud and Femininity*. London and New York: Routledge, 1992.

Brown, Janet. *Feminist Drama: Definition and Critical Analysis*. Metuchen, NJ: Scarecrow Press, 1979.

Butler, Judith. Gender Trouble: Feminism and the Subversion of Identity. London: Routledge, 1990.

Butler, Judith. Bodies that Matter: On the Discursive Limits of "Sex." New York and London: Routledge, 1993.

Caplan, Arthur, ed. *The Sociobiology Debate*. New York: Harper and Row, 1978.

Card, Claudia. "On Race, Racism, and Ethnicity." In *Overcoming Racism and Sexism*. Edited by Linda Bell and David Blumenfeld. Lanham, MD: Rowman and Littlefield, 1994.

Carson, Anne. "Putting Her In Her Place: Woman, Dirt, and Desire." In *Before Sexuality: The Construction of Erotic Experience in the Ancient Greek World*. Edited by David M. Halperin, John J. Winkler, and Froma I. Zeitlin. Princeton: Princeton University Press, 1990.

Case, Sue Ellen. *Feminism and Theatre*. New York, Routledge, 1988.

Chinoy, Helen Krich and Linda Walsh Jenkins. *Women in American Theatre*. New York: Crown Publishers, 1981.

Chodorow, Nancy. *The Reproduction of Mothering*. Berkeley: University of California, 1978.

Chomsky, Noam. *For Reasons of State*. New York: Vintage, 1973.

Cohen, Carl, *Against Racial Preference*. Lanham, MD: Rowman and Littlefield, 1995.

Cohen, G.A. *Karl Marx's Theory of History: A Defense*. Oxford: Oxford University Press, 1978.

Collier, Andrew. "Materialism and Explanation in the Human Sciences." In Mepham and Ruben, eds., *Issues in Marxist Philosophy* 2, *Materialism*.

Collins, Patricia Hill. "Learning to Think for Ourselves: Malcolm X's Black Nationalism Reconsidered." In *Malcolm X: In Our Own Image*. Edited by Joe Wood. New York: Doubleday, 1992.

Collins, Patricia Hill. "Sexuality, Television, and Death: A Black Gay Dialogue on Malcolm X." In *Malcolm X: In Our Own Image*. Edited by Joe Wood. New York: Doubleday, 1992.

Collins, Patricia Hill. *Black Feminist Thought*. London: Harper Collins Academic, 1990.

Comas-Diaz, Lillian. "An Integrative Approach." In *Women of Color: Integrating Ethnic and Gender Identities in Psychotherapy*. Edited by Lillian Comas Diaz and Beverly Greene. New York: The Guilford Press, 1994.

D'Souza, Dinesh. *The End of Racism*. New York: Free Press, 1995.

Davis, Angela. "Meditations on the Legacy of Malcolm X." In *Malcolm X: In Our Own Image*. Edited by Joe Wood. New York: Doubleday, 1992.

Davis, Ossie. "Our Shining Black Prince." In *Malcolm X: The Man and His Times*. Edited by John Hendrik Clarke. New York: Macmillan, 1969.

Davy, Kate. "Outing Whiteness: A Feminist/Lesbian Project," *Theatre Journal* 47 no. 2 (May 1995): 189–205.

Dickerson, Glenda. "The Cult of True Womanhood: Toward a Womanist Attitude in African-American Theatre," *Theatre Journal* 40 no. 2 (1988): 178–187.

Dinnerstein, Dorothy. *The Mermaid and the Minotaur*. New York: Harper Collophon, 1976.

Donkin, Ellen and Susan Clements, eds. *Upstaging Big Daddy: Directing Theater as If Gender and Race Matter*. Ann Arbor: University of Michigan Press, 1993.

Du Bois, W.E.B. *W.E.B. Du Bois: Writings*. New York: The Library of America, 1986.

Du Bois, W.E.B. *The World and Africa*. New York: International Publishers, 1965.

Dukes, Richard L. and Ruben Martinez. "The Impact of Ethgender Among Adolescents," *Adolescence*, 29, no. 113, (Spring 1994): 105–115.

Dworkin, Andrea. *Woman-Hating*. New York: Dutton, 1974.

Elkins, Stanley. *Slavery*. New York: Universal Library, 1963.

Elster, Jon. "Self-Realization in Work and Politics: The Marxist Conception of the Good Life." In Elster and Moene, eds., *Alternatives to Capitalism*.

Elster, Jon and Karl Ove Moene, eds. *Alternatives to Capitalism*. Cambridge: Cambridge University Press, 1989.

Engels, Frederich. "The Part Played by Labor in the Transition From Ape to Man." In Marx and Engels, *Selected Works*.

England, Paula. *Comparable Worth*. New York: Aldine De Gruyter, 1992.

Ezorsky, Gertrude. *Racism and Justice*. Ithaca: Cornell University Press, 1991.

Fanon, Franz. *Peau noire, masques blancs*. Paris: Éditions de Seuil, 1952. Translated into English, *Black Skin, White Masks*. Translated by Charles Lam Markmann. New York: Grove, 1967.

Fausto-Sterling, Ann. *Myths of Gender*. New York: Basic Books, 1986.

Feinberg, Leslie. *Stone Butch Blues*. Ithaca, NY: Firebrand Books, 1993.

Fields, Barbara. "Ideology and Race in American History." In *Region, Race, and Reconstruction*. Edited by J. Kousser and J. McPherson. New York: Oxford University Press, 1982.

Fishkin, James. *Justice, Equal Opportunity, and the Family*. New Haven: Yale University Press, 1983.

Forbes, J.D. "The Manipulations of Race, Caste, and Identity: Classifying Afro-Americans, Native Americans, and Red-Black People," *Journal of Ethnic Studies* 17 (1989): 1–51.

Forbes, J.D. *Black Africans and Native Americans*. Oxford: Basil Blackwell, 1988.

Freud, Sigmund. *Civilization and Its Discontents*. Standard edition. Translated and edited by James Strachey. New York: W.W. Norton & Company, 1961.

221

Frye, Marilyn. "Male Chauvinism: A Conceptual Analysis." In *Philosophy and Sex*. Edited by Robert Baker and Frederick Elliston. Buffalo: Prometheus, 1975. Reprinted in Bishop and Weinzweig, eds., *Philosophy and Women*.

Funderburg, L. Black, White, Other: Biracial Americans Talk About Race and Identity. New York: William Morrow and Company, Inc., 1994.

Garcia, J.L.A. "The Heart of Racism," *Journal of Social Philosophy*. Forthcoming.

Gates, Henry Louis, Jr. "Writing 'Race' and the Difference It Makes." In *"Race," Writing, and Difference*. Edited by Henry Louis Gates, Jr. Chicago: University of Chicago Press, 1986.

Geras, Norman. Marx and Human Nature: Refutation of a Legend. London: Verso, 1983.

Gibbs, J.T. "Biracial Adolescents." In *Children of Color: Psychological Interventions with Minority Youth*. Edited by J.T. Gibbs and L.N. Huang. San Francisco: Jossey-Bass, 1989.

Gibbs, J.T. "Identity and Marginality: Issues in the Treatment of Biracial Adolescents," *American Journal of Orthopsychiatry* 57 (1987): 265–278.

Giddings, Paula. When and Where I Enter: The Impact of Black Women on Race and Sex in America. New York: Bantam, 1984.

Gilligan, Carol. In a Different Voice: Psychological Theory and Women's Development. Cambridge, MA: Harvard University Press, 1982.

Gilroy, Paul, *The Black Atlantic*. Cambridge, MA: Harvard University Press, 1993.

Gleitman, Henry. *Psychology*. 2nd ed. New York: W.W. Norton & Company, Inc., 1986.

Goldberg, David Theo. *Racist Culture*. Cambridge: Blackwell, 1993.

Gordon, Lewis R. "'Critical' Mixed-Race?" *Social Identities* 1, no. 2 (1995): 381ƒ395.

Gordon, Lewis R. *Bad Faith and Antiblack Racism*. Atlantic Highlands, NJ: Humanities Press, 1995.

Gordon, Lewis R. Fanon and the Crisis of European Man: An Essay on Philosophy and the Human Sciences. New York and London: Routledge, 1995.

Gordon, Lewis R., ed. Existence in Black: An Anthology of Black Existential Philosophy. New York and London: Routledge, 1996.

Gordon, Lewis R., T. Denean Sharpley-Whiting, and Renée T. White, eds. *Fanon: A Critical Reader*. Oxford: Blackwell, 1996.

Gould, Stephen J. *Ever Since Darwin*. New York: Norton, 1977.

Gould, Stephen J. *The Mismeasure of Man*. New York: W.W. Norton, 1981.

Greene, B.A. "What Has Gone Before: The Legacy of Racism and Sexism in the Lives of Black Mothers and Daughters." In *Diversity and Complexity in Feminist Therapy*. Edited by L.S. Brown and M.P.P. Root. New York: Haworth Press, 1990.

Grosz, Elizabeth. *Volatile Bodies: Toward A Corporeal Feminism*. Bloomington: Indiana University Press, 1994.

Gutman, Herbert G. The Black Family in Slavery and Freedom, 1750ƒ1925. New York: Vintage, 1976.

Hacker, Andrew, *Two Nations*. New York: Ballantine Books, 1992.

Hackett, Clifford. "Comparable Worth: Better From a Distance," *Commonweal* May 31, 1985.

Hall, C.C.I. *The Ethnic Identity of Racially Mixed People: A Study of Black-Japanese*. Unpublished doctoral dissertation, University of California, Los Angeles, 1980.

Halperin, David, *Saint Foucault*. New York: Oxford University Press, 1995.

Hegel, G.W.F. *Science of Logic*. Translated by A.V. Miller. New York: Humanities Press, 1969.

222

Heiss, J. and S. Owens. "Self-Evaluations of Blacks and Whites," *American Journal of Sociology* 78 (1972): 360–370.

Heller, Agnes. *The Theory of Need in Marx*. London: Alison and Busby, 1976.

Hernton, Calvin C. *Sex and Racism in America*. New York: Anchor Books, 1988.

Hines, P. and L. Berg-Cross. "Racial Differences in Global Self Esteem," *Journal of Social Psychology* 113 (1981): 271–281.

Hölderlin, Friedrich. *Hölderlins Späte Hymnen*. München: R. Piper and Co., 1942.

Holmstrom, Nancy. "Do Women Have a Distinct Nature?," *Philosophical Forum* 14, no. 1 (Fall 1982). Reprinted in *Women and Values: Readings in Recent Feminist Philosophy*. Edited by Marjorie Pearsall. Belmont, California: Wadsworth, 1986.

Hook, Sidney. *From Hegel to Marx*. Ann Arbor: University of Michigan, 1962.

hooks, bell. "Sisterhood: Political Solidarity between Women." In *Feminist Philosophies*. Edited by Janet Kourany, James Sterba and Rosemarie Tong. Englewood Cliffs, NJ: Prentice-Hall, 1992.

hooks, bell. *Ain't I A Woman: Black Women and Feminism*. Boston: South End Press, 1981.

Horne, Gerald. "On the Criminalization of a Race," *Political Affairs* 73, no. 2 (February 1994): 26f30.

Hornsby, Jennifer. "Sexism." In *Oxford Companion to Philosophy*. Edited by Ted Honderich. New York: Oxford University Press, 1995.

Houston, V.H. "American Girl," *Pacific Citizen* (December 1985).

Hughes, Langston. *Selected Poems of Langston Hughes*. New York: Alfred A. Knopf, 1969.

Hull, Gloria T., et. al., eds. All the Women are White, All the Blacks Are Men, But Some of Us Are Brave: Black Women's Studies. New York: Feminist Press, 1982.

Hurston, Zora Neale. *The Sanctified Church*. Berkeley: Turtle Island, 1981.

Husserl, Edmund. *Phenomenology and the Crisis of Philosophy*. Translated and edited by Quentin Lauer. New York: Harper & Row, 1965.

Irigaray, Luce. *This Sex Which Is Not One*. Translated by Catherine Porter with Carolyn Burke. Ithaca: Cornell University Press, 1985.

Jaggar, Alison. "On Sexual Equality," *Ethics* 84 (1974). Reprinted in Bishop and Weinzweig, eds., *Philosophy and Women*.

Jaynes, Gerald and Robin Williams, eds. *A Common Destiny*. Washington, DC: National Academy Press, 1989.

Johnson, R.C. and C. Nagoshi. "The Adjustment of Offspring of Within-group and Interracial/Intercultural Marriages: A Comparison of Personality Factor Scores," *Journal of Marriage and the Family* 48 (1986): 279–284.

Johnson, James Weldon. Along This way: The Autobiography of James Weldon Johnson. New York: Penguin Books, 1990.

Jones, L. Bulletproof Diva: Tales of Race, Sex, and Hair. New York: Doubleday, 1994.

Joyce, Joyce Ann. Warriors, Conjurers, and Priests: Defining African-Centered Literary Criticism. Chicago: Third World Press, 1994.

Kaplan, Alexandra G. "Women's Self-Development in Late Adolescence." In *Women's Growth in Connection: Writings from the Stone Center*. Edited by Judith V. Jordan, Alexandra G. Kaplan, Jean Baker Miller, Irene P. Stiver, and Janet L. Surrey. New York: Guilford Press, 1991.

223

Kierkegaard, Søren. *Philosophical Fragments*. Translated by Howard V. Hong and Edna H. Hong. Princeton: Princeton University Press, 1985.

Kintz, Linda. The Subject's Tragedy: Political Poetics, Feminist Theory, and Drama. Ann Arbor: University of Michigan Press, 1992.

Kramarae, Cheris and Paula Treichler, eds. *A Feminist Dictionary*. Boston: Pandora, 1985.

Kripke, Saul. *Naming and Necessity*. Cambridge: Harvard University Press, 1972.

Lang, Helen S. "Aristotle and Darwin: The Problem of Species," *International Philosophical Quarterly* 23 (1983): 141–153.

Lang, Berel. *Act and Idea in the Nazi Genocide*. Chicago: University of Chicago Press, 1990.

Lerner, H. *The Creation of Patriarchy*. New York: Oxford University Press, 1986.

Levins, Richard and Richard C. Lewontin. *The Dialectical Biologist*. Cambridge, MA: Harvard University Press, 1985.

Lewontin, Richard C., Steven Rose and Leon J. Kamin. *Not in Our Genes*. New York: Pantheon Books, 1984.

Locke, Alain. *The Philosophy of Alain Locke: Harlem Renaissance and Beyond*. Edited by Leonard Harris. Philadelphia: Temple University Press, 1989.

Lorde, Audre. *Sister Outsider*. Trumansburg, NY: Crossing Press, 1984.

Lott, Tommy. "Du Bois on the Invention of Race," *Philosophical Forum* 24 nos. 1ƒ3 (FallƒSpring 1992ƒ93): 166ƒ187.

Loury, Glenn. "Self-Censorship in Public Discourse." In *One By One From the Inside Out*. Edited by Glenn Loury. New York: Free Press, 1995.

Lovibond, Sabina. "Feminism and Pragmatism: A Reply to Richard Rorty," *New Left Review* 178 (1989).

Lugones, Maria, "Playfulness, 'World'-Travelling, and Loving Perception." In *Cooking, Eating, Thinking*. Edited by Deane W. Curtin and Lisa M. Heldke. Bloomington: Indiana University Press, 1992.

MacKinnon, Catharine A. *Feminism Unmodified*. Cambridge MA: Harvard University Press, 1987.

Mahone, Sydne, ed. *Moon Marked and Touched by Sun: Plays by African-American Women*. New York: Theatre Communications Group, 1994.

Marsh, H.W. and R. Shavelson. "Self-Concept: Its Multifaceted Hierarchical Structure," *Educational Psychologist* 20: 107–123.

Martin, Jane Roland. "Methodological Essentialism, False Difference, and Other Dangerous Traps," *Signs* 19, no. 3 (1994): 630–657.

Martinez, Ruben and Richard L. Dukes. "Ethnic and Gender Differences in Self Esteem," *Youth & Society* 22, no. 3 (March 1991): 318–338.

Marx, Karl. *Capital I*. New York: International, 1967.

Marx, Karl and Frederich Engels. *Selected Works*. New York: International, 1968.

McDonald, G.F., ed. Perception and Identity: Essays Presented to A.J. Ayer With His Replies. Ithaca: Cornell University Press, 1979.

McLaughlin, Brian. "Exploring the Possibility of Self-Deception in Belief." In *Perspectives on Self-Deception*. Edited by Brian McLaughlin and Amelie Rorty. Berkeley: University of California Press, 1988.

Mepham, John and Dabid Hillel Ruben, eds. *Issues in Marxist Philosophy 2 Materialism*. Brighton: Harvester, 1979.

Merleau-Ponty, Maurice. *Phénoménologie de la Perception*. Paris: Gallimard 1945. Translated into English, *Phenomenology of Perception*. Translated by Colin Smith. New York and London: Routledge/Humanities Press, 1962.

Merleau-Ponty, Maurice. *The Visible and the Invisible*. Translated by Alphonso Lingis. Evanston: Northwestern University Press, 1968.

Miles, Robert. *Racism*. London: Routledge, 1989.

Miller, R. and B. Miller, B. "Mothering the Biracial Child: Bridging the Gaps Between African-American and White Parenting Styles," *Women and Therapy*, 10 (1990): 169–180.

Mills, Jane. Womanwords: A Dictionary of Words about Women. New York: Macmillan, 1989.

Molette, Carlton and Barbara Molette. *Black Theatre: Premise and Presentation*. Bristol, IN: Wyndham Hall Press, 1986.

Montague, Ashley. Man's Most Dangerous Myth: The Fallacy of Race. Cleveland: World, 1965.

Montague, Ashley. *Race, Science, and Humanity*. New York: Van Nostrand Reinhold, 1963.

Morrison, Toni, ed. Race-ing Justice, En-gendering Power: Essays on Anita Hill, Clarence Thomas and the Construction of Social Reality. New York: Pantheon Books, 1992.

Murray, Charles, "Affirmative Racism," *The New Republic*, December 31, 1984.

Natanson, Maurice. *Anonymity: A Study in the Philosophy of Alfred Schutz*. Bloomington: Indiana University Press, 1986.

National Conference of Catholic Bishops. Strengthening the Bonds of Peace: A Pastoral Reflection on Women in the Church and in Society. 1995.

Neal, A. and M.L. Wilson. "The Role of Skin Color and Features in the Black Community: Implications for Black Women and Therapy," *Clinical Psychology Review* 9 (1989): 323–334.

Nicholson, Linda. "Interpreting Gender," *Signs* 20 (Autumn 1994): 79–105.

Nokes, J. and G. Pridham, eds., *Nazism 1919–1945*. New York: Schocken, 1984.

Nozick, Robert. *Philosophical Investigations*. Cambridge: Harvard University Press, 1981.

Ollman, Bertell. *Alienation: Marx's Concept of Man in Capitalist Society*. Cambridge: Cambridge University Press, 1971.

Pallas, Aaron M., Doris R. Entwisle, and Karl L. Alexander. "Social Structure and the Development of Self-Esteem in Young Children," *Social Psychology Quarterly* 53, no. 4 (December 1990): 302–315.

Parfit, Derek. *Reasons and Persons*. Oxford: Oxford University Press, 1984.

Park, R.E. "Human Migration and the Marginal Man," *American Journal of Sociology* 33 (1928): 881–893.

Paul, Ellen. *Equity and Gender*. New Brunswick: Transaction Books, 1989.

Pittman, John P., ed. *African American Perspectives and Philosophical Traditions*. New York: Routledge, 1996.

Polachek, Solomon. "Women in the Economy." in *Comparable Worth: Issues for the 80's*. Washington, DC: U.S. Commission on Civil Rights, 1984).

Pyant, Carlton T. and Barbara J. Yanico. "Relationship of Racial Identity and Gender-Role Attitudes to Black Women's Psychological Well-Being," *Journal of Counseling Psychology* 38, no. 3 (1991): 315–322.

225

Quine, W.V.O. "Natural Kinds." In *Naming, Necessity, and Natural Kinds*. Edited by Stephen P. Schwartz. Ithaca: Cornell University Press, 1977.

Rawick, George P. From Sundown to Sunup: The Making of the Black Community. Westport, CT: Greenwood, 1977.

Reid, Pamela Trotman and Katherine Hulse Trotter. "Children's Self-Presentation with Infants: Gender and Ethnic Comparisons," *Sex Roles: A Journal of Research* 29, nos. 3/4 (1993): 171–181.

Reid, Pamela Trotman and Lillian Comas Diaz. "Gender and Ethnicity: Perspectives on Dual Status," *Sex Roles: A Journal of Research* 22 nos. 7/8 (April 1990): 397–407.

Roediger, David R. The Wages of Whiteness: Race and the Making of the American Working Class. London: Verso, 1992.

Root, M.P.P. "Disordered Eating in Women of Color," *Sex Roles* 22 (1990): 525–536.

Root, M.P.P. "Resolving 'Other' Status: Identity Development of Biracial Individuals." In *Diversity and Complexity in Feminist Therapy*. Edited by L.S. Brown and M.P.P. Root. New York: Haworth Press, 1990.

Root, M.P.P., ed. *Racially Mixed People in America.* Thousand Oaks, CA: Sage, 1992.

Root, M.P.P., ed. *The Multiracial Experience: Racial Borders as the New Frontier.* Thousand Oaks, CA: Sage Publications, 1996.

Rorty, Richard. *Contingency, Irony, Solidarity*. New York: Cambridge University Press, 1989.

Roscoe, Will. "How to Become a Berdache: Toward a Unified Analysis of Gender Diversity." In *Third Sex, Third Gender*. Edited by G. Herdt. New York: Zone Books, 1994.

Sartre, Jean-Paul. *L'être et le néant: essai d'ontologie phénoménologique*. Paris: Gallimard, 1943. Translated into English *Being and Nothingness: A Phenomenological Essay on Ontology*. Translated by Hazel Barnes. New York: Philosophical Library and Washington Square Press, 1956.

Schuyler, George. *Black No More*. New York: Negro Universities Press, 1931.

Seve, Lucien. Man in Marxist Theory and the Psychology of Personality. Brighton: Harvester, 1978.

Shoemaker, Sidney. *Self-Knowledge and Identity*. Ithaca: Cornell University Press, 1963.

Soper, Kate. *Humanism and Anti-Humanism*. LaSalle, IL: Open Court, 1986.

Sorenson, Elaine. "The Comparable Worth Debate." In *The Imperiled Economy, Book II*. Edited by Robert Cherry. New York: Union of Radical Political Economics, 1991.

Stepan, Nancy. The Idea of Race in Science: Great Britain, 1800–1950. London: Archon Books, 1982.

Stephan, C.W. "Ethnic Identity Among Mixed-Heritage People in Hawaii," *Symbolic Interaction* 14 (1991): 261–277.

Stephan, C.W., and W.G. Stephan. "After Intermarriage: Ethnic Identity Among Mixed-Heritage Japanese Americans and Hispanics," *Journal of Marriage and the Family* 51 (1989): 507–519.

Stiver, Irene P. "Beyond the Oedipal Complex: Mothers and Daughters." In Jordan, Kaplan, Miller, Stiver, and Surrey, eds., *Women's Growth in Connection*.

Stoller, R.J. "The Sense of Femaleness," *Psychoanalytic Quarterly* 7 (1968): 42–55.

Theatre Journal 37 no. 3 (October 1985): entire issue.

Thomas, Laurence. "Sexism and Racism: Some Conceptual Differences," *Ethics* 90 (1980): 239–250.

Tierney, Helen, ed. *Women's Studies Encyclopedia* 1. New York: Greenwood, 1989.

Timpanaro, Sebastiano. *On Materialism*. London: New Left Books, 1970.

Tucker, Richard C., ed. *The Marx-Engels Reader*. New York: Norton, 1978.

Ture, Kwame and Charles Hamilton. *Black Power*. New York: Vintage, 1992. Reissue, with new Afterwards, of 1967 edition.

Turner, C.B. and B.T. Turner. "Gender, Race, Social Class, and Self-Evaluations Among College Students," *The Sociological Quarterly* 23: 491–507.

Tuttle, Lisa, ed. *Encyclopedia of Feminism*. New York: Facts on File/Pletus, 1986.

Venable, Vernon. *Human Nature: The Marxian View*. Cleveland: World, 1966.

Verkuyten, Maykel. "Impact of Ethnic and Sex Differences on Global Self-Esteem Among Adolescents in the Netherlands," *Psychological Reports* 59 (1986): 446.

Von Altendorf, Alan and Theresa Von Altendorf. *Isms: A Compendium of Concepts, Doctrines, Traits, and Beliefs*. Memphis: Mustang, 1991.

Walker, Alice. *In Search of Our Mothers' Gardens*. San Diego: Harcourt Brace Jovanovich, 1967.

Walker, Margaret Urban. *Moral Understandings*. New York: Routledge, forthcoming 1996.

Warren, Karen. "The Power and Promise of EcoFeminism," *Environmental Ethics* (1990).

Warren, Mary Anne. *The Nature of Woman*. Inverness: Edgepress, 1980.

Wasserstrom, Richard. "Racism, Sexism, and Preferential Treatment: an Approach to the Topics," *UCLA Law Review* (February, 1977): 581–615. Reprinted, in part, as "Racism & Sexism," in Bishop and Weinzweig, eds., *Philosophy and Women*.

West, Cornel, *Race Matters*. New York: Vintage Books, 1994.

Wilkerson, Margaret B., ed. *Nine Plays by Black Women*. New York: New American Library, 1986.

Willett, Cynthia. *Maternal Ethics and Other Slave Moralities*. New York and London: Routledge, 1995.

Williams, Patricia J. *The Rooster's Egg: On the Persistence of Prejudice*. Cambridge, MA: Harvard University Press, 1995.

Wilson, T. "People of Mixed-Race Descent." In *American Mosaic: Selected Readings on America's Multicultural Heritage*. Edited by Y.I. Song and E.C. Kim. Sacramento, CA: Ethnicus—Center for Multicultural Studies, 1991.

Wittig, Monique. "One is Not Born a Woman," *Feminist Issues* 1 (1981): 47–54.

Wittig, Monique. "The Category of Sex," *Feminist Issues* 2 (1982): 63–8.

Wolin, Richard, ed. *The Heidegger Controversy*. Cambridge: MIT Press, 1992.

X, Malcolm (as told to Alex Haley). *The Autobiography of Malcolm X*. New York: Ballantine, 1973.

Zack, Naomi. *Race and Mixed Race*. Philadelphia: Temple University Press, 1993.

Zack, Naomi, ed. *American Mixed Race: The Culture of Microdiversity*. Lanham, MD: Rowman and Littlefield, 1995.

Zack, Naomi, *Bachelors of Science: Seventeenth Century Identity, Then and Now*. Philadelphia: Temple University Press, 1996.

ABOUT THE CONTRIBUTORS

Kwame Anthony Appiah is Professor of Afro-American Studies and Philosophy at Harvard University and the author of *In My Father's House: Africa in the Philosophy of Culture*, and *Necessary Questions: An Introduction to Philosophy, For Truth in Semantics*, and *Assertion and Conditionals*; as well as of three novels, of which the latest is Another Death in Venice (1995). He has been Chair of the Joint Committee on African Studies of the Social Science Research Council and is Chair of Harvard's African Studies Committee. His interests are reflected in the range of his journal publications: in the philosophy of language and mind, African philosophy, philosophical problems of race and racism, inter-cultural interpretation, and Afro-American and African literature and literary theory.

Judith Bradford is a graduate student at Fordham University who works in feminist epistemology. She has written articles on Wittgenstein and feminism (in Scheman, ed., *Rereading the Canon* series, Penn State Press, forthcoming) and on feminist epistemology of the family (in Nelson, ed., *Feminism and Families*, Routledge, forthcoming).

J. Angelo Corlett earned his Ph.D. in Philosophy at the University of Arizona in 1992. He is currently Assistant Professor of Philosophy in the Department of Philosophy at Georgia State University. He is the author of several articles in moral, social, and political philosophy, and epistemology, and of the book *Analyzing Social Knowledge* (Rowman & Littlefield, 1995); he is currently working on a book on the philosophy of Karl Marx. Corlett is also Editor-in-Chief of *The Journal of Ethics* (Kluwer), and Founding President of The Society for Ethics.

J.L.A. Garcia is Professor of Philosophy at Rutgers University. Since Yale University awarded him the doctorate in 1980, Prof. Garcia has published over forty scholarly articles on a variety of topics in moral philosophy and practical ethics, and his research has won fellowship support from the Ford Foundation, the National Endowment for the Humanities, and Harvard University. He has served as Senior Research Scholar at Georgetown University's Kennedy Institute of Ethics, as well as Fellow in Ethics at Harvard, and Visiting Fellow in Harvard's Division of Medical Ethics. Garcia has also taught philosophy at Georgetown and Notre Dame.

230

Freda Scott Giles earned her Ph. D in Theatre at the City University of New York Graduate School and is presently Assistant Professor of Drama at the University of Georgia. A historian, her special area of interest is the theatre and drama of the Harlem Renaissance. Her most recently published articles include "From Melodrama to the Movies: the Tragic Mulatto as a Type Character" (in Naomi Zack, ed., *American Mixed Race* (Rowman and Littlefield, 1995) and "Disparate Voices: African-American Theatre Critics of the 1920s" (in *Journal of American Drama and Theatre* 7, no. 1 (Winter 1995)). Giles is presently at work on a book about Harlem Renaissance dramatists.

Lewis R. Gordon teaches African-American Studies and Philosophy of Religion at Brown University, where he is also a member of the Center for the Study of Race and Ethnicity. He is author of *Bad Faith and Antiblack Racism* (Humanities Press); *Fanon and the Crisis of European Man: An Essay on Philosophy and the Human Sciences* (Routledge); and *Her Majesty's Other Children: Philosophical Sketches from a Neocolonial Age* (Rowland & Littlefield). He is also editor of *Existence in Black: An Anthology of Black Existential Philosophy* (Routledge), and co-editor of *Fanon: A Critical Reader* (Blackwell) and *Black Texts and Textuality: Constructing and De-Constructing Blackness* (Roman & Littlefield).

Helena Jia Hershel, Ph.D. is a psychotherapist in private practice in Oakland, California. Her clinical expertise is in working with individuals and couples, with a specialty in relationship and multi-cultural issues. She is a Professor of Clinical Psychology teaching in the areas of cross-cultural psychology and psychoanalytical theory at The Center For Psychological Studies in Albany, California. She has also published numerous articles and is a frequent lecturer on women's issues and cross-cultural topics.

Nancy Holmstrom is Associate Professor of Philosophy at Rutgers University in Newark. Her early interests were in Metaphysics and Philosophy of Mind, but then turned to social and political philosophy, a continuing theme being the nature and conditions of human freedom. She has published numerous articles on Marxist and feminist theory.

Berel Lang is Professor of Philosophy and Humanistic Studies at the State University of New York, Albany. Among his books are *Mind's Bodies: Thought in the Act* (1995); *Writing and the Moral Self* (1991); and *Act and Idea in the Nazi Genocide* (1990).

Kevin Thomas Miles is Assistant Professor of Philosophy at Villanova University. He recently received his Ph.D. from DePaul University, and his dissertation develops a discussion of the form of justice Aristotle identifies as "equity" in the *Nicomachean Ethics*. Presently he is teaching ancient Greek philosophy and ethics.

John P. Pittman (Ph.D., CUNY) teaches philosophy at John Jay College of Criminal Justice in New York City. He has edited an anthology *African-American Perspectives and Philosophical Traditions* (The Philosophical Forum, 1992; reprint by Routledge, 1996). He is writing a book on social constructivism.

Maria P.P. Root, Ph.D., is Associate Professor in the Department of American Ethnic Studies at the University of Washington in Seattle and a clinical psychologist in private practice. She has edited the award-winning book, *Racially Mixed People in America* (Sage, 1992), and most recently, *The Multiracial Experience: Racial Borders as the New Frontier* (Sage, 1996).

Crispin Sartwell is Assistant Professor of Philosophy at the University of Alabama. He is the author of *The Art of Living: Aesthetics of the Ordinary in World Spiritual Traditions* and *Obscenity, Anarchy, Reality* (State University of New York Press, 1995 and 1996). He is working on a book about African-American autobiography.

Laurie Shrage is Associate Professor of Philosophy and an adjunct faculty member in Ethnic and Women's Studies at California State Polytechnic University, Pomona. She is the author of *Moral Dilemmas of Feminism: Prostitution, Adultery, and Abortion* (Routledge, 1994) and of articles on topics in ethics, aesthetics, and feminist theory. She is currently completing a children's book on transgender issues titled *Brad Whose Name Used To Be Barbara.*

James P. Sterba (Ph.D. University of Pittsburgh) is Professor of Philosophy at the University of Notre Dame, where he teaches ethics and political philosophy. He has written more than 130 articles and published 15 books, most recently *Feminist Philosophies* (1992), *Contemporary Social and Political Philosophy* (1994), *Morality and Social Justice* (1994), and *Morality in Practice,* 5th ed. (1995). He is past president of the North American Society for Social Philosophy, past president of Concerned Philosophers for Peace, and past president of the International Society for Philosophy of Law and Social Philosophy (American Section), and he has lectured widely in the United States and Europe.

Naomi Zack (Ph.D. Columbia University) is the author of *Race and Mixed Race* (Temple University Press, 1993) and *Bachelors of Science: Seventeenth-Century Identity, Then and Now* (Temple, 1996); and the editor of *American Mixed Race: The Culture of Microdiversity* (Rowman & Littlefield, 1995). She is Assistant Professor of Philosophy at the University at Albany, State University of New York.

INDEX